grace today

J. MARK MARTIN

grace today

365 daily devotions through the bible
VOLUME ONE

J. MARK MARTIN

GRACE
UPON GRACE

Grace Upon Grace Productions
Phoenix, Arizona

GRACE TODAY
365 Daily Devotions through the Bible
Volume One
published by Grace Upon Grace Productions
Phoenix, Arizona

Copyright © 2009 by J. Mark Martin
International Standard Book Number 978-0-9710828-6-1

These devotions include edited excerpts from *Grace Mail*, a daily e-devotional
by J. Mark Martin. These are used with the author's permission.

Cover and graphic design by Shawn Landis.

Printed in the United States of America

www.calvaryphx.com

ISBN 978-0-9710828-6-1

grace today

Dedication

To my two precious daughters, Emily and Ellie, and to Daniel, the best son in the whole-wide world. I love the three of you dearly. May you always continue to love one another and grow in God's grace.

"I could have no greater joy than to hear that my children are walking in the truth." 3 John 4

Preface

This book was written to give you a dose of encouragement every day.

For years I've read various devotional books and have often been surprised at how frequently God will speak to my heart in an especially relevant way while reading through a daily selection.

I've written *Grace Today* praying that, through the pages of this book, God will do the same for you and lead you to find encouragement and practical, personal application of the Bible.

I hope that *Grace Today* opens the windows and lets the light of God's Word stream into your life. God will revitalize your soul and frame your day with encouraging truths from His Word.

grace today

"That is why I tell you not to worry about everyday life—whether you have enough food and drink, or enough clothes to wear. Isn't life more than food, and your body more than clothing? Look at the birds. They don't plant or harvest or store food in barns, for your heavenly Father feeds them. And aren't you far more valuable to him than they are?" (Matthew 6:25-26).

Jesus is saying that needless worry goes against the lessons of nature. If the natural world around us isn't worrying, neither should the children of God! Our loving Father in Heaven is watching over us and this day's needs are in His hands.

"So don't worry about tomorrow, for tomorrow will bring its own worries. Today's trouble is enough for today" (Matthew 6:34).

Giving our cares and worries to God helps us to live a SUPER-natural life. If that old crow in the back yard trusts God, so can you!

"Can all your worries add a single moment to your life?" (Matthew 6:27).

I bet you know this, but worrying isn't good for you. When we torment ourselves over things that might happen or we allow ourselves to fixate on some dreaded thing, we're actually sabotaging our peace. Jesus is clearly saying that when we worry, we add nothing to our lives; we actually lose something, something is subtracted—our peace.

Grace today

Worry steals our peace by robbing us of the moment we're living in. God's plan is to give you peace for this minute. Worry demands a week or a month's worth of peace for that moment, and that will never be delivered. God's grace is always enough for right now, and right now is where we're living. Jesus has promised, "I'll be with you... day after day after day, right up to the end of the age" (Matthew 28:20, MSG).

3 JANUARY

"And why worry about your clothing? Look at the lilies of the field and how they grow. They don't work or make their clothing, yet Solomon in all his glory was not dressed as beautifully as they are. And if God cares so wonderfully for wildflowers that are here today and thrown into the fire tomorrow, he will certainly care for you. Why do you have so little faith?" (Matthew 6:28-30).

What if your mirror could talk? What would it say? "How do I look?" "What am I going to wear?" "I look fat!" "Why isn't my hair curly?" "I wish my hair was straight!" "I wish I *had* some hair!"

If mirrors echoed what they hear us say, we might be more aware of how much energy we spend to project a physical image of ourselves, and how little time we spend dressing ourselves spiritually every day. If how you looked on the outside was directly proportional to how much time you spend with God each morning, how would you look right now? (It's okay to laugh! I'm having some hilarious images come to my mind too!).

Let's spend more time grooming the inside; the results are sure to show on the outside.

Paul's words to the Colossian Christians seem especially appropriate today: "It wasn't long ago that you were doing all that stuff and not knowing any better. But you know better now, so make sure it's all gone for good: bad temper, irritability, meanness, profanity, dirty talk. Don't lie to one another. You're done with that old life. It's like a filthy set of ill-fitting clothes you've stripped off and put in the fire. Now you're dressed in a new wardrobe. Every item of your new way of life is custom-made by the Creator, with his label on it. All the old fashions are now obsolete" (Colossians 3:7-10, MSG).

JANUARY 4

"So don't worry about these things, saying, 'What will we eat? What will we drink? What will we wear?' These things dominate the thoughts of unbelievers, but your heavenly Father already knows all your needs" (Matthew 6:31-32).

You're not on your own, you don't have to take care of yourself, you're not an orphan! You have a loving Father in Heaven who is going to take care of your needs. When we worry, we're living like we're on our own.

When you start to worry:
- Remember, you're part of the family—the Father's family. You're not alone. God has promised to care for those who are living for Him.
- Think, "How big a deal is this in the light of eternity?"
- Turn off the static. Worry is like listening to static all the time. It's annoying and exhausting. The best way to deal with it is not to try to fine tune the station and figure out all the reasons for your anxiety, but to turn it off! Worry

would love to play over all the activities of your life. Turn it off by trusting Jesus' words.

- Cast if off by getting quiet with the Lord and writing everything down that is worrying you. Then take that piece of paper and throw it away! You're actually obeying God's Word which says for you to cast "...the whole of your care [all your anxieties, all your worries, all your concerns, once and for all] on Him, for He cares for you affectionately and cares about you watchfully" (1 Peter 5:7, AMP).

5 JANUARY

"But seek first His kingdom and His righteousness, and all these things will be added to you" (Matthew 6:33, NASB).

We may have many "wants" and we all share basic "needs," but Jesus says that "The thing you should want most is God's kingdom and doing what God wants. Then all these other things you need will be given to you" (NCV).

Putting God first; this is a basic and necessary part of being a Christian.

The Message paraphrase refreshes these words for us: "Steep your life in God-reality, God-initiative, God-provisions. Don't worry about missing out. You'll find all your everyday human concerns will be met." Jesus is telling us to keep the main thing the main thing. God's kingdom, God's will and God's Word come first in a believer's life. All other things must be ordered after this priority, and when we live this way, we can be confident of God's provision.

Here's the practical stuff:

How do believers today practice Matthew 6:33? We will start with our time, and put God first every day. This means time for prayer and reading the Word. We will put God first in every week, attending the house of God faithfully. We will put God first every payday, paying the tithe to the Lord. We will put God first in our choices, making no decision that would leave God out. Lot left God out of his decisions and ended up in the darkness of a cave, practicing terrible sin![1]

JANUARY 6

"So don't worry about tomorrow, for tomorrow will bring its own worries. Today's trouble is enough for today" (Matthew 6:34).

One Christian woman shares, "How many mistakes I have made with the children because I was 'fretting'—concerned to the point of worry. And invariably it prompted me to unwise action: Sharpness, unfair punishment, unwise discipline... even my attitude and tone of voice. But a mother who walks with God knows He only asks her to take care of the possible and to trust Him with the impossible; she does not need to fret."

David says, "Don't give in to worry or anger; it only leads to trouble" (Psalm 37:8, TEV).

grace today

7 JANUARY

"The seed that fell among thorns stands for those who hear, but as they go on their way they are choked by life's worries, riches and pleasures, and they do not mature" (Luke 8:14, NIV).

Several years ago *USA Today* published the results of a poll that asked adults to look back over their lives and share what they most regret wasting time on. Topping the list, 67% of those questioned responded that they regretted they had spent time "worrying."[2]

Worrying disturbs the peace, the peace of our souls. When you worry, you're not going to grow. You'll be doing well to hold your ground, if you can even do that. The loss of your peace should always be a sign that there is something else going on. In His book, *The Fight*, John White reminds us, "If you lack peace, it is because something is hindering the work of the Holy Spirit in your life... Peace is a kind of signal. Any lack of it is an alarm telling you that things have gone wrong." It's not always sin in your life, though it could be. Sometimes it's simply not taking care of your physical needs or a matter of not realizing that you're in more of a spiritual battle than you think.

8 JANUARY

"Don't worry about anything; instead, pray about everything. Tell God what you need, and thank him for all he has done. Then you will experience God's peace, which exceeds anything we can understand. His peace will guard your hearts and minds as you live in Christ Jesus" (Philippians 4:6-7).

Have you ever noticed that 95 percent of the things you spend so much time worrying about never happen? What a huge waste of time and emotional energy.

The Bible tells us that we can spare ourselves a whole lot of stress and honor God a lot more by turning our problems into prayers.

Obviously, God is big enough to handle our cares. He's much more experienced at solving problems than we are.

I read of a weary Christian who was lying awake one night trying to hold the world together by his worrying. Then he heard the Lord gently say to him, "Now you go to sleep, Jim, I'll sit up."

"Praise the Lord; praise God our savior! For each day he carries us in his arms" (Psalm 68:19).

JANUARY 9

"Don't let your hearts be troubled. Trust in God, and trust also in me" (John 14:1).

If you're still a confirmed worrier and continue to be plagued by this struggle, here are some things not to worry about—use your worrying time for better things.

Don't worry about:
- Things out of your control – There's nothing you can do about them anyway... there's nothing you can do about them anyway... there's nothing you can do about them

Grace today

anyway... there's nothing you can do about them anyway... get the point!

- Things that are insignificant – Think, "What difference will this make in five years?"
- Water under the bridge – What's happened has happened. God says that if you love Him, He will "work all things together for good" (Romans 8:28).
- Tomorrow – Most of what you worry about for tomorrow won't happen, and you can't control what does happen; that is God's job, not yours.

Irrational, habitual worrying has to be submitted to the Lordship of Jesus Christ. We have to stand up in faith and discipline our feelings and emotions and say, "Regardless of how things look, what I feel, or what I fear, God is the One who controls my destiny!" Say that with me, "Regardless how things look, what I feel, or what I fear, God is the One who controls my destiny!" Even in the midst of his pain and loss, Job trusted his life and future to God: "But once he has made his decision, who can change his mind? Whatever he wants to do, he does. So he will do to me whatever he has planned. He controls my destiny" (Job 23:13-14).

10 JANUARY

"When Abram was ninety-nine years old, the LORD appeared to him and said, 'I am God Almighty; serve me faithfully and live a blameless life'" (Genesis 17:1).

You're never too old to serve the Lord! God calls us to serve Him faithfully and to live a holy life, not just in our early years, but also in our latter days.

As we age we become more dependent. Instead of hopping over the fence, you open the gate. You mosey, rather than hurry. Large print and bright lights attract you. Instead of jumping into your pants, you carefully sit down and put one leg in at a time. People start to call you "Sir" or "Ma'am" and even open the door for you! When you think about wrinkles, the first thing that comes to mind isn't your shirt!

Growing older can bring with it scary and stressful times. That's why it's so good to know that to a man who was just about to celebrate his 100th birthday God revealed himself to be "God Almighty" or "El Shaddai." El Shaddai means "God All-Sufficient," "God of complete provision."

You may be aging, but the Ageless One is there to provide for all your needs. May you find refreshment and renewal in the everlasting arms of God our Savior.

"Therefore we do not become discouraged (utterly spiritless, exhausted, and wearied out through fear). Though our outer man is [progressively] decaying and wasting away, yet our inner self is being [progressively] renewed day after day" (2 Corinthians 4:16, AMP).

January 11

"Now that I am old and gray, do not abandon me, O God. Let me proclaim your power to this new generation, your mighty miracles to all who come after me" (Psalm 71:18).

I love to see older Christians on fire for the Lord. Though sometimes they battle health crises and obstacles that their

grace today

younger brethren are clueless to really understand, their love for Christ is contagious and inspiring.

John Wesley was the founder of the Methodist Church. In its prime it was once a growing, going, evangelical movement that transformed England and North America. John Wesley was a man who kept going. He was full of energy and enthusiasm for Christ. After riding 250,000 miles on horseback, and after preaching 40,000 sermons, writing 400 books, and mastering 10 languages at age 83, he complained in his diary that he was angered because he could no longer write longer than 15 hours a day without his eyes beginning to hurt. At 86 he had to drop back to preaching just two times a day, seven days a week! At 88 his journal again reveals that he complained that he was finding a tendency to sleep-in in the morning, until 5:30 A.M.!

There's a new generation coming up that needs to hear from you! Press on, keep on the course. While you're here, the Lord has a plan for you.

"But," maybe you're thinking, "I'm too old. How can I serve the Lord?"

Here are a few ideas:
- Share your testimony with those the Lord brings your way.
- Memorize Scriptures and share them.
- Give God your best.
- Spend extra time with your children, grandchildren and "greats."
- Listen to the Bible and spiritual books on CD or tape.
- Cook for people – there's a whole lot of "religion" in good food!
- Go to a nursing home and pray for and encourage those who don't have what you have.

- Join a letter-writing or email ministry. Encourage people. Your experience with Christ is a treasure—share it!
- Write encouraging notes to spiritual leaders.
- Offer sleepless hours to the Lord, spend a chunk of that time in intercessory prayer.
- When a part of your body hurts, pray for the Body of Christ, the problems in the Church or the persecuted Church.

January 12

"I rejoice in your word like one who discovers a great treasure" (Psalm 119:162).

Someone asked Billy Graham what he would do if he could live his life over again. Many were shocked by his response. A lot of people thought he would talk about how he would go more places and reach more people for the Lord, but you know what he said? He said that if he could live his life over, he would spend more time with the Lord, reading and studying the Word of God.

David says in Psalm 19:10 that God's Word is "...more desirable than gold, even the finest gold... sweeter than honey, even honey dripping from the comb."

This means that God's Word is life! It is very important for us to eat the Word of God. We must take it in, understand it, absorb it, and make it part of our very being. From God's Word comes life itself.

Come to the Bible with a sense of expectation. Realize that God promises to meet you in His Word!

grace today

The Bible says that "…God… rewards those who sincerely seek him" (Hebrews 11:6). God promises that if we draw near to Him, He will draw near to us! (James 4:8a).

"He feels pity for the weak and the needy, and he will rescue them" (Psalm 72:13).

13 January

"For the word of God is alive and powerful. It is sharper than the sharpest two-edged sword, cutting between soul and spirit, between joint and marrow. It exposes our innermost thoughts and desires" (Hebrews 4:12).

Calvin Coolidge once remarked, "People criticize me for harping on the obvious. Yet if all the folks in the United States would do the few simple things they know they ought to do, most of our big problems would take care of themselves."

Coolidge's comments apply very well to our getting more out of the Bible. Every Christian knows that he or she should spend daily time with the Lord, but most of us would admit to some degree of frustration with our actual doing what we know we should do.

You have to open the Bible and read it to get blessed by it! It's not a four-leaf clover! It's not a good-luck charm! It won't bless you by osmosis! In order for it to get into you, you've got to get into it! As Isaiah the prophet says: "Get and read GOD's book…" (Isaiah 34:16a, MSG).

"But the time is coming—indeed it's here now—when true worshipers will worship the Father in spirit and in truth. The Father is looking for those who will worship him that way. For God is Spirit, so those who worship him must worship in spirit and in truth" (John 4:23-24).

God is seeking you! He wants fellowship with you!

The Bible is God's way of talking to us, and good listening will heighten our intimacy with God.

The Bible clearly illustrates the connection between knowing God and knowing Scripture. Through the prophet Isaiah, God says that He looks with favor on humble people who tremble at His Word (Isaiah 66:2, 5).

The Holy Spirit uses the Word of God to speak to our hearts. This is the primary way that the Lord communicates to and directs you as a believer.

I've heard it illustrated this way. It's like starting a car. "God's Spirit is the engine, your will serves as the ignition key, and God's Word acts as fuel. If you have an engine without fuel, you can turn the ignition key all you want, but the car will not start. Without the Word, the power of the Holy Spirit will go un-ignited. You can have the best of engines, and a tank full of the best fuel, but until the ignition is turned there will be no energy. So the Holy Spirit and the Word without the cooperation of the human will are essentially dormant."

grace today

Just as God used to speak to Moses as a friend (Exodus 33:11), so God wants to speak to you through His Word as *your* special Friend.

Jesus made it clear that intimacy with Him cannot be attained away from His Word: "Those who accept my commandments and obey them are the ones who love me. And because they love me, my Father will love them. And I will love them and reveal myself to each of them" (John 14:21).

15 JANUARY

"In the secret place of His tent He will hide me..." (Psalm 27:5, NASB).

God will talk to you while you're on the run, but you'll hear more when you sit down and listen. Christians for thousands of years have credited having a daily quiet time with God, a daily appointment with God, as the source of their spiritual growth and peace.

By spending time with God each day you are making a declaration of your dependence on God. You're saying, "My rebellious, independent days are over!"

Here's some "Quiet Time Helps":
- Make it special – It may be a corner of the living room or a desk in the family room, or just a lazy-boy somewhere, but find a space that becomes a familiar place for meeting with God.

- Be creative – Susannah Wesley had 19 children. You know how she had her quiet time? She would sit down in a chair and pull her apron over her head—and woe to the child that disturbed her! Jewish men take their prayer room with them, they pray under a tallit, or prayer-shawl.
- Let music enhance, but not distract – Christian music can set a tone of worship and praise. I find that instrumental praise music distracts me less than really upbeat contemporary Christian music. Remember, the purpose of this time is to have God speak to your heart through His Word.
- Believe that God is going to meet with you – "Every morning you'll hear me at it again. Every morning I lay out the pieces of my life on your altar and watch for fire to descend" (Psalm 5:3, MSG).

JANUARY 16

"Therefore, since we are surrounded by such a huge crowd of witnesses to the life of faith, let us strip off every weight that slows us down, especially the sin that so easily trips us up. And let us run with endurance the race that God has set before us. We do this by keeping our eyes on Jesus, the champion who initiates and perfects our faith" (Hebrews 12:1-2a).

There was a sign at the airport runway, which read: "Keep moving, if you stop you are a danger to those who are flying."

Those who run races always do better when someone is watching. Remember as you run this race, the Lord is watching. Keep your focus on the Lord.

grace today

Corrie Ten Boom was a former concentration camp prisoner and author of *The Hiding Place*. She said:

> Look within and be depressed.
> Look without and be oppressed.
> Look at Jesus and be at rest.

17 JANUARY

"After you have read this letter, pass it on to the church at Laodicea so they can read it, too. And you should read the letter I wrote to them" (Colossians 4:16).

When someone asks you what kind of a Bible you read, tell them you can only read an opened Bible! Bible reading is a major factor in Christian growth.

Here are some ways to get more out of your Bible reading:

- Read extensively – Read through the Bible. Read through a book of the Bible. Get the whole counsel of God's Word.
- Read intensively – Read a single Bible book over and over again. Read it in as many translations as you can get a hold of. You'll find great reward in mastering even a small part of God's Word, and you'll find that it masters you! R. A. Torrey used to say that he made it a rule to read enough of the Bible to enable him to turn one page of the Bible every twenty-four hours.
- Read defensively – By this I mean, watch for the concentration robbers. They'll try to wreck your time in God's Word, but don't be discouraged by them. Here's a simple way to handle distractions; keep a notepad to write things that you think of that you should do. Read aloud.

You'll be surprised how much this will help you get more out of the Word, and you'll remember it better because you're getting input, not just from your eyes, but also from your ears!

* Read carefully – Read for the whole context. Read enough to develop the continuity of thought. Sometimes that means you read a few more verses, other times you'll need to read the whole chapter.

It's exciting to see God develop a hunger in your heart for His Word!

JANUARY 18

"Open my eyes to see the wonderful truths in your instructions" (Psalm 119:18).

When the Bible is approached with reverence and love, you will see its message unfold. Prayer is the password that opens the Word. The Bible should have "Handle With Prayer!" stamped on its cover.

Let's pray and ask the Lord to open up His Word to us: "Father, thank You for giving us Your living Word, it's more necessary to us than food. Please give us an increased desire for it and an increased capacity to understand it. Thank You for meeting us in Your Word. In Jesus' Name, Amen."

"O my people, listen to my instructions. Open your ears to what I am saying..." (Psalm 78:1).

grace today

19 JANUARY

"You yourselves know, dear brothers and sisters, that our visit to you was not a failure. You know how badly we had been treated at Philippi just before we came to you and how much we suffered there. Yet our God gave us the courage to declare his Good News to you boldly, in spite of great opposition" (1 Thessalonians 2:1-2).

One of the essential, elemental truths of serving the Lord that you'd better learn early on, is that when you serve the Lord, you're going to encounter opposition!

The Apostle Paul expected opposition. It's that way in our lives, too, isn't it? Every opportunity to serve God is met by some kind of opposition.

Behind all this opposition stands our adversary, our opponent— the devil. Paul says, "There are many adversaries," (NASB) or those "who oppose me," (NIV).

As the Lord opens up opportunities for us to infiltrate Satan's dark kingdom, opportunities at work, at school, in our homes, our families and in our community, we can expect opposition. G. Campbell Morgan said, "If you have no opposition in the place you serve, you're serving in the wrong place."

20 JANUARY

"If I must boast, I would rather boast about the things that show how weak I am" (2 Corinthians 11:30).

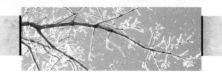

The secret of pioneer missionary to China, Hudson Taylor's peace of mind was his refusal to look at secondary causes of conflicts and adversities of life. As he labored on the mission field, he knew that his steps were all ordered by the Lord, and that nothing could happen without His loving approval.

Referring to the biblical character Job, Taylor remarked that even Satan had to get God's permission before he could afflict Job with pain and sorrow. And even though the adversary did bring about great calamities, Job was right in recognizing that his trials were ultimately a part of God's plan for his life.

"To be sure," said Taylor, "The patriarch [Job] was deeply distressed and perplexed, but he never wavered in his confidence that the Lord's hand was upon him. He knew that he was not the helpless victim of chance."

We can have peace knowing that God controls this day and this week. Nothing can touch us that hasn't first passed through His love.

JANUARY 21

"With your unfailing love you lead the people you have redeemed..." (Exodus 15:13a).

When Rowland Bingham, founder of the Sudan Interior Mission, was injured in a car crash, he was rushed to the hospital in critical condition. He suffered a severe laceration on his head and had a number of broken bones. The next day as he regained consciousness, he asked his nurse what he was doing there. "Be very quiet," said the nurse, "You've been in a serious accident."

"Accident?" Bingham responded, "There are no accidents in the life of a Christian. This is just an *incident* in God's perfect leading."

You need to know that God doesn't make any mistakes! If you think God makes mistakes—you're mistaken! Live this day securely in His love.

"But he led his own people like a flock of sheep, guiding them safely through the wilderness" (Psalm 78:52).

22 JANUARY

"We always thank God for all of you and pray for you constantly. As we pray to our God and Father about you, we think of your faithful work, your loving deeds, and the enduring hope you have because of our Lord Jesus Christ" (1 Thessalonians 1:2-3).

When a person is really saved there is evidence of God's work in their lives. Today's text lists some of the evidences of salvation that Paul saw shining in the lives of the Thessalonian Christians.

First, they were faithfully working for the Lord. They weren't working *for* salvation, but they were working *since* they were saved.

Second, they were known for their loving deeds. The things they did were prompted by a genuine love for Jesus and for other people.

Sometimes on the radio or TV you'll hear a disclaimer: "The views and opinions expressed do not necessarily reflect those

of the management or ownership of this station." But we can't separate our love for God from our service for His people. We can't put a disclaimer on the end of our day and say, "The way I have not lived whole-heartedly for the Lord and not served Him and His people does not necessarily reflect the *real* love I have in my heart for Jesus!"

Thirdly, they lived in the continual anticipation of the return of our Lord Jesus Christ! This anticipation and hope continuously recalibrates our lives and keeps eternal things in focus.

Let's pray that as we work for Jesus and share His love this day, that it will be the day that He returns!

JANUARY 23

"Obviously, I'm not trying to win the approval of people, but of God. If pleasing people were my goal, I would not be Christ's servant" (Galatians 1:10).

The Bible teaches us that the bondage of people-pleasing can keep us from fully serving Christ. Paul always sought to please God. He always wanted God's smile, even if that meant he wouldn't have the smile of the world.

Let's determine, because we have God's acceptance, to live our lives looking only for the Lord's smile and approval. We can live with man's disapproval as long as we know that we have the Lord's approval and smile.

The way to become free of controlling people is to live as a servant of God.

grace today

24 JANUARY

"Your old life is dead. Your new life, which is your real life—even though invisible to spectators—is with Christ in God. He is your life" (Colossians 3:3, MSG).

Knowing who you are in Christ frees you from being manipulated by people. Christian Herter was running hard for re-election as governor of Massachusetts, and one day he arrived late at a barbecue. He'd had no breakfast or lunch, and he was famished. As he moved down the serving line, he held out his plate and received one piece of chicken.

The governor said to the serving lady, "Excuse me, do you mind if I get another piece of chicken? I'm very hungry." The woman replied, "Sorry, I'm supposed to give one piece to each person." He repeated, "But I'm starved!" And again she said, "Only one to a customer."

Herter was normally a modest man, but he decided this was the time to use the weight of his office and said, "Madam, do you know who I am? I am the governor of this state." She answered, "Do you know who I am? I'm the lady in charge of chicken. Move along, Mister!"

That was a lady who knew who she was and who knew her position. She was the "lady in charge of chicken," and she wasn't about to be intimidated or manipulated by anyone!

When we know who we are in Christ, when we know how loved and accepted we are in Him, we will break free from being manipulated by people.

Jesus said, "And you will know the truth, and the truth will set you free... So if the Son sets you free, you are truly free" (John 8:32, 36).

JANUARY 25

"Even though we had some standing as Christ's apostles, we never threw our weight around or tried to come across as important, with you or anyone else" (1 Thessalonians 2:6, MSG).

God uses people who are humble. An old rancher was interviewed and asked what made him so successful as a rancher. With a twinkle in his eye he told the reporter, "It's been about 50 percent weather, 50 percent good luck, and the rest is brains." Here's a man who lives with both feet on the ground!

Evangelist Billy Graham's life has modeled the kind of humility that honors God. Early in his ministry he said, "The one thing I want you to pray for is this: That I will not take credit for the successes of these things whatsoever, because if I do, my lips will turn to clay." Longtime Graham organization board member, Allan Emery comments, "He never did take any credit. He never let anybody make him a big shot. It's humility I have never seen in anybody else... he had a tremendous sense of humility, and does have. Yet he also has what a friend of mine calls 'command presence.' When Billy comes into a room, you know something's very unusual. His voice just makes you want to listen. Yet he understands it's a gift the Lord bestowed on him."[3]

Let's have our prayer be that the Lord will use us, and as He does that all the glory will go to Him!

grace today

26 JANUARY

"This is my commandment: Love each other in the same way I have loved you. There is no greater love than to lay down one's life for one's friends. You are my friends if you do what I command. I no longer call you slaves, because a master doesn't confide in his slaves. Now you are my friends, since I have told you everything the Father told me. You didn't choose me. I chose you. I appointed you to go and produce lasting fruit, so that the Father will give you whatever you ask for, using my name. This is my command: Love each other" (John 15:12-17).

Notice what Jesus says, He "commands" us twice in these six verses to love one another. The writer of Hebrews also exhorts, "Keep on loving each other as brothers and sisters" (Hebrews 13:1).

This love we have for other Christians is evidence that we are born again. "We know that we have passed over out of death into Life by the fact that we love the brethren (our fellow Christians). He who does not love abides (remains, is held and kept continually) in [spiritual] death" (1 John 3:14, AMP).

Let me share 3 practical ways we can put our love into practice. We can show our love by:
- Caring.
- Covering.
- Confronting.

27 JANUARY

"But we don't need to write to you about the importance of loving each other, for God himself has taught you to love

one another... Make it your goal to live a quiet life, minding your own business and working with your hands, just as we instructed you before" (1 Thessalonians 4:9, 11).

Paul is saying that one of the ways we show our love is by caring for other Christians. We care enough to help other believers and we care enough not to burden other believers by working to support ourselves. As we work, or prepare ourselves for a career someday, we are not only taking care or our own needs, but also we will have something to share with others.

In Ephesians 4:28 Paul said, "Let him who steals steal no longer; but rather let him labor, performing with his own hands what is good, in order that he may have something to share with him who has need" (NASB). Caring for those among us who have material needs of food, clothing or housing shows the authentic love of Christ.

"Teach those who are rich in this world not to be proud and not to trust in their money, which is so unreliable. Their trust should be in God, who richly gives us all we need for our enjoyment. Tell them to use their money to do good. They should be rich in good works and generous to those in need, always being ready to share with others" (1 Timothy 6:17-18).

Apply the text by asking these questions:
- Who do I know that needs financial help?
- Will the career choices I am making be pleasing to God?
- Am I ready to share?
- Am I prone to take advantage of other believers' generosity?

28 JANUARY

"And now I make one more appeal, my dear brothers and sisters. Watch out for people who cause divisions and upset people's faith by teaching things contrary to what you have been taught. Stay away from them. Such people are not serving Christ our Lord; they are serving their own personal interests. By smooth talk and glowing words they deceive innocent people" (Romans 16:17-18).

There are times when we show our love for each other by confronting wrongdoing and marking wrongdoers. This is not pleasant, but love without boundaries isn't love at all.

People who attack other Christians or Christian ministries are walking in the flesh at best, and may not even be saved. People who cause divisions show that they love themselves and their opinions and even their cause more than they love the Body of Christ. God hates them and their work: "There are six things the LORD hates—no, seven things he detests: ...a person who sows discord in a family" (Proverbs 6:16; 19b).

The wolves are after you. Years ago, the May 1987 edition of National Geographic included an article about the arctic wolf. Author L. David Mech described how a seven-member pack had targeted several musk-oxen calves who were guarded by eleven adults. As the wolves approached their potential victims, the musk oxen would gather in an impenetrable semicircle, their deadly rear hooves facing out. All the calves remained safe during a long standoff with the enemy. But then a single ox broke rank, and the rest of the herd scattered into nervous little groups. A skirmish ensued, and the adults finally fled in panic, leaving the calves to the merciless predators. Not a single calf survived.

In Acts 20 the Apostle Paul warned the Ephesian elders that vicious wolves would come and not spare the flock. Though the wolves continue to attack the church today, they cannot penetrate and destroy when unity is maintained.

JANUARY 29

"For there must also be factions among you, so that those who are approved may become evident among you" (1 Corinthians 11:19, NASB).

You might be thinking, "What kind of a devotional is this?" I share it because for most of us our church family is one of the most important parts of our life. We love the church that we are part of and don't want anything to happen to the sweetness of the unity and fellowship that we experience, but what happens when that sweetness and unity is challenged? It happened in the New Testament Church, and it will happen today. The Bible tells us that many times these situations are opportunities for God to show whom He approves.

Here's some advice:
- Generally, if your church hits stormy water, stay in the boat – It will become evident who is walking in the love of Jesus and following His Word, and who is not. Don't jump ship too soon. Commenting on a situation like this, the Apostle John says, "These people left our churches, but they never really belonged with us; otherwise they would have stayed with us. When they left, it proved that they did not belong with us. But you are not like that, for the Holy One has given you his Spirit, and all of you know the truth" (1 John 2:19-20).

Grace today

- Reject divisive, factious people – Most divisive people thrive on attention, and are drawing attention to themselves and not to Jesus. Paul gives this clear command: "Reject a factious man after a first and second warning, knowing that such a man is perverted [some translations say, 'warped' or 'corrupted'] and is sinning, being self-condemned" (Titus 3:10-11, NASB).
- Stay sweet – Romans 12:17-21 sums it up: "Never pay back evil with more evil. Do things in such a way that everyone can see you are honorable. Do all that you can to live in peace with everyone. Dear friends, never take revenge. Leave that to the righteous anger of God. For the Scriptures say, 'I will take revenge; I will pay them back,' says the LORD. Instead, 'If your enemies are hungry, feed them. If they are thirsty, give them something to drink. In doing this, you will heap burning coals of shame on their heads.' Don't let evil conquer you, but conquer evil by doing good."

30 JANUARY

"But how can we sing the songs of the LORD while in a pagan land?" (Psalm 137:4).

Nothing will cause you to lose your joy faster than disobedience to God. Because God's people forsook His Word, they experienced the tragic consequences of the destruction of Jerusalem and deportation to Babylon. In the process they lost their song and bitterness took hold of their hearts.

Hang onto your song by staying close to the Composer, our Lord Jesus Christ! F. B. Meyer, commenting on this Psalm said,

"How shall we sing... in a strange land? 'The Lord's song' is only possible in the Lord's house, where his presence is manifested and felt. To be separated from Zion was to be separated from God; and to lose God was to lose all. When we have lost the sense of God's presence, having been led captive by our sins, we too are sure to lose our joy, and peace, and blessedness. The land of the stranger and the song of the Lord can never be found together."[4]

"I waited patiently for the LORD to help me, and he turned to me and heard my cry. He lifted me out of the pit of despair, out of the mud and the mire. He set my feet on solid ground and steadied me as I walked along. He has given me a new song to sing, a hymn of praise to our God. Many will see what he has done and be amazed. They will put their trust in the LORD" (Psalm 40:1-3).

Remember: Grace is the key that unlocks the chain of unforgiveness.

JANUARY 31

"Dear brothers and sisters, honor those who are your leaders in the Lord's work. They work hard among you and give you spiritual guidance. Show them great respect and wholehearted love because of their work. And live peacefully with each other" (1 Thessalonians 5:12-13).

Our spiritual leaders need our prayers. Would you pray today for those who teach you and lead you in your church?

The Book of Hebrews exhorts us to "Remember your leaders who taught you the word of God. Think of all the good that

has come from their lives, and follow the example of their faith" (Hebrews 13:7).

Here are three ways to show your spiritual leaders you love them:

- Respect them – The Bible says that they "...have charge over you in the Lord" (1 Thessalonians 5:12, NASB). They're also going to have to give an account for us before the Judgment Seat of Christ.
- Appreciate them – "But we request of you, brethren, that you appreciate those who diligently labor among you..." (1 Thessalonians 5:12, NASB). This means that if they are feeding us and leading us in the Lord, we should value them highly and place a high estimate on them. In God's kingdom they are valuable. They work hard because they love you.
- Show your love to them – Verse 13 says, "Show them great respect and wholehearted love because of their work." To "honor" means "to esteem them very highly" (NASB) or to "hold them in the highest regard in love" (NIV). It literally means to love them "super abundantly," "extravagantly," or "excessively." Let your love for your spiritual leaders be excessive, extravagant—a visible outpouring of Christian love.

"And you are helping us by praying for us. Then many people will give thanks because God has graciously answered so many prayers for our safety" (2 Corinthians 1:11).

Paul knew the power of prayer to affect the pagan world around him, so he was quick to ask believers to "cover" him with a shield of prayer.

When we pray for those who spiritually feed us and lead us, we actually become spiritual partners with them! "Join me in my struggle by praying to God for me" (Romans 15:30, NIV).

Here's a guide for praying for spiritual leaders:
- Pray for the proclamation of the Word – "Finally, brethren, pray for us that the word of the Lord will spread rapidly and be glorified, just as it did also with you" (2 Thessalonians 3:1, NASB).
- Pray for the protection of the leader – Anyone sharing the Word of God becomes a special target for spiritual attack (1 Corinthians 16:9).
- Pray that their work will be pleasing – "Now I urge you, brethren, by our Lord Jesus Christ and by the love of the Spirit, to strive together with me in your prayers to God for me, that I may be delivered from those who are disobedient in Judea, and that my service for Jerusalem may prove acceptable to the saints" (Romans 15:30-31, NASB).
- Pray that they will have times of refreshing – "...strive together with me in your prayers to God for me, ...that I may come to you in joy by the will of God and find refreshing rest in your company" (Romans 15:30, 32, NASB).

2 February

"The LORD appeared to him from afar, saying, 'I have loved you with an everlasting love; therefore I have drawn you with lovingkindness' " (Jeremiah 31:3, NASB).

Your comfort and hope is anchored in God's love. God has proven His love for you, and His Word tells us that it's a love that never ends. God's love for you was demonstrated at the cross (Romans 5:8; 1 John 4:9-10). John comments on Jesus' love by saying, "...having loved His own who were in the world, He loved them to the end" (John 13:1, NASB).

Jesus loves you so much that He will never become discouraged with you. The prophet Isaiah says: "He will not crush the weakest reed or put out a flickering candle. He will bring justice to all who have been wronged" (Isaiah 42:3).

The NIV puts it this way: "A bruised reed he will not break, and a smoldering wick he will not snuff out" (verse 3a) which means that if you are kind of obnoxious, like a smoky candle, His heart is not to blow you out, His heart is to help you burn brightly.

"Thank You, Lord, for never getting tired of me and for not getting frustrated with my failures. I want to burn brightly for You today. In Jesus' Name, Amen!"

3 February

"Of Benjamin he said, 'The beloved of the LORD dwells in safety. The High God surrounds him all day long, and dwells between his shoulders' " (Deuteronomy 33:12, ESV).

Today's verse gives us a wonderful picture of the kind of love God has for us: "About Benjamin he said: 'Let the beloved of the LORD rest secure in him, for he shields him all day long, and the one the LORD loves rests between his shoulders'" (NIV). Some Bible commentators have had a hard time accepting this verse for what it says. They try to explain it away, saying that the Hebrew word normally meaning "shoulders" or "shoulder blades" may mean something else like "weapons" or "hills!"

What Moses is saying is that Benjamin enjoys the Lord's special protection and love. "And the one the LORD loves rests between his shoulders" (literally, "he shall dwell between his shoulders"). The Lord is shown as carrying Benjamin on His back like a father carries his dearly-loved child!

What a fantastic place for each beloved child of God! How comforting and encouraging it is to think of dwelling safely on our Heavenly Father's shoulders, high above all that would threaten us! We are being carried on His shoulders like a father carries a child.

Make it your desire and your ambition to know more of the reality and the blessing of Benjamin's place and portion. Don't be satisfied with anything short of this kind of intimate place close to your Heavenly Father.

FEBRUARY 4

"Just as a father has compassion on his children, So the LORD has compassion on those who fear Him" (Psalm 103:13, NASB).

God delights in you! He is a loving Father. This is hard for some people to comprehend because they did not have a father who

loved them. Without a human example, such a child has a hard time seeing God as his or her Father.

But God is a Father who dearly loves us! The Bible gives us some insights into just how much our Heavenly Daddy loves us. The love of our Heavenly Daddy is not based on what we can do for Him, and it is not conditioned by our obedience. It is based on His love for us!

Look again at what Psalm 103:13 says: "Just as a father has compassion on his children, so the LORD has compassion on those who fear Him."

The NKJV translated this verse: "As a father pities..." Translators really don't know what to do with this because the Hebrew word is *racham*, which means, "to be soft toward, to handle or touch lovingly, to tenderly caress, to cuddle, or to snuggle or stroke."

Could it possibly be true? Does God love us like that? Yes, He does! Wow! What a picture of our Heavenly Father! He delights in us! He cares for us! He wants to take us into His arms and snuggle and love on us!

Think about the implications of this truth:
- God is my Father.
- God loves me and enjoys me.
- God wants 'to be soft toward' me.

5 FEBRUARY

"God the Father knew you and chose you long ago, and his Spirit has made you holy. As a result, you have obeyed him and

have been cleansed by the blood of Jesus Christ. May God give you more and more grace and peace" (1 Peter 1:2).

The truth that you are really loved by God is demonstrated by the fact that God has chosen you! Your salvation was initiated by God. We're not saved merely because we want to be; that is only part of the picture. The Bible also tells us we're saved because God wants us to be saved! What a wonderful thing to think about, God really wants you!

God, in love, chose you "before the foundation of the world..." (Ephesians 1:4, NASB). His choice of you was based on His foreknowledge (1 Peter 1:2a).

You may have overheard believers sometimes arguing over whether or not they're saved by their believing or by God's choosing. Rather than getting into that fruitless argument, believe both, because the Bible teaches both. We're saved both by God's choosing us and by our believing in the Lord Jesus Christ (1 Peter 1:1-2; Isaiah 55:1-3; 6-7; John 3:16; John 7:37-39; Isaiah 1:18; Matthew 11:28-30; Romans 10:9-13).

Evangelist D. L. Moody explained it well when he said that "Outside and over the door to salvation is a sign and as you approach the door you can see that it says, 'Whosoever will, let him take the water of life freely.' When you receive Jesus Christ as your Savior you walk through the door and above the door on the salvation side it reads: 'Chosen from before the foundation of the world.' "

grace today

6 FEBRUARY

"May the Lord direct your hearts into the love of God and into the steadfastness of Christ" (2 Thessalonians 3:5, NASB).

The word "direct" means "to guide," or "to direct completely." It's translated "to guide our feet into the way" in Luke 1:79, (NASB). This word means to open up the way by removing obstacles so that you can get to the place you want to go. In this case, into the love of God and the steadfastness of Christ.

The truth here is tremendous! This is saying the Lord is at work in our lives removing the obstacles and roadblocks that keep us from fully, completely resting, rejoicing and comprehending His love for us!

This could be translated, "May the Lord bring you into an ever-deeper understanding of the love of God and of the endurance of Christ."

Paul is clearly praying that the Lord will open up the way for each of us to directly enjoy and live in the knowledge of God's love for us. He's asking the Lord to remove the roadblocks that keep us from living in God's love.

What are some of the things that are blocking you from fully enjoying the love of God?

Let's ask the Lord to begin removing them right now: "Father, thank You for Your desire to move the things aside that are keeping me from knowing You better and serving You fully. Please move the roadblocks. In Jesus' Name, Amen!"

"God blesses those who mourn, for they will be comforted" (Matthew 5:4).

The NIV translates this verse: "Blessed are those who mourn, for they will be comforted."

There are nine different Greek words used to speak of sorrow in the New Testament, but the one Jesus chose to use is the strongest, the most intense. It speaks of the deepest, heart-wrenching grief and is generally only used for speaking about the death of a loved one. When we remember that the word "blessed" means "happy," we realize that Jesus is actually saying, "Happy are the sad!"

Jesus is talking about the kind of sadness that we have when we see our own spiritual poverty and are led to mourn over our condition. There is a genuine progression here. As we see the Lord high and lifted up, we see ourselves as we ought—nothing to be proud about! Remember what C. S. Lewis said, "The real test of being in the presence of God is that you either forget about yourself altogether, or you see yourself as a small dirty object." Spiritual poverty leads to godly sorrow; the poor in spirit become "those who mourn."

Whenever we come to the Lord with repentant hearts, mourning over our sin, we will leave comforted.

Those who come to the Lord with broken hearts will not leave with broken hearts. "The high and lofty one who lives in eternity, the Holy One, says this: 'I live in the high and holy place

Grace today

with those whose spirits are contrite and humble. I restore the crushed spirit of the humble and revive the courage of those with repentant hearts' " (Isaiah 57:15).

What might hinder you from entering into the happiness that God offers?
- Hanging onto known sin.
- Hiding your sin.
- Refusing God's comfort.

8 FEBRUARY

"Then Christ will make his home in your hearts as you trust in him. Your roots will grow down into God's love and keep you strong. And may you have the power to understand, as all God's people should, how wide, how long, how high, and how deep his love is. May you experience the love of Christ, though it is too great to understand fully. Then you will be made complete with all the fullness of life and power that comes from God" (Ephesians 3:17-19).

I'm praying that the Lord Jesus guides your heart into an ever-deeper understanding of His love. I like the way The Message puts it: "You'll be able to take in with all followers of Jesus the extravagant dimensions of Christ's love. Reach out and experience the breadth! Test its length! Plumb the depths! Rise to the heights! Live full lives, full in the fullness of God."
This kind of a grasp of God's love will:
- Maintain you – It will root you and ground you (Ephesians 3:17).

- Mature you – And you'll bear much fruit to God's glory! "When you produce much fruit, you are my true disciples. This brings great glory to my Father. 'I have loved you even as the Father has loved me. Remain in my love'" (John 15:8-9).
- Motivate you – To serve Christ like nothing else. "For the love of Christ controls and urges and impels us, because we are of the opinion and conviction that [if] One died for all, then all died" (2 Corinthians 5:14, AMP). The NIV says the love of Christ "compels" us.

Grasping God's love is a life-changing experience!

FEBRUARY 9

"He went out and cried and cried and cried" (Matthew 26:75, MSG).

Have you ever failed? I know it's a silly question, but what do you do when you fail? What's the biblical perspective on failure? Lots of Christians would say that the biblical perspective is simple: DON'T. But I see the Bible showing us that failure is a part of everyone's life. It gives us ways to meet defeat and overcome our mistakes.

Winston Churchill said, "Success is going from failure to failure without loss of enthusiasm." I think this could have been the Apostle Peter's motto. His life is not a model of constant victory, it's a model of what God can do with someone who knows how to meet defeat.

Peter's biggest failure, recorded for all eternity, is that he denied knowing Jesus at the hour of the Lord's greatest need. You can

read about this in Matthew 26:69-75. Someone else failed that same night. Judas betrayed Jesus to His enemies for thirty pieces of silver. Judas hung himself. Peter wept in repentance. Failure always has two options. We can either place our failures in the Lord's hands, or we can hold onto them and be paralyzed or even destroyed by them.

Ron Allen writes: "George Elliot said, 'Failure after a long perseverance is grander than never to have a striving good enough to be a failure.' Disaster is not the worst thing that could ever happen. On April 25, 1915, Australian and New Zealand soldiers landed on the beaches of the Gallipoli peninsula. It was part of a plan to storm Istanbul. The plan was misconceived. The troops had no hope. From atop the cliffs that rose sharply from the beach, the Turks mowed down the hapless allies with heavy machine gun fire. The campaign was sustained for months but was eventually aborted after 8,000 Australians had died. For a thinly populated country, this bloodbath was a major catastrophe. Yet, today, Australians celebrate the event. Not because it was a success, but because values of sacrifice and mateship were forged there. A young country saw in the valor and disciple of its defeated men, values to build a nation with."[5]

Only through the grace of Christ can we celebrate our defeats. Through His transforming power He can take our messes and turn them into masterpieces.

What you do with your failures and defeats is up to you. You can either see the hand of the Lord working through your failures, or you can step into despair. The choice is yours.

"So, if you think you are standing firm, be careful that you don't fall!" (1 Corinthians 10:12, NIV).

This verse is treated well in The Message: "Don't be so naive and self-confident. You're not exempt. You could fall flat on your face as easily as anyone else. Forget about self-confidence; it's useless. Cultivate God-confidence."

There are lots of things that can trip us up in our walk with the Lord. Never assume you're beyond falling. Here are some things to watch out for, using the acronym DEFEAT:

    D – Distraction – from the things of God.
    E – Entanglement – with the world.
    F – Forgetfulness – of what God has done for you.
    E – Entertainment – that tempts you and tears you down.
    A – Absence – from fellowship with God's people.
    T – Troubles – that won't go away.

These things spell defeat for many believers. Be alert today for any of these things that might trip you up. I'm praying for you!

"If he stumbles, he's not down for long; GOD has a grip on his hand" (Psalm 37:24, MSG).

Yesterday we talked about reasons for defeat in our lives. Today let me share with you how to meet defeat, because what you do when you fail is almost more important than what you do when you succeed. When you fail, refuse to be beat! We have the victory in Jesus!

grace today

Helpful ways to respond to DEFEAT:

   D – Dedication – delight yourself in the Lord.
   E – Examination – ask yourself what went wrong. What should you add to your walk with the Lord?
   F – Fear the Lord. Someday we are going to stand before the Lord. Walk like it.
   E – Endure hardship. God is working in your life in these rough times.
   A – Armor is essential. God has given you everything you need (Ephesians 6:10-18).
   T – Trust that God is still working in your life.

12 FEBRUARY

"God blesses those who hunger and thirst for justice, for they will be satisfied" (Matthew 5:6).

I'm used to the way the New American Standard Bible translates this verse: "Blessed are those who hunger and thirst for righteousness, for they shall be satisfied."

Whenever you see the word "righteousness" used this way, you could just about insert the word "Jesus" because He is "righteousness" personified. Your hunger and thirst for Jesus will always be satisfied.

E. M. Blaiklock tells of the incredible incident that occurred during the liberation of Palestine in World War I. The allied British, Australian, and New Zealand soldiers were closely pursuing the Turks as they retreated from the desert. As the allied troops moved northward past Beersheba, they began to outdistance their water-carrying camel train. When the

water ran out, their mouths got dry, their heads ached, and they became dizzy and faint; their eyes became bloodshot, their lips swelled and turned purple, and mirages became common.

They knew that if they did not make the well of Sheriah by nightfall, thousands of them would die—as hundreds already had done. Literally fighting for their lives, they managed to drive the Turks from Sheriah.

As water was distributed from the great stone cisterns, the more able-bodied were required to stand at attention and wait for the wounded and those who would take guard duty to drink first. It was four hours before the last man had his drink. During that time the men stood no more than twenty feet from thousands of gallons of water, to drink of which had been their consuming passion for many agonizing days. It is said that one of the officers who was present reported, "I believe that we all learned our first real Bible lesson on the march from Beersheba to Sheriah Wells. If such were our thirst for God, for righteousness and for His will in our lives, a consuming, all-embracing, preoccupying desire, how rich in the fruit of the spirit would we be!"[6]

"You're blessed when you've worked up a good appetite for God. He's food and drink in the best meal you'll ever eat" (MSG).

FEBRUARY 13

"God blesses those who are humble, for they will inherit the whole earth" (Matthew 5:5).

grace today

The NIV says, "Blessed are the meek, for they will inherit the earth."

For a lot of us this is a hard concept to swallow, because we equate meekness with weakness. We think that Jesus is saying, "Blessed are the doormats, for they shall inherit the earth!"

Jesus is not saying that! The whole idea of "meekness" or "gentleness" is all about tremendous strength. The word "meek" was used in Greek literature to speak of the breaking of a horse. That stallion was a powerful animal, but once it was broken, it's strength was under control.

This is so vital in a believer's life. The Book of Proverbs says: "Like a city that is broken into and without walls is a man who has no control over his spirit" (Proverbs 25:28, NASB). An unbroken animal is useless. So, strength, without control, is useless in the Christian life. In fact, it can be a real detriment to a godly life.

Meekness is the opposite of getting even or inflicting violence on someone. Biblical gentleness or meekness is power completely surrendered to God's control. We see this perfectly illustrated for us when Jesus was on the cross and His enemies were torturing and mocking Him. We know He had the power to vaporize them, but instead He prayed, "Father forgive them, for they do not know what they are doing."

You can be meek and still be strong; your strength is controlled by the Holy Spirit. You will inherit the earth!

"May the Lord lead your hearts into a full understanding and expression of the love of God and the patient endurance that comes from Christ" (2 Thessalonians 3:5).

The Bible tells us that the Lord is at work right now to clear the path so that you can enter into God's awesome love!

The only way we can live a satisfying and God-glorifying life is to allow the Lord to remove the things that keep us from knowing His love. Sometimes boulders of guilt, shame or feeling unworthy can be obstacles that keep us from fully resting and rejoicing in the love the Lord has for us.

You may be thinking, "I'm not worthy for God to love me." That's a huge roadblock, but you know what? God removes that by making His love for you unconditional. God's love for you can't be earned or deserved. God doesn't love you because of something you're doing, so He won't stop loving you if you stop doing something! He doesn't love you because you're so loveable. He loves you because HE is love.

Jesus died on the cross for the wrong things that you have done. His death was the just payment for those things. When we trust in Him, the guilt of our sin is removed and we have right standing before God.

"But now God has shown us a way to be made right with him without keeping the requirements of the law, as was promised in the writings of Moses and the prophets long ago. We are made right with God by placing our faith in Jesus Christ. And this is true for everyone who believes, no matter who we are. For everyone has sinned; we all fall short of God's glorious standard. Yet God, with undeserved kindness, declares that we

grace today

are righteous. He did this through Christ Jesus when he freed us from the penalty for our sins. For God presented Jesus as the sacrifice for sin. People are made right with God when they believe that Jesus sacrificed his life, shedding his blood. This sacrifice shows that God was being fair when he held back and did not punish those who sinned in times past... Can we boast, then, that we have done anything to be accepted by God? No, because our acquittal is not based on obeying the law. It is based on faith" (Romans 3:21-25; 27).

15 FEBRUARY

"God blesses those who are poor and realize their need for him, for the Kingdom of Heaven is theirs" (Matthew 5:3).

The word "blessed" means "happy." Happiness is the most sought after thing in the world! But people are looking for happiness in all the wrong places. Jesus indicates that happiness, real blessing, only comes from knowing Him. When we realize our need for Him and see that we're utterly bankrupt and broken spiritually, then the Lord opens up our eyes to see who He is and what He can do for us.

"Blessed are the poor in spirit, for theirs is the kingdom of heaven" (Matthew 5:3, NASB).

"This year, Lord, I want to get my eyes off of myself and onto You. I realize my need for You, and I ask that You show Yourself to me in a clear and poignant way. I want to live differently — dependently on You. In Jesus' Name, Amen!"

"You're blessed when you're at the end of your rope. With less of you there is more of God and his rule" (Matthew 5:3, MSG).

"God blesses those who work for peace, for they will be called the children of God" (Matthew 5:9).

You're a peacemaker when you promote peace, not only seeking to keep the peace, but desiring to bring other people into peace with each other. The great Bible translator, William Tyndale, translated this, "Blessed are the maintainers of peace." The happiest Christians are the reconcilers.

Psalm 120:6-7 says, "I am tired of living among people who hate peace. I search for peace; but when I speak of peace, they want war!"

Oswald Sanders said, "There is a world of difference between passively keeping peace and actively making peace. Jesus has in view not a passive virtue but a sacrificial activity."[7]

Generally, there is no peace without sacrifice. It took a cross for God to make peace with us, and often you'll find there's a cross involved when we make peace with each other. Peace always is purchased through sacrifice.

Sometimes we're called to lay down our lives, even to the point of allowing our peace to be broken, like Jesus allowed His peace to be broken to make peace with other people.

Though Romans 12:18 admonishes us, "Do all that you can to live in peace with everyone," we understand that even Jesus couldn't be at peace with everyone! Many found fault with Him and always will. It will be no different for you.

grace today

17 FEBRUARY

"God blesses those who are persecuted for doing right, for the Kingdom of Heaven is theirs. God blesses you when people mock you and persecute you and lie about you and say all sorts of evil things against you because you are my followers. Be happy about it! Be very glad! For a great reward awaits you in heaven. And remember, the ancient prophets were persecuted in the same way" (Matthew 5:10-12).

How can we be happy when we're being persecuted?

To the Lord's Jewish audience this must have been a very startling new concept because they had been taught that persecution was to be viewed as a curse from God. To be told that it could be a source of joy or happiness and even blessing must have been revolutionary!

In 2 Timothy 3:12 the Apostle Paul says, "Indeed, all who desire to live godly in Christ Jesus will be persecuted" (NASB). Jesus isn't asking us to enjoy the pain of persecution, but we are to be happy about the fruit that it bears in our lives.

Persecution teaches us to resist caving in to pressure to conform to this world's ways. Maybe you're being held back from following the Lord because you've been more concerned about what people think of you than what God thinks of you.

"Dear friends, don't be surprised at the fiery trials you are going through, as if something strange were happening to you. Instead, be very glad—for these trials make you partners with Christ in his suffering, so that you will have the wonderful joy of seeing his glory when it is revealed to all the world. So be happy when

you are insulted for being a Christian, for then the glorious Spirit of God rests upon you. If you suffer, however, it must not be for murder, stealing, making trouble, or prying into other people's affairs. But it is no shame to suffer for being a Christian. Praise God for the privilege of being called by his name!" (1 Peter 4:12-16).

FEBRUARY 18

"I will very gladly spend and be spent for your souls..." (2 Corinthians 12:15a, NKJV).

The Message puts it this way: "I'd be most happy to empty my pockets, even mortgage my life, for your good..."

Recently I read about Michelangelo, one of history's greatest sculptors and painters. His works are masterpieces of art and are priceless. Just about everyone's heard of Michelangelo, but have you ever heard of a man named Lorenzo? He discovered Michelangelo early on and took him into his home, treated him as a son, and coached him in the art.

I read that some consider Lorenzo's ability greater than Michelangelo's, but even if that were so, no one would have even known about Michelangelo if Lorenzo had not taken the time to pour his life and his knowledge and his passion for art into Michelangelo. Because of what he did, the whole world has been blessed![8]

19 FEBRUARY

"For God has not given us a spirit of fear and timidity..."
(2 Timothy 1:7a).

Preacher E. Stanley Jones said, "Fear is the sand in the machinery of life." When you think about it, the Apostle Paul and Timothy could have feared many things: persecution, not having enough money, critics, false teachers, or even dying all alone.

Though Paul and Timothy had many things that they might be frightened about, Paul takes his eyes off those things and places them on the Lord! I want to encourage you to do the same. In order to stand firm in spite of the difficulties and the fears we face, there are three weapons we can use to fight fear. Ralph Waldo Emerson said, "The wise man in the storm prays to God, not for safety from danger, but for deliverance from fear. It is the storm within which endangers him, not the storm without."

"For God has not given us a spirit of fear and timidity, but of power, love and self-discipline." The "spirit" (in verse 7) that God has given us is the Holy Spirit who will never generate fear in us. Tomorrow we will look at God's antidotes for fear!

20 FEBRUARY

Power, love, and discipline are God's antidotes for fear. The Holy Spirit will give you power so that you can stand in His strength and not your own. God's love casts out fear. "There is no fear in love; but perfect love casts out fear" (1 John 4:18a, NASB). The third spiritual weapon we're given to fight fear with is discipline, which speaks of self-control.

The antidote for fear is knowing God's love. Oswald Chambers said, "The remarkable thing about fearing God is that when you fear God, you fear nothing else, whereas if you do not fear God, you fear everything else."

"This is a wise, sane Christian faith: that a man commit himself, his life, and his hopes to God; that God undertakes the special protection of that man; that therefore that man ought not to be afraid of anything."[9]

Go forward today despite your fears. Songwriters Bill and Gloria Gaither express the confidence we have in God with the words:

Because He lives I can face tomorrow,
Because He lives all fear is gone;
Because I know He holds the future.
And life is worth the living just because He lives.

Love casts out fear. The only power that is strong enough to resist fear is the power of love!

The cure for fear is faith in God and in His Word and a realization that today, and every day, Jesus is always right beside you. You are not on your own!

F. B. Meyer said, "God incarnate is the end of fear; and the heart that realizes that he is in the midst... will be quiet in the midst of alarm."

"I waited patiently for the LORD to help me, and he turned to me and heard my cry. He lifted me out of the pit of despair, out of the mud and the mire. He set my feet on solid ground and

steadied me as I walked along. He has given me a new song to sing, a hymn of praise to our God. Many will see what he has done and be amazed. They will put their trust in the LORD" (Psalm 40:1-3).

21 FEBRUARY

"Make the LORD of Heaven's Armies holy in your life. He is the one you should fear. He is the one who should make you tremble" (Isaiah 8:13).

One of the main tactics our spiritual enemy, the devil, uses is fear. Often he will try to instill in us a fear of people. Here are some encouraging Scriptures I've gathered to share with you.

The fear of people:
- Isaiah 51:12-15 – "I, yes I, am the one who comforts you. So why are you afraid of mere humans, who wither like the grass and disappear? Yet you have forgotten the LORD, your Creator, the one who stretched out the sky like a canopy and laid the foundations of the earth. Will you remain in constant dread of human oppressors? Will you continue to fear the anger of your enemies? Where is their fury and anger now? It is gone! Soon all you captives will be released! Imprisonment, starvation, and death will not be your fate! For I am the LORD your God, who stirs up the sea, causing its waves to roar. My name is the LORD of Heaven's Armies."
- Psalm 118:6-8 – "The Lord is on my side; I will not fear. What can man do to me? The Lord is on my side and takes my part, He is among those who help me; therefore shall I see my desire established upon those who hate me. It

is better to trust and take refuge in the Lord than to put confidence in man" (AMP).

- Proverbs 29:25 – "The fear of man brings a snare, but whoever leans on, trusts in, and puts his confidence in the Lord is safe and set on high" (AMP). Here's how The Message paraphrases it: "The fear of human opinion disables; trusting in God protects you from that."

FEBRUARY 22

Today, let's look at some of the "fear nots" from the Bible:

- Isaiah 51:7 – "Listen to Me, you who know righteousness, a people in whose heart is My law; do not fear the reproach of man, nor be dismayed at their revilings" (NASB).
- Lamentations 3:57 – "You drew near when I called on You; You said, 'Do not fear!' " (NASB).
- Isaiah 59:19b – "When the enemy comes in like a flood, the Spirit of the LORD will lift up a standard against him" (NKJV).
- Isaiah 37:6 – "Don't be afraid because of words" (paraphrased).
- Isaiah 12:2b – "I will trust in him and not be afraid."
- Isaiah 44:8a – "Do not tremble; do not be afraid."
- Jeremiah 1:8 – "Do not be afraid of them" (paraphrased).
- Jeremiah 23:4b – "They will never be afraid again."
- Acts 27:24 – Jesus tells Paul not to be afraid.
- Hebrews 13:6 – "So we can say with confidence, 'The LORD is my helper, so I will have no fear. What can mere people do to me?' "

grace today

23 FEBRUARY

"For this reason I also suffer these things, but I am not ashamed; for I know whom I have believed and I am convinced that He is able to guard what I have entrusted to Him until that day" (2 Timothy 1:12, NASB).

A few years ago a survey showed that 45% of adults in America believe they have a responsibility to share their religious beliefs with those of other faiths. But only 3 in 10 had actually done so in that last year.[10]

The one thing the majority of the population fears the most is speaking in public. I think that's why some of us are afraid to speak up for Jesus!

I read a funny story about a Christian in the time of the Roman Empire who was thrown to a hungry lion in the coliseum. As the bloodthirsty spectators cheered on, the lion pounced on the Christian. But the Christian quickly whispered something in the lion's ear, and the huge beast backed away in terror. After this happened several times, the emperor sent a centurion to find out what magic spell could make a ferocious lion cower in fear. A few minutes later the guard returned and said, "The Christian told the lion, 'After dinner you'll be required to say a few words.' "

Don't be afraid to *talk* about Jesus. Think about what you're doing and the "ripple effect" it could have! You can be shaking like a leaf and still shake the world.

"Let the children come to me. Don't stop them! For the Kingdom of God belongs to those who are like these children" (Mark 10:14b).

Have you ever thought that your sharing the Gospel won't make any difference? I hope that you'll never see things the same after hearing this story I recently read.

A Sunday school teacher named Edward Kimball, like a lot of us, wasn't always sure his life had made much of a difference. But in 1858, he at least was able to lead a shoe clerk to Christ. The clerk, Dwight L. Moody, became an evangelist, and in 1879 Moody awakened an evangelistic zeal in the heart of F. B. Meyer, then the pastor of a small church in New England. Meyer, preaching on a college campus, won a student named J. Wilbur Chapman to Christ.

While Chapman was involved in YMCA work, he employed a former baseball player named Billy Sunday to help with evangelistic meetings. Sunday held a series of services in the Charlotte, North Carolina area, and a group of local men were so excited by the meetings that they planned another series of meetings. This time they brought preacher Mordecai F. Ham to town.

During one of his meetings, a young man named Billy Graham yielded his life to Christ. Since then, millions have heard the gospel through Graham's ministry. Kimball had started quite a ripple effect! You never know the ripple effect you're having for eternity!

grace today

A recent survey showed that the time to reach people for Jesus Christ is while they're still young:

Before age 6 – 6%
Ages 6-9 – 24%
Ages 10-12 – 26%
Ages 13-15 – 15%
Ages 16-19 – 10%
Age 20 and Older – 23%

The time to reach people for Jesus Christ is while they're still young. 75% come to Christ before they are 20! You can see how important it is to share the Gospel with everyone, especially with kids! Many thanks to the hundreds of you who are involved in Calvary's Children's Ministries and Student Ministries. Big reward is coming!

25 FEBRUARY

"For Christ's love compels us, because we are convinced that one died for all, and therefore all died. And he died for all, that those who live should no longer live for themselves but for him who died for them and was raised again" (2 Corinthians 5:14-15, NIV).

I like the way J. B. Phillips translates verse 14. He says, "The very spring of our actions is the love of Christ..."

D. L. Moody, America's foremost evangelist during the 19th century, also preached the Gospel powerfully in London and other cities of Great Britain 120 years ago. But some clergymen, who were jealous of this uneducated Yankee, wanted to know

his secret. So they knocked on the door of his hotel room and greeted him by saying, "Mr. Moody, we would like to have a word with you. You've come here to London, you have a sixth-grade education, you speak horrible English, your sermons are terribly simple, and yet thousands of people are converted. We want to know, how do you do it?"

Moody invited his guests into his room and walked over to a window. "Tell me," he said, "what do you see?" One gentleman looked out and said, "I see a park and some children playing." "Anything else?" Moody asked. Another man said, "I see about the same thing except there is an older couple walking hand in hand, enjoying the evening." A third clergyman added that he saw a young couple, and then he asked, "Mr. Moody, what do you see?"

As Moody stood there staring out the window, tears began to roll down his cheeks onto his gray beard.

"Mr. Moody, what are you looking at?" One of his curious guests asked. "What do you see?" "When I look out the window, I see countless thousands of souls that will one day spend eternity in hell if they do not find the Savior," Moody said. That was his secret.

Moody had compassion for those who did not know Jesus Christ. That compassion governed his life, and he gave his life over to evangelism to rescue people from hell.[11]

26 February

"Anyone who wants to live all out for Christ is in for a lot of trouble; there's no getting around it" (2 Timothy 3:12, MSG).

I was reading about William Booth, founder of the Salvation Army. The early Salvationists were greatly persecuted in London. When, with his early corps of workers, he began preaching in front of saloons and dens of vice, mobs of ruffians and drunks were instigated to disrupt and, if possible, stop the efforts. Booth and his workers often returned to their quarters with bloodied faces and rotten egg-spattered uniforms. But they kept right on.

The Religious Tract Society reported: In various places gangs sprung up "composed of the worst hooligans of the district, who, primed with drink, followed and brutally ill-treated the defenseless Salvationists. Magistrates withheld police protection. Salvationists were blamed, frequently sent to prison and fined, for breaches of the peace caused entirely by their enemies. Mocking detractors once pelted them with live coals or dead cats as they sang outside saloons. At least they were noticed. Today, Salvation Army officers complain of public apathy over their preaching."[12]

Thomas A Kempis (c.1380-1471) said, "It is preferable to have the whole world against you, than Jesus offended with you."

"Have mercy on me, O God, because of your unfailing love. Because of your great compassion, blot out the stain of my sins. Wash me clean from my guilt. Purify me from my sin" (Psalm 51:1-2).

"For God saved us and called us to live a holy life. He did this, not because we deserved it, but because that was his plan from before the beginning of time—to show us his grace through Christ Jesus. And now he has made all of this plain to us by the appearing of Christ Jesus, our Savior. He broke the power of death and illuminated the way to life and immortality through the Good News" (2 Timothy 1:9-10).

Jesus has broken the power of death! The Greek word for "broke" means "to abolish" or "to render idle, unemployed, inactive, inoperative" and "to make of none effect."

In John 11:25-26 Jesus comforted Martha whose brother had died with these words: "...I am the resurrection and the life. Anyone who believes in me will live, even after dying. Everyone who lives in me and believes in me will never ever die. Do you believe this, Martha?"

The Bible actually says that because of what Jesus has done for us, WE SHALL NOT SEE DEATH: "But I do not seek My glory; there is One who seeks and judges. Truly, truly, I say to you, if anyone keeps My word he will never see death" (John 8:50-51, NASB).

The word "see" in John 8:51 is *theoreo* and means "to look at with interest and attention." The dying believer has his interest and attention so fixed on the Lord Jesus and the glories of heaven, that the dark specter, death, is only on the periphery of his consciousness.

grace today

28 FEBRUARY

"...Our Savior Christ Jesus ...annulled death and made it of no effect and brought life and immortality (immunity from eternal death) to light through the Gospel" (2 Timothy 1:10b, AMP).

Out of the depth of his pain, Job exclaims, "But as for me, I know that my Redeemer lives, and that he will stand upon the earth at last. And after my body has decayed, yet in my body I will see God! I will see him for myself. Yes, I will see him with my own eyes. I am overwhelmed at the thought!" (Job 19:25-27).

The Bible says that Jesus has brought life and immortality to light (verse 10c). The Greek word, "brought to light" is *photizo* which means "to cause something to exist and thus come to light and become clear to all." "Immortality" speaks of incorruption and perpetuity.

When the great Christian and scientist Sir Michael Farady was dying, journalists questioned him about his speculations for a life after death. "Speculations!" he said, "I know nothing about speculations. I'm resting on certainties. 'I know that my redeemer lives,' and because He lives, I shall live also."

We are promised eternal life, an unending life through faith in Jesus. "But these have been written that you may believe that Jesus is the Christ, the Son of God; and that believing you may have life in His name" (John 20:31, NASB).

"Don't let the world around you squeeze you into its own mould, but let God re-mould your minds from within, so that you may prove in practice that the plan of God for you is good, meets all his demands and moves towards the goal of true maturity" (Romans 12:2, Phillips).

Just like today, the early believers felt a tremendous pressure to lay aside their convictions and conform to the world around them. Roman society was quite accepting of just about every religion. There were dozens of gods and goddesses, and scores of philosophies circulating and being accepted at the time. To be "open-minded" was considered a virtue. There were no firm convictions on what was right and what was wrong.

The only thing first century Rome had little time for was a group of people who claimed to have found the only way to God, and they were willing to sacrifice anything, even life itself for it! The early Christians were under definite pressure to let go of truth, but it was not up for grabs! Because they took a stand, we're standing today!

Years ago F. B. Meyer said, "Everywhere men are trying to win the smile of the world, and the 'well-done' of Christ."[13]

"Retain the standard of sound words which you have heard from me, in the faith and love which are in Christ Jesus. Guard, through the Holy Spirit who dwells in us, the treasure which has been entrusted to you" (2 Timothy 1:13-14, NASB).

We don't have to take the tactic of making the church as close to the world as we can, hoping to win the world, because those tactics won't work long-term. Whenever the church becomes insecure and intimidated by the culture surrounding her, she waffles on the truth and weakens.

History shows that after the church was legalized in the fourth century, it slowly took the tactic of accepting paganism into the church in order to win pagans. As the church marketed itself to the pagan world by trying to be like the pagan world, it did gain numbers, but it also became worldly and spiritually weak. There were more bodies in services, but hearts were not changed. Though spoken years ago, F. B. Meyer's words sound contemporary, "The Church which admits the world into its circle will find that it will get worldly quicker than the world will become Christian."[14]

If you're part of a Bible-teaching church that will boldly and clearly talk about the Good News of Jesus, stand by it and support it. The Holy Spirit is still writing chapters to the Book of Acts. Find where He's working and get into the flow of the Spirit.

3 MARCH

"As you know, all the Christians who came here from Asia have deserted me..." (2 Timothy 1:15a, TLB).

How many times have you been rejected? Perhaps even now you feel deserted and all alone. Paul was all alone in Nero's prison. Some of you may not be in a literal prison, but you find yourself in the prison of circumstances, with bars of trials.

Who hasn't ever been tempted to give up? Who hasn't ever been tempted to lose heart? If you have, you join the great company of those men and women who have served God, but encountered obstacles, sorrows and trouble, pain, persecution and trials. Join the company of Moses and David, Elijah, Isaiah and Jeremiah, and Paul. Discouragement comes to everyone.

Sometimes even when all you want to do is serve the Lord, all your friends desert you, or at least it seems that way. I was thinking of some of the things you may be experiencing right now, some very trying times:

- Times of illness.
- Times when you are all alone, separated from loved ones.
- Times when friends misunderstand you or your motives.
- Times when you're alienated from those you love.

In times like these, the Lord has promised us His comfort and strength. The Apostle Paul experienced God's special comfort. He says, "God... comforts the depressed" (2 Corinthians 7:6, NASB).

MARCH 4

Jesus knows what it's like to be deserted. The experience of being "left" or "deserted" happened repeatedly in His ministry. At one point in His ministry the Bible says that "...many of His disciples withdrew and were not walking with Him anymore" (John 6:66, NASB). Jesus experienced desertion and a friend's betrayal.

Because Jesus knows what it's like to be deserted and left alone, His words take on a special force when He says, "...I will never leave you nor forsake you" (Hebrews 13:5, ESV).

grace today

I think the way the Amplified Version translates this verse is awesome: "...I will not in any way fail you nor give you up nor leave you without support. [I will] not, [I will] not, [I will] not in any degree leave you helpless nor forsake nor let [you] down (relax My hold on you)! [Assuredly not!]"

This gives us confidence and security; look at the next verse: "So that we confidently say, 'The Lord is my helper; I will not fear; what can man do to me?' " (verse 6, ESV).

5 MARCH

"...I will be with you; I will not fail you or forsake you" (Joshua 1:5b).

The Lord encouraged the governor of Judah and the High Priest of Israel through the prophet Haggai, saying: "...take courage, ...take courage, ...take courage, and work; for I am with you" (Haggai 2:4b).

Jesus gives us the encouragement of His presence. "...I am with you always, even to the end of the age" (Matthew 28:20b).

When David Livingstone returned to his homeland of Scotland after 16 very difficult years as a missionary in Africa, he was one very weak and sick man. During those years of service his body was emaciated by the effects of 27 fevers. One arm hung useless at his side, the result of being mangled by a lion.

He was speaking to the students at Glasgow University and the core of his message to the young men and women gathered there was this: "Shall I tell you what sustained me during the hardship

and loneliness of my exile? It was Christ's promise, 'Lo, I am with you always, even unto the end.' "[15]

This promise is ours as well!

MARCH 6

"The Lord is on my side; I will not fear. What can man do to me?" (Psalm 118:6, AMP).

David is saying, "The Lord is on my side; I will not fear. What can man do to me?" Let me share what protestant reformer, Martin Luther, said of this Psalm in 1512:

> This is my psalm, my chosen psalm. I love them all; I love all Holy Scripture, which is my consolation and my life. But this Psalm is nearest my heart, and I have a familiar right to call my own. It has saved me from many a pressing danger, from which nor emperor, nor kings, nor sages, nor saints could have saved me. It is my friend; dearer to me than all the honors and power of the earth.[16]

In Deuteronomy 31:8, Moses told Joshua, "The LORD is the one who goes ahead of you; He will be with you. He will not fail you or forsake you. Do not fear or be dismayed" (NASB).

Here are some special promises for you:
- "And the LORD replied, 'I will personally go with you, Moses, and I will give you rest—everything will be fine for you' " (Exodus 33:14).
- "The LORD will work out his plans for my life—for your faithful love, O LORD, endures forever" (Psalm 138:8).

Grace today

- "Never doubt in the darkness what God has shown you in the light."[17]
- "That Your beloved may be delivered, save with Your right hand, and hear me" (Psalm 60:5, NKJV).

7 MARCH

"In a wealthy home some utensils are made of gold and silver, and some are made of wood and clay. The expensive utensils are used for special occasions, and the cheap ones are for everyday use. If you keep yourself pure, you will be a special utensil for honorable use. Your life will be clean, and you will be ready for the Master to use you for every good work" (2 Timothy 2:20-21).

What's your destiny? I read how Lloyd's of London followed 100,000 paper clips and found that only about 2,000 were used to hold papers together. The bank said 14,163 clips were bent and twisted during telephone conversations. Another 19,143 were used as chips in card games. Another 7,200 were used to clip together clothing. Another 5,434 became toothpicks or ear scratchers. Another 5,308 were converted into nail cleaners. Another 3,916 cleaned pipes. The rest fell ingloriously to the floor and were swept away.[18]

How could such an ingenious invention, and so useful, be so misused and wasted? Maybe that's the question Paul has on his mind as he pens this message to Timothy.

"Why do people waste their lives when they have been created with so much eternal potential?"

What do you want to *be* for the Lord? What do you want to *do*

for the Lord? A paper plate, a Styrofoam plate, a paper cup? Or do you want to be a piece of fine china, ready to be used in the honored, sacred service of the Lord!

Something pretty important the Lord is saying here is that we have the power to choose what we're going to be. Paul doesn't say that some are predestined to dishonor. He says that "If you keep yourself pure, you will be a special utensil for honorable use."

MARCH 8

"Because we have these promises, dear friends, let us cleanse ourselves from everything that can defile our body or spirit. And let us work toward complete holiness because we fear God" (2 Corinthians 7:1).

What's your "DASH"? Do you know?

Let me tell you what I'm talking about. In a cemetery most gravestones have a date when the person was born and a date when he or she died. In between those two dates is a dash. That dash represents what that person did with his or her life.

What is your dash? Going to school? Getting married? Is it working? Perhaps retiring? Friends?

Will your dash count for eternity? Will you make a mark that is eternal?

Someone I know thought about writing out their obituary. It really made them think about what their priorities were and how they were spending their life. It might not be a bad exercise.

I want your dash to be a life well-spent for Jesus!

grace today

9 MARCH

"Joyful are people of integrity, who follow the instructions of the Lord" (Psalm 119:1).

Reproductions, they are everywhere! It's kind of nice in many ways. You can get copies of just about anything. You can buy a copy of a Monet masterpiece on canvas for under $100. You can buy cloned Rolexes and "engineered" marble and granite-like countertops. For years we have seen furniture covered with thin veneers of wood or paper made to look like wood. "Leather-like," "marble-like," "gold-tone," "silver-tone," "created stone," and "faux" have become words that we use all the time to describe the stuff we surround ourselves with. How often have you told a friend, "It looks just as good as the real thing!"

It's fine to cut corners in many areas of life and enjoy the creative efforts of some to make cheap copies of real things. But real spiritual life can't be faux or made into a cheap veneer. There can never be a "faux-Christian." There's no such thing as "Christian-tone," or "Christian-like." A Christian is either real or not real. Authentic Christianity is 100 percent Christian through and through. Live an authentic life for Jesus everywhere you go. Live that authentic life at home, at school, in your workplace, and yes, even on the freeways! Live that authentic life even when no one is watching (see 1 Peter 3:12).

10 MARCH

"Run from anything that stimulates youthful lusts. Instead, pursue righteous living, faithfulness, love, and peace. Enjoy the companionship of those who call on the Lord with pure hearts" (2 Timothy 2:22).

This is nearly identical to what Paul had written Timothy in his first letter: "But flee from these things, you man of God, and pursue righteousness, godliness, faith, love, perseverance and gentleness" (1 Timothy 6:11, NASB).

This word, pursue, has the strong meaning of quickly, determinedly, running after something. It means to hotly pursue something; to seek eagerly and earnestly.

The application of the truth here is that we do not stop intensely pursuing our goal until we've achieved it! We don't ever give up until we've reached the goal!

There are four things we're called to pursue:
1. Righteousness – There's an old Latin proverb that says "God takes notice of clean hands, not full hands." Pursue righteousness.
2. Faith – Notice he doesn't say, "Analyze your faith," "Measure your faith," "Exercise your faith." He simply says, "Pursue faith." Faith's virtue is in its OBJECT! Live by this motto: "I will not allow what I do know to be shaken and disturbed by what I do not know."
3. Love – See 1 Peter 3:8.
4. Peace – We're not just to desire peace, but as believers we are to actively pursue it. We're to go after it (1 Peter 3:11, Hebrews 12:14).

Thomas A Kempis said, "All men desire peace, but very few desire those things that make for peace."

11 MARCH

"Carrying the cross by himself, he went to the place called Place of the Skull (in Hebrew, Golgotha). There they nailed him to the cross. Two others were crucified with him, one on either side, with Jesus between them" (John 19:17-18).

The cross, what makes it so special?

At one time in AD 70 during the Jewish revolt, just before the conquest of Jerusalem and the destruction of the second Jewish Temple, the Romans were crucifying about 500 people a day on the Mount of Olives, outside of Jerusalem. They finally ran out of wood and space. The Jewish historian Josephus says that the Romans crucified half the Jewish population of Jerusalem.

People ask, "So why was the crucifixion of Jesus so historically significant?" This kind of execution, in a minor Roman province, might have been nothing more than a cruel, commonplace event. Instead, it became the turning point of human history!

You can't fully understand Jesus' life apart from His death. In fact, to really understand Jesus' life, you have to first begin with His death. It's not until we look at Jesus' suffering and death that we begin to understand what Jesus' life is all about.

"God proved his love on the cross. When Christ hung, and bled, and died it was God saying to the world—I love you" (Billy Graham).

"A servant of the Lord..." (2 Timothy 2:24a).

Albert Schweitzer said, "I don't know what your destiny will be, but one thing I know; the only ones among you who will be really happy are those who have sought and found how to serve."

It's significant that Paul uses a term in our text that actually means, "bond-servant." This is a term with a rich background and full of meaning. It signifies a certain kind of slavery that was unique in the ancient world. Some people were born slaves. Others became slaves because they were captured in war or were sold into slavery because of debt. But, a bond-servant was a slave because of love (Exodus 21:2-6). A bond-servant served because, as Exodus says, "he loved his master."

The use of the analogy of us being Jesus' bond-servants is used repeatedly in the New Testament. We are not serving God out of fear, or for what we can get out of it. We're serving God for the sake of love!

> Because I love You
> I will serve You
> Because I love You
> I'll do Your will
> I will worship and praise You
> All of my days
> I will because I love You
>
> I will keep Thy commandments
> Unto others good things shall I do
> I will pray and be faithful to Your house
> I will because I love You[19]

grace today

13 MARCH

I read that at Taylor University when graduates walk by to get
their diplomas, they walk by a man who gives them a towel.
Warren Wiersbe said, "Serving God isn't punishment; it's
nourishment." Jesus said, "My food...is to do the will of Him
who sent Me, and to finish His work" (John 4:34, NIV).

This verse is so good! Let me share it with you from a couple of
translations:

- "...My nourishment comes from doing the will of God,
  who sent me, and from finishing his work."
- "...My food (nourishment) is to do the will (pleasure) of
  Him Who sent Me and to accomplish and completely
  finish His work" (AMP).
- "...The food that keeps me going is that I do the will of the
  One who sent me, finishing the work he started" (MSG).

14 MARCH

"I thank Christ Jesus our Lord, who has strengthened me,
because He considered me faithful, putting me into service"
(1 Timothy 1:12, NASB).

I read a great illustration of faithfulness recently.

As the ancient city of Pompeii had been excavated, they found
an interesting thing. The volcanic ash preserved the form of
many of the people who were in the city. Many of them were
found fleeing the city as Mt. Vesuvius was erupting. The hot soot
and the poisonous gases overcame these people and they were
actually encased in a volcanic cast.

Amidst the remains there have been many very interesting and touching findings. But one bears special significance here. A Roman sentinel who was guarding the city was found at the city gate right where he'd been placed by his captain. He refused to desert his post even though it seemed as though the world was coming to an end. Through cinders and ash, he remained faithfully at his post; and that's where he was found by archeologists 1000 years later!

Now, if you're serving the Lord in children's ministry, no one's expecting you to stand still and be burned to ashes by a bunch of hyperactive four to five year olds, but you are expected to be trustworthy and dependable.

This applies to wherever you serve the Lord!

MARCH 15

"But Jesus called them together and said, 'You know that the rulers in this world lord it over their people, and officials flaunt their authority over those under them. But among you it will be different. Whoever wants to be a leader among you must be your servant, and whoever wants to be first among you must become your slave. For even the Son of Man came not to be served but to serve others and to give his life as a ransom for many'" (Matthew 20:25-28).

D. L. Moody once said, "The measure of a man is not how many servants he has, but how many men he serves."

One pastor put it so well:

> A servant is one who accepts a position, task, or role that allows him to meet the needs of other people. A true servant must be willing to accept a position that others may consider to be beneath them.
>
> These kinds of servants are the ones who work in the nursery or teach Sunday school. They cook the food for a high school banquet or provide transportation for the elderly. They disciple new believers, set up the coffee or sound system, or put away chairs. They pick up after their children, make copies for a coworker, or help their neighbor mow the lawn. They are willing to accept any task, no matter how lowly, if it is an opportunity to minister to others.[20]

Let's join Jesus in serving His people!

16 MARCH

"You should know this, Timothy, that in the last days there will be very difficult times" (2 Timothy 3:1).

The Apostle Paul is saying, "Listen my child in the faith, and those who follow Jesus as His disciples, there are no easy days ahead! Mark my words, terrible, trying, difficult times are coming." Paul wanted to emphasize to Timothy that opposition to the truth is not a passing situation, but a permanent characteristic of this age!

Desperate times are predicted in the last days. And over the past 2,000 years many difficult times have come for the Church of

Jesus Christ. Jesus said, "I will build My church; and the gates of Hades will not overpower it" (Matthew 16:18, NASB). That implies the enemy will resist and attack Jesus' Church.

Though we read some very sobering things, know this: God is in control. None of this is catching God by surprise. Our comfort in the last days is that we know the ending. It's like going to a movie, but you've already read the book! You know the script; knowing how it ends can get you through some very scary times.

God doesn't want us living in fear. He wants us to live in faith and to be bold and courageous! When asked how she handled difficulty, Corrie Ten Boom replied, "Well, at first I try to walk past it. If that does not help, I try to climb over it; and when I cannot climb over it, to crawl underneath. And when that is not possible I go straight through—God and I!"[21]

MARCH 17

"For people will love only themselves and their money..." (2 Timothy 3:2a).

One of the ways we see how attached we are to our money is by asking ourselves: "Who or what do we put first?"

I heard a story told over the radio about a man who was being encouraged by his pastor to begin giving to the Lord. The pastor assured the man that the Lord had promised to bless those who give to Him. They talked a little bit more and then the pastor went on to say, "I will personally guarantee you that if you give to the Lord and then at the end of the month have a shortage of funds, I will make it up for you, whatever the amount! I just

want you to step out and do what the Lord says and experience His blessings."

The man agreed. Then the pastor said, "Do you realize what you've just done? You are going to give to God because I, a man with limited resources, a man who could die today, a man who might not even keep his promises, have promised to make up any shortfall for you. Yet, God has promised in His Word to bless those who give to Him!"

One way to combat greediness and selfishness is to give to God! Not just what you have left over, but give God the first of what you earn. Put Him at the top of your budget.

18 MARCH

"...Malicious gossips..." (2 Timothy 3:3b, NASB).

Paul says the end time world will be filled with malicious gossips. Watch out for gossips today. The Greek word for gossip is *diaboloi*, which literally means "devils," "slanderers!"

Writer William Wilderson once said the anatomy of any organization includes different kinds of "bones." Wishbones who wish someone else would do the work; Knucklebones who knock what everyone else does; Backbones who actually do the work; and Jawbones who talk incessantly, but do little else. Gossips fall into this last category.

A Gossip usually doesn't think he or she is a gossip and likes to makes a mountain out of a mole hill by adding some dirt.

They say that hell for Gossips is a place where people are forced to mind their own business! Have you ever noticed how difficult it is for Gossips to do just that?

MARCH 19

"Lead me by your truth and teach me, for you are the God who saves me" (Psalm 25:5a).

Einstein was once traveling from Princeton on a train when the conductor came down the aisle, punching the tickets of each passenger. When he came to Einstein, Einstein reached in his vest pocket. He couldn't find his ticket, so he reached in his other pocket. It wasn't there, so he looked in his briefcase, but couldn't find it. Then he looked in the seat by him. He couldn't find it. The conductor said, "Dr. Einstein, I know who you are. We all know who you are. I'm sure you bought a ticket. Don't worry about it." Einstein nodded appreciatively.

The conductor continued down the aisle punching tickets. As he was ready to move to the next car, he turned around and saw the great physicist on his hands and knees looking under his seat for his ticket. The conductor rushed back. "Dr. Einstein, don't worry," he said. "I know who you are. No problem. You don't need a ticket. I'm sure you bought one."

Einstein said, "Young man, I too know who I am. What I don't know is where I'm going."

Can you say, "I know who I am and I know where I'm going?"

Jesus said, "I am the way, the truth, and the life. No one can come to the Father except through me" (John 14:6).

grace today

20 MARCH

"Therefore be patient, brethren, until the coming of the Lord...
You too be patient; strengthen your hearts, for the coming of the
Lord is near" (James 5:7a, 8, NASB).

Do you ever feel like God isn't working fast enough in your life?
Believe me, you're not the first to feel this way! The great New
England preacher Phillips Brooks was noted for his poise and
quiet manner. At times, however, even *he* suffered moments of
frustration and irritability. One day a friend saw him feverishly
pacing the floor like a caged lion. "What's the trouble, Mr.
Brooks?" he asked. "The trouble is that I'm in a hurry, but God
isn't!"[22]

Every Christian I know has felt this way! The Bible exhorts us
to be patient and allow the Lord to work in our lives, on His
schedule. "Friends, when life gets really difficult, don't jump
to the conclusion that God isn't on the job. Instead, be glad that
you are in the very thick of what Christ experienced. This is a
spiritual refining process, with glory just around the corner"
(1 Peter 4:12-13, MSG).

I know the Lord is speaking in a special way to your heart today.
Trust Him, He is in control!

21 MARCH

The Lord Jesus told His disciples that "...They ought to pray and
not to lose heart..." (Luke 18:1b, NASB).

Throughout the years many people have shared with me the frustration they've felt with unanswered prayer:

- "What's the use of praying? I pray, but my prayers are never answered."
- "My prayers don't seem to get higher than the ceiling."
- "I feel like my prayers aren't on target..."

We'll pray more when we see our prayers are being answered, and our prayers will be answered when they are offered in a way that they hit the target.

Prayer hits the target when we pray "in fellowship" with God.

Jesus said: "If you abide in Me, and My words abide in you, ask whatever you wish, and it will be done for you" (John 15:7, NASB). This is living in dependence on God, living like there is a God.

The Apostle James says that many Christians forget to ask God for simple things: "You do not have because you do not ask" (James 4:2b, NASB).

R. A. Torrey said, "Prayer is the hand that takes to ourselves the blessings that God has already provided in His Son."

But in Psalm 66:18 David says: "If I regard wickedness in my heart, the Lord will not hear" (NASB).

Basically this is saying, "If I have not confessed the sin in my heart, the Lord will not listen..." The Lord is saying we can't go any farther until we get things straightened out here.

grace today

22 MARCH

The Lord Jesus told His disciples that "...They ought to pray and not to lose heart..." (Luke 18:1b, NASB).

As Jesus' disciples we desire to pray and not lose heart, and we will do this more and more as our prayers hit the target.

Yesterday, we saw that our prayers do hit the target when we pray "in fellowship" with God.

Today, we see that prayer also hits the target when we "ask in faith."

James 1:6-8 makes it clear that coming to God, with trust in God, is very important in prayer:

> "But when you ask him, be sure that your faith is in God alone. Do not waver, for a person with divided loyalty is as unsettled as a wave of the sea that is blown and tossed by the wind. Such people should not expect to receive anything from the Lord. Their loyalty is divided between God and the world, and they are unstable in everything they do."

Notice also that faith implies a persistence:

> "Keep on asking, and you will receive what you ask for. Keep on seeking, and you will find. Keep on knocking, and the door will be opened to you" (Matthew 7:7).

I was encouraged to continue to pray when I realized:

> "Prayer is not overcoming God's reluctance; it is laying hold of God's willingness" (Martin Luther).

The Lord Jesus told His disciples that "...They ought to pray and not to lose heart..." (Luke 18:1b, NASB).

This sure sounds like effective prayer. But how can my prayers be effective? Our prayers hit the target when we:
- Pray in fellowship with God.
- Ask in faith.
- Pray God's will.

What really revolutionized my prayer life was when I realized the purpose of prayer.

I'd always been taught to believe that the purpose of prayer was to tell God what I needed or wanted and try to convince Him to do it.

But the purpose of prayer is not to get MY will done, it's to get God's will done. When Jesus taught His disciples to pray, He said to pray this way: "...Our Father who is in heaven, Hallowed (Holy) be Your name. Your kingdom come. Your will be done, on earth as it is in heaven" (Matthew 6:9-10, NASB).

God will always bless His will!

Listen, God always answers prayers. Just not the way we might expect. He answers prayers:
- "Yes"
- "No"
- "Wait"
- And sometimes, "You've got to be kidding!"

grace today

But we do have such a special promise from God about our prayers found in I John 5:14: "This is the confidence which we have before Him, that, if we ask anything according to His will, He hears us"(NASB).

I like reading this from the New Living Translation; "And we are confident that he hears us whenever we ask for anything that pleases him."

24 MARCH

"I am bent over and racked with pain. All day long I walk around filled with grief" (Psalm 38:6).

Pain is a pain. You're well acquainted with pain. It can be a very troublesome companion. The Bible tells us that we can counter pain with praise music.

"Don't be drunk with wine, because that will ruin your life. Instead, be filled with the Holy Spirit, singing psalms and hymns and spiritual songs among yourselves, and making music to the Lord in your hearts. And give thanks for everything to God the Father in the name of our Lord Jesus Christ" (Ephesians 5:18-20).

"Sing psalms and hymns and spiritual songs to God with thankful hearts" (Colossians 3:16b).

It's interesting that recent research suggests that music reduces pain! "Sixty-six elderly arthritis patients took part in a study recently reported in the Journal of Advanced Nursing. Half of the participants sat quietly and listened to twenty minutes of

Mozart tunes each day for two weeks. The other half just sat quietly, or read something, for the same period of time. Those in the music group experienced steadily decreasing pain scores over the 14 days, while those in the control group did not."[23]

If listening to Mozart can help ease arthritis pain, what do you think praise music could do for you? Why don't you try adding some praise songs to other pain-management techniques you employ?

"For you are my hiding place; you protect me from trouble. You surround me with songs of victory" (Psalm 32:7).

MARCH 25

"The godly walk with integrity; blessed are their children who follow them" (Proverbs 20:7).

Just a few years ago a national survey of high school students revealed that they want character in leaders, but they have a really difficult time finding role models in public figures. Here's what the survey, reported in *USA Today*, showed:

> ...High school students (in order of preference) want a leader who cares about average people (33%), is consistent in his or her beliefs (30%), has strong leadership skills and career experience (29%) and has high ethical values (22%), as well as being a good communicator (22%). But a majority of students could not name a single public figure—in government or outside it—with such qualities.[24]

Dad, mom, grandma, grandpa, you're being watched by a couple of generations who are looking for role models and heroes. We can't let them down!

The great Bible teacher Henrietta C. Mears said, "Your influence is negative or positive, never neutral."

26 March

"Run from anything that stimulates youthful lusts..."
(2 Timothy 2:22a).

When we allow the Lord to clean up our lives then we'll be ready for the Master to use us for every good work. We'll be utensils or instruments "...for honor, sanctified, useful to the Master, prepared for every good work" (2 Timothy 2:21, NASB).

You know what? That's what I want to be! I want to be a vessel God can use for His purpose! I want to be ready for the Master to use at any moment!

Paul gives the practical command in verse 22: "Run from anything that stimulates youthful lusts." This is talking about a continuous action as a habit of life.

Are there things in your life that stir up lust? Maybe the TV programs you watch or the places you go online? Do you read books or magazines that cause you to stumble? Sometimes the people we're hanging out with cause us to stumble into lust. The Bible says to continually run from anything that stimulates youthful lust.

MARCH 27

"All you who fear the LORD, trust the LORD! He is your helper and your shield" (Psalm 115:11).

It was pioneer missionary to China, J. Hudson Taylor, who said "God's work, done in God's way, will never lack God's supply." I think of the encouragement this is to us as we do God's work together and trust Him for provision.

Sometimes we get our work confused with God's work. What I mean is, we can be convinced something is God's will when it isn't. You've experienced the disappointment of discovering that you had plans that God didn't have! I've watched people get bitter and upset with God during those times. I've also seen many who have bowed to God's will, and the Lord has led them on to some very special places.

"God gives His very best to those who leave the choice with Him" (J. Hudson Taylor).

MARCH 28

"Yes, even when I am old and gray-headed, O God, forsake me not, [but keep me alive] until I have declared Your mighty strength to [this] generation, and Your might and power to all that are to come" (Psalm 71:18, AMP).

A lot of people figure that if they retire they can't do much for the Lord. "I can't learn as well as I used to." "I forget a lot of things." "I don't have the energy I used to." Of course all of these things can be true, but don't sell yourself short. God used a lot of

grace today

men and women who were above the age of retirement! Help me remember some of them:

- Abraham
- Sarah
- Moses
- Caleb
- Joshua
- Anna

I can't remember all of them, but the Lord can still use me!

Arthur Morgan said, "Preparation for old age should begin not later than one's teens. A life which is empty of purpose until sixty-five will not suddenly become filled on retirement."

29 MARCH

"Don't let anyone think less of you because you are young. Be an example to all believers in what you say, in the way you live, in your love, your faith, and your purity" (1 Timothy 4:12).

"Joash was seven years old when he became king" (2 Kings 11:21).

"Uzziah son of Amaziah began to rule over Judah... He was sixteen years old when he became king, and he reigned in Jerusalem fifty-two years..." (2 Kings 15:1-2).

"Josiah was eight years old when he became king, and he reigned in Jerusalem thirty-one years..." (2 Kings 22:1).

"So Jehoshaphat ruled over the land of Judah. He was thirty-five

years old when he became king, and he reigned in Jerusalem twenty-five years..." (2 Chronicles 20:31).

Isaac was in his twenties when He submitted to the test of faith on Mount Moriah.

Joseph was in his twenties when the Lord used Him to deliver His people.

Obviously, the Lord calls people to serve Him and uses people who are young! My earliest memory is sitting in church and reading Jeremiah 1:4-10 and thinking that the Lord was calling me to serve Him! If you are young and have a sense of God's call for ministry, missions, or some other specific kingdom calling, pursue it! You will always be glad you did. Do everything you can to prepare yourself now for what the Lord is going to do in, with, and through your life.

MARCH 30

"Do not gloat over me, my enemies! For though I fall, I will rise again. Though I sit in darkness, the LORD will be my light" (Micah 7:8).

Erwin Lutzer, pastor of Moody Bible Church in Chicago, once said, "Failure is the backdoor to success." If we were to fill out a survey and were asked, "Have you ever failed?" You and I would have to check "yes." There's no way around it. Life is filled with failure.

Think about failure every time you shop at Macy's. R. H. Macy failed seven times before his store in New York City caught on.

grace today

As you struggle in high school or college, think about Thomas Edison. He was thrown out of school in his early grades because his teachers believed he couldn't do the work.

Next time you strike out think about Babe Ruth, who, though he hit 714 home runs, struck out 1,330 times!

Peter failed big time. But Jesus wouldn't let him stop there. Jesus made special efforts to restore and encourage Peter; and the Lord's work through Peter went on to change the course of history and your life. Think about it: a failure named Peter preached the first message that ultimately brought the Good News of the Gospel to you!

Chuck Swindoll writes, "Great accomplishments are often attempted but only occasionally reached. Those who reach them are usually those who missed many times before. Failures are only temporary tests to prepare us for permanent triumphs."

31 MARCH

"But Caleb tried to quiet the people as they stood before Moses. 'Let's go at once to take the land,' he said. 'We can certainly conquer it!' But the other men who had explored the land with him disagreed. 'We can't go up against them! They are stronger than we are!' So they spread this bad report about the land among the Israelites: 'The land we traveled through and explored will devour anyone who goes to live there. All the people we saw were huge. We even saw giants there, the descendants of Anak. Next to them we felt like grasshoppers, and that's what they thought, too!' " (Numbers 13:30-33).

The "grasshopper complex" is contagious! Watch out, people are catching it everywhere!

Paul Harvey told the story of the most remarkable knight in the court of King Charles I; His name was Sir Jeffrey Hudson. Hudson has been immortalized in the art and literature of the 17th century. He was not merely a legend; his deeds of valor, his life of adventure and romance are a matter of historical fact!

From a very early age, Jeffrey Hudson was destined to royal favor. When he was only nine years old he entered the service of the Duke and Duchess of Buckingham. He was trained there and was later presented to the King and Queen of England.

When he was eleven years old he was accepted into the British diplomatic service. His first mission involved a trip to France; the return voyage was interrupted by pirates! The bravery he demonstrated throughout that attack would typify him in later years. His life of adventure was just beginning!

When he was still in his teens, reports of his courage spread, and at the age of nineteen Jeffrey was welcomed in his homeland as a hero. He was knighted Sir Jeffrey Hudson. The ladies of the royal court fought for his attention. A book was written about him!

Sir Jeffrey became a captain in the King's army and fought bravely against the Puritans who were seeking to overthrow Charles I. When Charles was ousted, he escaped with the Queen to France. From that time until the day he died, he experienced an incredible succession of exploits: Duels to the death, unjust imprisonment and escape, world travel, battles with pirates, and slavery among the Turks.

grace today

At thirty-nine he returned to England and the friendly court of Charles II. For seven years he maintained his reputation as a gallant knight before retiring to the quiet life of a country squire.

We'll see the "rest of the story" tomorrow...

Continued from yesterday's reading...

But retirement was too quiet for this guy! So, in 1679, at the age of sixty, he left the comfort of his country home and pension to join the secret service of the King.

Sir Jeffrey encountered many perils, but there was one time when he narrowly escaped with his life. While he had easily survived battle on land and sea, one day, in a very embarrassing way, Sir Jeffrey nearly drowned in the washbasin!

How could this be? The reason is found in the portraits we have of him that survive to this day. Portraits of Sir Jeffrey and the Queen hang in Hampton Court to this day. And his clothing has been preserved in the Ashmolean Museum in Oxford.

How could he almost drown in the washbasin? Well, the courageous Sir Jeffrey Hudson, the Knight who was one of the bravest, brightest, and most famous heroes of the seventeenth century, this incredible soldier, this valiant warrior, Sir Jeffrey Hudson, in his stocking feet was only eighteen inches tall![25]

Now, what if Hudson had succumbed to a "grasshopper complex" generated by comparing himself with other people? What if he had lived in constant fear? Instead, he lived life boldly, courageously and fearlessly. He did things no one would have ever expected him to do.

Maybe you've been measuring yourself by the wrong standard. One person, with the Lord on his or her side, is mightier than a thousand without the Lord's help!

grace today

"Through God we will do valiantly, and it is He who shall tread down our adversaries" (Psalm 108:13, NASB).

2 APRIL

"As we pray to our God and Father about you, we think of your faithful work, your loving deeds, and the enduring hope you have because of our Lord Jesus Christ" (1 Thessalonians 1:3).

Fifty years ago Winston Churchill asked a young minister, "Young man, can you give me any hope?"

Lots of people are asking that same question today. They're looking to you for the answer. An event is coming that will leave the world stunned and confused. Worldwide network news teams will report the disappearance of millions of people. To the world it will be a mystery, but for Christians it will be another great fulfillment of biblical prophecy. Jesus will fulfill His promise!

This event is the rapture of the church. The word "rapture" doesn't appear in the English versions of the Bible, but comes from the Latin translation of the Scripture for the phrase "caught up" in 1 Thessalonians 4:17. The word "caught up" in Latin is *rapere,* which transliterated in English is "rapture."

But though this word "rapture" is not in the Bible, the concept is absolutely biblical.

The Bible teaches that Jesus will return in the air to catch away all believers and take them to be with Him forever.

Having this blessed hope of Jesus' return changes the way we face this day. I made a sign that I keep around so that I see it; it simply says, "PERHAPS TODAY!"

APRIL 3

There are times when our weaknesses and inadequacies are all part of God's plan for our lives.

"...My power works best in weakness" (2 Corinthians 12:9b).

Sometimes, as in Paul's situation, our weakness is a great asset. Oswald Chambers said, "God comes in where my helplessness begins." Our weaknesses make us appreciate God's strength!

"Each time he said, 'My grace is all you need. My power works best in weakness.' So now I am glad to boast about my weaknesses, so that the power of Christ can work through me. That's why I take pleasure in my weaknesses, and in the insults, hardships, persecutions, and troubles that I suffer for Christ. For when I am weak, then I am strong" (2 Corinthians 12:9-10).

A friend shared this insight with me; see if it fits you. "If part of the Holy Spirit's job in the past has been to create something out of nothing, then to create something out of your life is not going to be His most difficult task! I am frustrated by people who have no difficulty believing that God could create the universe, but do have difficulty believing God can do something worthwhile with them. The One who brought things into being in the first place will live within you and make your life His workshop."[26]

grace today

4 APRIL

The only way to stay energized as a believer is to stay "plugged-in."

In Romans 15 Paul tells us that the power for his life and ministry didn't come from himself, it came from the Holy Spirit.

"Now may the God of hope fill you with all joy and peace in believing, so that you will abound in hope by the power of the Holy Spirit... sanctified by the Holy Spirit... in the power of signs and wonders, in the power of the Spirit..." (Romans 15:13, 16b, 19a, NASB).

The Christian life is a supernatural life and can only be lived in supernatural power. Our great need is to stay "plugged in" through Bible study, fellowship with one another, the breaking of bread and prayer (Acts 2:42). God is not calling us to serve Him in our own strength and from our own supply! He is calling us to plug into Him and His supply!

I remember my wife, Leslie, telling me that she saw some geese flying. They were flying along in a "V" formation. Studies have been made on why geese fly the way they do. Those studies tell us a lot about the importance of fellowship with one another.

As each bird flaps its wings, it creates "uplift" for the bird immediately following it. By flying in a "V" formation, the whole flock has at least seventy-one percent greater flying range than if each bird flew on its own.

When people share a common direction and sense of community, they can get where they are going more quickly and easily. They are traveling on the thrust of one another.

Stay plugged in to the Word and in fellowship with other believers!

"Answer me when I call, O God of my righteousness! You have relieved me in my distress; be gracious to me and hear my prayer" (Psalm 4:1, NASB).

The word "relieved" in Hebrew means "to enlarge." God enlarges us in our distress. In times of distress He enlarges life (James 1:2-4) and faith. Faith is increased as we are forced to rely more on the Lord and His provision. "Pressure on the outside makes us bigger on the inside" (Warren Wiersbe).

Great tests usually precede a great testimony! One commentator says, "Great perils commonly precede great preferments. David found it so. The way to any great attainment is usually steep and rough. This is true in everything. It is especially true in moral attainments. Let not the children of God be discouraged through the greatness of their way. No strange thing has happened to them."[27]

"When I call, give me answers. God, take my side! Once, in a tight place, you gave me room; now I'm in trouble again: grace me! hear me!" (Psalm 4:1, MSG).

"All of your works will thank you, LORD, and your faithful followers will praise you. They will speak of the glory of your kingdom; they will give examples of your power" (Psalm 145: 10-11).

grace today

6 APRIL

"For it is You who blesses the righteous man, O LORD, You surround him with favor as with a shield" (Psalm 5:12, NASB).

Martin Luther, whom the Lord used to start the Protestant Reformation, was commanded to appear before Cardinal Cajentan, who demanded the Reformer to give an answer for what the Catholic church thought were his heretical beliefs.

When he was asked by one of the Cardinal's officials where he could find a shelter if his patron, the Elector of Saxony, should desert him, Luther replied, "Under the shield of heaven!" When the official heard Luther's reply, he walked out of the room and didn't say another word!

Our Lord shuts the mouth of our enemies and delivers us from the lion's mouth!

"Thank You, Lord, for Your protection over my life, my family, and my church. In Jesus' Name, Amen!"

"...Joyful are those who have the God of Israel as their helper, whose hope is in the LORD their God" (Psalm 146:5).

7 APRIL

"Do not fret because of evildoers, be not envious toward wrongdoers" (Psalm 37:1, NASB).

This entire Psalm is an acrostic, an alphabetical Psalm, in which verses or groups of verses begin with successive letters of the Hebrew aleph-bet.

Today, I'd like to share some Bible study notes on this Psalm:

Verse 1 – "Fret not," from the Hebrew word, *charah*, which means "to be hot, to glow or grow warm, to blaze up in anger or jealousy." Don't get heated up with anger.

Realize that what the wicked gain is quickly lost. They sprout up and blossom and bloom, but just as quickly dry up.

Always ask yourself, "Ten years from now, what would I wish I had done in this situation?" Risk all you are and have for God and the pursuit of obedience. We find our lives only when we lose them. John 12:24-25 says, "...unless a kernel of wheat falls to the ground and dies, it remains only a single seed. But if it dies, it produces many seeds. The man who loves his life will lose it, while the man who hates his life in this world will keep it for eternal life" (NIV).

Verse 4 – "Delight yourself in the Lord" could actually be translated, "Luxuriate!"

Verse 5 – "Commit" means "to roll away." The right response to fretting or worrying about wrong-doers is to focus on the Lord, "Luxuirate" in Him and roll your burdens onto the Lord. "...the LORD's delight is in those who fear him, those who put their hope in his unfailing love" (Psalm 147:11).

APRIL 8

Transformation is a difficult process! Change is hard!

They had been married for fifty years! Fifty long, miserable years! For fifty years this now elderly couple had fought and argued every day of their lives.

GRace today

It was the typical marriage standoff: She said that she would change when he changed, and he said he'd change when she changed. The couple's children threw a very nice fiftieth anniversary party for them. And after the celebration had ended and the guests were gone, the wife turned to her husband and said, "We've lived together for fifty years, but it's been miserable. We've fought every day." Then she paused... "Now I think it's time to change. In fact, I've been praying that things would change. I've been praying that the Lord would take one of us home. And when He answers my prayer... I'm going to go live with my sister in Grand Rapids!"

Change is hard! As this story illustrates! Transformation can be very difficult. But today we're going to see how real transformation can take place.

"With eyes wide open to the mercies of God, I beg you, my brothers, as an act of intelligent worship, to give him your bodies, as a living sacrifice, consecrated to him and acceptable by him. Don't let the world around you squeeze you into its own mould, but let God re-mould your minds from within, so that you may prove in practice that the plan of God for you is good, meets all his demands and moves towards the goal of true maturity" (Romans 12:1-2, Phillips).

I like the way this translation translates the phrase: "Don't let the world around you squeeze you into its own mould..." (verse 2a). This word "squeeze," translated "conform" in other translations, means to be "fashioned according to someone else's pattern." This carries the meaning of appearing to be on the outside what you are not on the inside!

Here the context is speaking of people who look like the world on the outside, but are really Children of God on the inside.

There is a lot of pressure on you to conform to the world's standards. There's pressure to cheat, be unfaithful, lie, steal, dress like the world, talk like the world, or to hide your witness for Jesus. Knowing the pressure is there, we resist it and decide the world's going to have to conform to us!

Think about it:
- Where is the world squeezing me?
- Where do I feel the pressure to conform the most?

We're no longer like the world! We must remember who we are in Christ!

APRIL 9

"All Scripture is inspired by God and is useful to teach us what is true and to make us realize what is wrong in our lives. It corrects us when we are wrong and teaches us to do what is right. God uses it to prepare and equip his people to do every good work" (2 Timothy 3:16-17).

There's awesome power in the Word of God to transform your life!

The verses we are reading today are telling us that God's Word is powerful because it comes directly from God! It is inspired! The Greek word for inspiration means "God-breathed." The Bible has come from God to us. Jesus said, "...the words that I have spoken to you are spirit and are life" (John 6:63b NASB).

grace today

Since God has "breathed" His Word, then every part of it is entirely, absolutely and perfectly consistent with who He is!

One Bible teacher has put it this way: "Because God is wise, the Bible is wise. Because He is perfect, His Book is flawless. Because He is eternal, the Scriptures are never outdated. In every point and in every way, God's Word is completely consistent with His character."[28]

"Thank You, Lord, for giving us the joy of spending time with You and Your Word every day! We love our time with You! Thank You for drawing us close to You. In Jesus' Name, Amen."

10 APRIL

"Therefore, we never stop thanking God that when you received his message from us, you didn't think of our words as mere human ideas. You accepted what we said as the very word of God—which, of course, it is. And this word continues to work in you who believe" (1 Thessalonians 2:13).

Because God's Word is powerful, it is able to work a transformation in your life!

The transformation God's Word makes in a life is real and practical!

A truck driver was giving his testimony about the change Christ had made in his life. He was asked to think of some specific way in which he was changed. After a pause he said, "Well, when I find somebody tailgating my truck I no longer drive on the shoulder of the road to kick gravel on him."

I really want to share with you how the Amplified Bible translates today's passage, particularly the last phrase!

"And we also [especially] thank God continually for this, that when you received the message of God [which you heard] from us, you welcomed it not as the word of [mere] men, but as it truly is, the Word of God, which is effectually at work in you who believe [exercising its superhuman power in those who adhere to and trust in and rely on it]" (1 Thessalonians 2:13, AMP).

Stay in the Word. It will do a supernatural work in your life! God's Word is powerful!

APRIL 11

"Before the mountains were created, before the earth was formed, you are God without beginning or end" (Psalm 90:2, TLB).

God is altogether different than anything He has created. He is uncreated and has always been! The Bible tells us that He is eternal.

Someone has said, "About the closest any of us get to an encounter with eternity is being twenty minutes late for an important appointment and having to wait at another red light!"

God has always been. Before there was anything, before there was time, there was God! God is eternal!

He is called the "Eternal God" in Romans 16:26.

grace today

"Lord, You have been our dwelling place in all generations. Before the mountains were born or You gave birth to the earth and the world, even from everlasting to everlasting, You are God" (Psalm 90:1-2, NASB).

It's interesting that the Bible never tries to prove God's existence or explain where He came from. It just matter-of-factly states: "In the beginning God created the heavens and the earth."

You have a Father in Heaven who is much bigger than any need you will ever have! He is in control of this day. Trust Him to take care of every detail of this day and the rest of this week. He loves you eternally!

12 APRIL

" '...You are witnesses that I am the only God,' says the LORD. 'From eternity to eternity I am God. No one can snatch anyone out of my hand. No one can undo what I have done' " (Isaiah 43:12b-13).

The Bible shows us that God is eternal, He has always existed. He did not have a beginning and has no end (1 Corinthians 2:7). Before anything was created, God existed; before "day one," God was there! "Wow, that just boggles my mind!" Well, if God were small enough for our minds to comprehend, He wouldn't be big enough to meet our needs!

Richard L. Strauss captured the essence of the truth of the eternality of God very well in his book, *The Joy of Knowing God*, look at what he said:

Because God is eternal, He is self-existent, that is, He is the only being who does not owe His existence to somebody else. He is independent of any other being or cause. He is over and above the whole chain of causes and effects. He is uncreated, unoriginated, without beginning, owing His existence to no one outside Himself. He has life in and of Himself. As Jesus put it, 'For just as the Father has life in Himself, even so He gave to the Son also to have life in Himself' (John 5:26). Were it any other way He would not be God. An eternal being must be self-existent.[29]

"...I will sing praise to the name of the LORD Most High" (Psalm 7:17b).

APRIL 13

"Trust in the LORD always, for the LORD GOD is the eternal Rock" (Isaiah 26:4).

What difference does it make if God is eternal or not?

Here's one difference: The God who watches over you doesn't wear a watch! He is blessedly outside of time, in control of all time and space!

2 Peter 3:8 – "But do not forget this one thing, dear friends: With the Lord a day is like a thousand years, and a thousand years are like a day" (NIV).

Revelation 4:8 – "Each of these living beings had six wings, and their wings were covered all over with eyes, inside and out. Day after day and night after night they keep on saying, 'Holy, holy,

grace today

holy is the Lord God, the Almighty—the one who always was, who is, and who is still to come.' "

You can always trust God to be on time! God lives outside of time and is not affected by it! You don't need to go to astrologers, you don't need your fortune read, because God is in your future right now!

"Can God predict the future?" Yes and No. Well, He doesn't have to predict the future, because He already knows it. Isn't that mind-blowing? God is so awesome.

So, I'm not going to worry about tomorrow. God is already in my future right now!

"O LORD, our Lord, your majestic name fills the earth! Your glory is higher than the heavens" (Psalm 8:1).

14 APRIL

Because God is eternal, He is dependable!

We can count on Him to do what He has said. He can be trusted to do, and be able to do, what He has said. God is not growing weary, He's not aging. He is the same today as He was yesterday!

"...Have you never understood? The LORD is the everlasting God, the Creator of all the earth. He never grows weak or weary..." (Isaiah 40:28b).

You can place your trust in the Lord. He will never let you down.

"Trust in the LORD forever, for the LORD, the LORD, is the Rock eternal" (Isaiah 26:4, NIV).

APRIL 15

"All honor and glory to God forever and ever. He is the eternal King, the unseen one who never dies; he alone is God. Amen" (1 Timothy 1:17).

Since God is the Eternal One, how should we respond to Him?
- By Worshiping Him – "To the only God our Savior, through Jesus Christ our Lord, be glory, majesty, dominion and authority, before all time and now and forever. Amen" (Jude 25, NASB).
- By Serving Him – Everything exists for Him: "For by Him all things were created, both in the heavens and on earth, visible and invisible, whether thrones or dominions or rulers or authorities—all things have been created through Him and for Him" (Colossians 1:16, NASB). Whatever we do in word or deed, do all for the glory of God.
- By Declaring Him – There are a lot of things in this world that try to usurp God's rightful place: People, philosophies, policies, false religions. We declare the truth about the true and the Living God.

You can help spread the Word about God around the world through prayer, your personal witness and giving. The investment of your resources into the work of the Kingdom of God will bring about eternal dividends. You will accrue eternal interest. What an opportunity!

Grace today

16 APRIL

"Understand, therefore, that the LORD your God is indeed God. He is the faithful God..." (Deuteronomy 7:9).

Another unique characteristic of your Heavenly Father, The Living God, is that He is faithful. That is what He is, it's a part of His nature! "If we are unfaithful, he remains faithful, for he cannot deny himself" (2 Timothy 2:13). Our Heavenly Father is characterized by His faithfulness.

The word "faithful" (*aman*) literally means "firm, established, lasting, reliable, sure." It's basically the same word as "AMEN!"

Look at how the "Song of Moses" refers to the faithfulness of God: "For I proclaim the name of the LORD; ascribe greatness to our God! The Rock! His work is perfect, for all His ways are just; a God of faithfulness and without injustice, righteous and upright is He" (Deuteronomy 32:3-4, NASB).

God's faithfulness distinguishes Him from all other so-called "gods." All the other "gods" are fickle, undependable, but GOD is faithful!

Because God is unchanging and eternal:
- He is faithful.
- He is totally reliable.
- He will never let you down!

Now don't get that confused with always getting what you want or expect.

God is the One Person whom you can depend upon to be stable and trustworthy, no matter what! If He has said He will do something, He will do it! You can count on that!

"I trust in the LORD for protection" (Psalm 11:1a).

APRIL 17

"Your unfailing love, O LORD, is as vast as the heavens; your faithfulness reaches beyond the clouds" (Psalm 36:5).

God's faithfulness is abundant and immeasurable.

Psalm 89:8 (NASB) says that "Faithfulness surrounds" the Lord and Isaiah the prophet says that "...faithfulness [is] the belt about His waist" (Isaiah 11:5b, NASB). God's faithfulness is the basis of our confidence in Him. God is just as faithful today as He has always been!

Having a faithful God is such a blessing to us. God is faithful in what He says.
- Titus 1:2 says God is the "...God, who cannot lie..." (NASB).
- Hebrews 6:18 says that "...it is impossible for God to lie..."

God is faithful in what He does. God would never lie to you. What He says is backed up by His faithfulness. Read the Bible to find out all God has promised you.

"The LORD's promises are pure, like silver refined in a furnace, purified seven times over" (Psalm 12:6).

grace today

18 APRIL

"But the Lord is faithful; he will strengthen you and guard you from the evil one" (2 Thessalonians 3:3).

God is faithful in what He does. He's faithful to forgive us.

"If we say that we have no sin, we are only fooling ourselves and refusing to accept the truth. But if we confess our sins to him, he can be depended on to forgive us and to cleanse us from every wrong..." (1 John 1:8-9, TLB).

God is also faithful to strengthen and protect us.

"But the Lord is faithful, and He will strengthen you and protect you from the evil one" (2 Thessalonians 3:3, NASB).

This is especially true during times of temptation and trial. When you are tempted, the Lord will always provide a way for you to escape falling into sin. This is the promise we have in 1 Corinthians 10:13: "No temptation has overtaken you but such as is common to man; and God is faithful, who will not allow you to be tempted beyond what you are able, but with the temptation will provide the way of escape also, so that you will be able to endure it" (NASB).

The term, "way of escape," was used of a narrow mountain pass through which a trapped army might escape from an enemy who would destroy them. God always has a way of escape. When we yield to temptation, it is because we have either ignored or refused His provision of escape.

Our faithful God will strengthen you, protect you, and provide for your victory today.

"I know, O LORD, that Your judgments are righteous, And that in faithfulness You have afflicted me" (Psalm 119:75, NASB).

God is a faithful God. He is faithful to forgive us and to strengthen and protect us. Another way God shows His faithfulness to us is that He faithfully disciplines us.

God lovingly corrects us to train us as His children. The reason why God disciplines us is because He is faithful!

There was a farmer who had three sons: Jim, John, and Sam. No one in this family ever attended church or had any time for God. The pastor and the others in the Christian community had tried for years to interest the family in the things of God, to no avail.

Then, one day Sam was bitten by a rattlesnake. The doctor was called, and he did all he could to help Sam, but the outlook for Sam's recovery was not very good at all. So, this family who never had any time for the Lord, frantically called the local pastor and asked him to pray whatever he thought was best. He looked at what was happening and began to pray this prayer:

"O wise and righteous Father, we thank Thee that in Thy wisdom Thou hast sent this rattlesnake to bite Sam. He has never been inside the church, and it is doubtful that he has, in all this time, ever prayed or even acknowledged Thine existence. Now, we trust that this experience will be a valuable lesson to him and will lead to his genuine repentance and change. And now, O Father, wilt Thou send another rattlesnake to bite Jim; and another to bite his brother John; and another really big one to bite the old man. For years we have done everything we know

to get them to turn to Thee, but all in vain. It seems, therefore, that what all our combined efforts could not do, this rattlesnake has done. We thus conclude that the only thing that will do this family any real good is rattlesnakes; so, Lord, send us bigger and better rattlesnakes. Amen."

20 APRIL

"He who calls you is faithful; he will surely do it"
(1 Thessalonians 5:24, ESV).

God is faithful to preserve us. Corrie Ten Boom stated this truth so succinctly: "In God's faithfulness lies eternal security."

I love the way Erwin Lutzer, Pastor of Moody Memorial Church in Chicago has put it, "God's investment in us is so great He could not possibly abandon us."

Now, it's one thing to know about the faithfulness of God, and another thing to live by it! We all have times in our lives when, based on outward conditions and external situations, it is difficult to believe that God is faithful when:
- We're disappointed.
- We're suffering.
- We feel everything is hopeless.

Father in Heaven may allow us to suffer, but He can never forget us because He is faithful! God is faithful! That is our encouragement!

"The faithful love of the LORD never ends! His mercies never cease. Great is his faithfulness; his mercies begin afresh each morning" (Lamentations 3:22-23).

Thomas Obediah Chisholm (1866-1960) was born in a crude log cabin in Franklin, Kentucky. From this humble beginning and without the benefit of high school or advanced education, he somehow began his career as a school teacher at the age of sixteen in the same country school where he had received his elementary training. After accepting Christ as Savior, he became editor of The Pentecostal Herald and later was ordained as a Methodist minister. Throughout his long lifetime, Mr. Chisholm wrote more than 1200 sacred poems, many of which have since become prominent hymn texts.

While many enduring hymns are born out of a particular dramatic experience, this was simply the result of the author's "morning by morning" realization of God's personal faithfulness in his daily life. Shortly before his death in 1960, Thomas Chisholm wrote:

> "My income has never been large at any time due to impaired health in the earlier years which has followed me on until now. But I must not fail to record here the unfailing faithfulness of a covenant keeping God and that He has given me many wonderful displays of His providing care which have filled me with astonishing gratefulness."[30]

grace today

GREAT IS THY FAITHFULNESS

Great is Thy faithfulness, O God my Father!
There is no shadow of turning with Thee;
Thou changest not; Thy compassions, they fail not:
As thou hast been Though forever wilt be.

Summer and winter, and springtime and harvest,
Sun, moon, and stars in their courses above,
Join with all nature in manifold witness
To Thy great faithfulness, mercy and love.

Pardon for sin and a peace that endureth,
Thine own dear presence to cheer and to guide,
Strength for today and bright hope for tomorrow,
Blessings all mine, with ten thousand beside.

Great is Thy faithfulness!
Great is Thy faithfulness!
Morning by morning new mercies I see;
All I have needed Thy hand has provided,
Great is Thy faithfulness, Lord, unto me.

22 APRIL

"I can never escape from your Spirit! I can never get away from
your presence! If I go up to heaven, you are there; if I go down
to the grave, you are there. If I ride the wings of the morning, if
I dwell by the farthest oceans, even there your hand will guide
me, and your strength will support me. I could ask the darkness
to hide me and the light around me to become night—but even
in darkness I cannot hide from you. To you the night shines as

bright as day. Darkness and light are the same to you" (Psalm 139:7-12).

The Bible clearly teaches that there is no place in the world, there is no place in this universe, where God is not. God is not limited by space; He is not in space, just as He is not in time. This is because He created both space and time, and He *WAS* before there was space or time!

The Bible teaches that God is omnipresent; this means that God is present everywhere. God is everywhere at once. There is no place, no space, where He cannot be found!

God is everywhere in the universe. "Am I a God who is only in one place and cannot see what they are doing? Can anyone hide from me? Am I not everywhere in all of heaven and earth?" (Jeremiah 23:23-24, TLB).

Where are you today? Where will you be tonight? God is already there, waiting for you!

APRIL 23

"But will God really live on earth? Why, even the highest heavens cannot contain you. How much less this Temple I have built!" (1 Kings 8:27).

This was King Solomon's dedicatory prayer. As he prayed, he understood that God could never be contained in one place.

What does this mean for you? This means that God is always accessible! There is no place in the world, or the universe, that

grace today

God is inaccessible. As A. W. Tozer said, "God is everywhere here, close to everything, next to everyone."[31]

We don't have to travel to a particular place for God to be accessible to us. God is bigger than any of the boxes we build for Him locally or mentally.

God is right here with you. Enjoy His presence throughout this day.

24 APRIL

"Am I a God who is only in one place and cannot see what they are doing? Can anyone hide from me? Am I not everywhere in all of heaven and earth?" (Jeremiah 23:23-24, TLB).

We cannot hide from God. Proverbs says, "The eyes of the LORD are in every place, watching the evil and the good" (Proverbs 15:3, NASB).

The writer of Hebrews reminds us that because God is everywhere, all the time, "Nothing in all creation is hidden from God. Everything is naked and exposed before his eyes, and he is the one to whom we are accountable" (Hebrews 4:13).

The Lord sees everything we do. There is nothing He does not see. He is everywhere. He sees and knows everything! We need to remind ourselves of this! Be conscious of God's presence before you sin! He is here. He sees. God knows all our sins. Moses wrote: "You spread out our sins before you—our secret sins—and you see them all" (Psalm 90:8). David writes: "O God, You know my foolishness; and my sins are not hidden from You" (Psalm 69:5, NKJV).

Lots of people try in vain to evade God, but God cannot be evaded in time, nor in space, nor in eternity.

Because God is everywhere and sees all things, one day all things will be brought to light.

"In times of trouble, may the LORD answer your cry..." (Psalm 20:1a).

April 25

"It is God who enables us, along with you, to stand firm for Christ" (2 Corinthians 1:21).

In years past, when shipbuilders were planning on making a great ship, they knew that the life of the crew and the safety of the cargo depended upon the ship's mainmast.

To make the mainmast, they would find a straight, tall tree on the top of a mountain near the coast. Then they would cut down all the other trees around it so that it would be exposed to the full force of the angry winds and mighty gusts that blow off the sea. After many years of exposure to such harshness, the tree would become stronger and stronger, its very fiber being strengthened by the intense buffeting it was experiencing day after day. Finally, after many testing storms alone on the mountaintop, the tree was ready to be trusted as the mainmast of a great ship.

Do you feel like that tree, singled out and everything around you cut away? Maybe you thought you were being picked on or "judged" by God. Instead, it might be that God has marked you out for a great purpose in His kingdom plan.

grace today

26 APRIL

"It is God who enables us, along with you, to stand firm for Christ" (2 Corinthians 1:21).

In yesterday's reading, the storms that the tree endured built it up. God allows storms in our lives, not to destroy us, but to strengthen us. Alan Redpath, the former pastor of the Moody Memorial Church in Chicago, shared his insight on God's master plan for our lives:

> There is nothing—no circumstance, no trouble, no testing—that can ever touch me until, first of all, it has gone past God and past Christ, right through to me. If it has come that far, it has come with great purpose, which I may not understand at the moment; but as I refuse to become panicky, as I lift my eyes up to Him and accept it as coming from the throne of God for some great purpose of blessing to my own heart, no sorrow will ever disturb me, no trial will ever disarm me, no circumstance will cause me to fret, for I shall rest in the joy of what my Lord is.[32]

This paragraph is something that you'll want to forward to a friend. Copy it and put it where you'll see it often.

27 APRIL

"...Every plant not planted by my heavenly Father will be uprooted..." (Matthew 15:13a).

"The wicked are overthrown and are no more, but the house of the righteous will stand" (Proverbs 12:7, NASB).

Another way a mighty tree's fiber is strengthened is by having its roots go deep into the soil, and cling to the underground rocks and boulders. Not long ago I read about a three hundred foot redwood tree that had fallen down during one of Northern California's recent deluges. It was thousands of years old and had survived forest fires and outlived scores of generations of people. Why did it fall? Its roots were only six inches under the ground! Redwood trees have one weakness. Though they stand nearly impervious to insect infestation and to disease, and they are naturally fire-resistant, they have shallow roots. Loving the redwoods as I do, I mourned the loss of this natural giant and noticed a spiritual application for my life.

I began thinking about a lot of Christians I had known that had fallen into sin. Prior to their fall, they looked so spiritually strong and massive, but when the stormy blasts of temptation and sin came into their lives, they fell. The kind of tree that doesn't fall over in a storm, no matter how saturated the soil becomes, is one that has an invisible means of support. Its roots, hidden underground, grip rocks and boulders that no eye sees. Christians who end up standing through the storms of life have an invisible Source of strength. Jesus Christ is their Rock, and no matter how the wind blows, they stand firm. We must have a deep foundation in the Word of God.

God bless you as you stand in the Lord. "But grow in the grace and knowledge of our Lord and Savior Jesus Christ. To Him be the glory, both now and to the day of eternity. Amen" (2 Peter 3:18, NASB).

28 APRIL

"This suffering is all part of the work God has given you. Christ, who suffered for you, is your example. Follow in his steps" (1 Peter 2:21, TLB).

Jesus has set an example of perseverance for us.

He patiently suffered many things. The Greek word for "endurance" or "perseverance" is *hupomone,* a compound word made of *hupo,* "under," and *meno,* "to remain," or "to abide." It means to remain under trouble and trial. It speaks of a steadfastness, a "hanging-in-there-ness," no matter the cost.

This kind of perseverance [hupomone] is talking about enduring hard circumstances. Another word, "longsuffering," (*machrothumia*), is the word that means putting up with tough people, longsuffering or patience shown to people.

Perseverance or endurance means we stand bravely in faith even though all sorts of things may be against us.

The patient suffering of Christ is our example:
- In tribulation – Romans 5:3-4.
- In reproach – Romans 15:4, 5.
- In suffering – 2 Corinthians 1:6.
- In affliction – 2 Corinthians 6:4.
- In persecution and distress – 2 Corinthians 12:12, 2 Thessalonians 1:4, 1 Timothy 6:11-12.

Jesus is coming soon! Hang in there! Run to win the race!

As we enjoy God's love and learn to rely upon it, we can wait in patience for the day when all our trials will be ended, and the Lord Jesus will come to take us to be forever with Himself.

APRIL 29

You are on this planet to please God and not to please people. "Therefore also we have as our ambition, whether at home or absent, to be pleasing to Him" (2 Corinthians 5:9, NASB).

Whoever you are living to please is your God. Most Christians who would never fall down and worship an idol are caught red-handed in idolatry!

People-pleasing is a kind of idolatry. Why do we fall into people-pleasing? Because of fear! Often we're afraid of the consequences of not pleasing them! The Lord wants to set us free from fearing people. He doesn't want us fearing anyone but Him!

Proverbs 29:25 says, "The fear of man brings a snare" (NASB).

In Isaiah 51:7-8 God says, "Listen to Me, you who know righteousness, a people in whose heart is My law; do not fear the reproach of man, nor be dismayed at their revilings. For the moth will eat them like a garment, and the grub will eat them like wool. But My righteousness shall be forever, and My salvation to all generations" (NASB).

"But," someone says, "if I follow the Lord, people will make fun of me, or they may jump all over me!" It doesn't matter! You obey, and let the Lord deal with the results. That's His department!

Grace today

Someone has said, "Reputation is what people think about you. Character is what God knows you are!"

Jesus said, "...do not fear those who kill the body, but are unable to kill the soul; but rather fear Him who is able to destroy both soul and body in hell" (Matthew 10:28, NASB).

30 APRIL

"Once God has spoken; twice I have heard this: That power belongs to God" (Psalm 62:11, NASB).

"He fills his hands with lightning bolts and hurls each at its target" (Job 36:32).

A single stroke of lightning, which is usually three to four miles long, travels at speeds of up to 100,000 miles per second, or half the speed of light! At that speed it's impossible to see that the bolt is actually traveling from the ground up to the clouds. But in a single flash, it can carry 100 million volts of electricity and reach a temperature of 55,000 degrees Fahrenheit, five times hotter than the surface of the sun! Earth is struck by at least 100 strokes of lightning every second. That's more than 8.6 million strikes a day!

Talk about the power of God!

Your Father in Heaven has unlimited power at His disposal, all the time, to help you in any way you need. So don't sweat the small stuff (which is all stuff from God's perspective!).

"...For I know the one in whom I trust, and I am sure that he is able to guard what I have entrusted to him until the day of his return" (2 Timothy 1:12b).

God's almighty power secures us. We are made secure by the exercise of God's mighty power.

"For I am confident of this very thing, that He who began a good work in you will perfect it until the day of Christ Jesus" (Philippians 1:6, NASB).

This is not the language of uncertainty, is it? There is a remarkable passage in Isaiah that I'd like you to look at:

"And the work of righteousness will be peace, and the service of righteousness, quietness and confidence [security, assurance] forever" (Isaiah 32:17, NASB).

The righteousness spoken of here is not our righteousness. This is the righteousness of God, revealed in the Gospel and given to us through faith in Jesus Christ. It is the righteousness of faith.

Because of God's power, you can have assurance of your salvation.

Because of this, if you are a believer, you should have assurance of salvation. Look up these three references in your Bible that emphasize the security we have in God's great power: John 1:12-13, 1 John 5:12-13, Hebrews 10:22.

2 MAY

"Hallelujah! For the Lord our God, the Almighty, [omnipotent, KJV] reigns" (Revelation 19:6b, NASB).

God's almighty power secures us!

One of the former pastors of First Baptist Church in Dallas, Texas, George W. Truett, told the story about how he once had to perform the funeral of a young wife and mother from his congregation.

After the service, friends gathered around the young husband and the little girl who were left. His friends urged him to go with them to their homes for a few days, but he refused. He said that he would have to face reality of life without his wife sooner or later, and he might as well begin now.

He took his little girl back to what now seemed to be a very lonely, empty house where everything reminded him of his wife. His precious little daughter sensed something was wrong with her daddy, but she was not old enough to understand what was going on, and she kept going through the house calling for her mother.

She didn't make it any easier by constantly reminding her daddy that he was not feeding her or putting her to bed like her mother did. When he finally tucked her in bed, he went into his bedroom and began to cry.

He thought she had fallen right sleep. So he just poured out his heart to God saying, "O God, it is dark down here."

But she was not asleep, and she began to cry when she heard that and she said, "Daddy, it is dark over here, too. Take me in bed with you." So he took his precious little one into bed with him as he tried to comfort her.

After a little while she reached over in the darkness and felt for the face of her father. When she touched him she said, "Daddy, I can go to sleep if your face is toward me."

Being assured that his face was toward her, she soon dropped off into peaceful slumber.

Her father thought about what she said, and then he tearfully prayed again, "Oh God, it is dark down here, but I can bear it if I know your face is toward me." Soon, he too was sound asleep. God's face was toward him.

God is for us! His face is toward us! We are kept in His powerful hand. Jesus said, "I give them eternal life, and they will never perish. No one can snatch them away from me, for my Father has given them to me, and he is more powerful than anyone else. No one can snatch them from the Father's hand" (John 10:28-29).

God never lets go of us, He never relaxes His hold on us. We are secure in His hand. I can know that God's face is towards me. His power keeps me securely.

MAY 3

"This means that anyone who belongs to Christ has become a new person. The old life is gone; a new life has begun!" (2 Corinthians 5:17).

grace today

The Christian life is a changed life!
- A change of habits.
- A change of heart.
- A change of enjoyments.
- A change of loves.
- A change of thinking and mind.
- And ultimately, a change of address!

Another way to look at it, is there will be the evidence of love in your life. You love God's Word and you have a hunger for it. You love God's people and you have a sincere affection for them.

You love God's fellowship and you love to please the Lord!

4 MAY

"God saved you by his grace when you believed. And you can't take credit for this; it is a gift from God. Salvation is not a reward for the good things we have done, so none of us can boast about it" (Ephesians 2:8-9).

It's like buying a house. If you buy a new house and move into it, it doesn't matter if you feel like it's your new house; it's yours, because of a contract. Our salvation is based on a covenant, a contract that Almighty God has made with us, the New Covenant!

Emotional experiences may quickly accompany salvation, but they can just as quickly leave. Emotions are great when they are on your side, but when they aren't, don't worry. "Be my feelings what they will, Jesus is my Savior still."

MAY 5

Unconfessed sin can really ding a person's sense of security as a believer. In fact, this is one of the biggest reasons Christians lack assurance.

Proverbs 28:13 says, "People who conceal their sins will not prosper, but if they confess and turn from them, they will receive mercy."

Confession of sin is important. It reminds us of Christ's forgiveness, and it keeps us tuned to God's will.

Back during the cold war, a Soviet archaeological expedition in Egypt found a mummy. The mummy was sent back to the former USSR for study, and the first thing they wanted to do was determine its age. The scientists, however, were pushed aside by the secret police who shouted, "Leave it to us; we will find out!" Forthrightly, the secret police announced that the mummy's age was 4,840 years. "Amazing," the soviet scientists said. "How did you determine it?" "Easy," said the secret police. "The mummy confessed."

Now, God isn't going to make you confess, but by being honest with God, you help yourself and your spiritual growth.

God promises to forgive us!

"If we claim we have no sin, we are only fooling ourselves and not living in the truth. But if we confess our sins to him, he is faithful and just to forgive us our sins and to cleanse us from all wickedness. If we claim we have not sinned, we are calling God a liar and showing that his word has no place in our hearts" (1 John 1:8-10).

grace today

6 MAY

Do you ever struggle with comparing yourself with someone else? It can go both ways, sometimes motivated by pride, other times feeling like you can't do anything really well.

The Apostle Paul had the antidote for this one. Listen to how he responded to those who wanted to get him into the mire of comparing himself with others:

"Oh, don't worry; we wouldn't dare say that we are as wonderful as these other men who tell you how important they are! But they are only comparing themselves with each other, using themselves as the standard of measurement. How ignorant!" (2 Corinthians 10:12).

This is the best perspective I've ever heard. It's the eternal perspective! Jesus is the standard.

Here's the rest of Paul's perspective: "Our goal is to measure up to God's plan for us, and this plan includes our working there with you... As the Scriptures say, 'If anyone is going to boast, let him boast about what the Lord has done and not about himself.' When someone boasts about himself and how well he has done, it doesn't count for much. But when the Lord commends him, that's different!" (2 Corinthians 10:13b,17-18, TLB).

When you're tempted to look around and compare, look at Jesus!

7 MAY

"And we know that God causes everything to work together for the good of those who love God and are called according to his purpose for them" (Romans 8:28).

There are a lot of things that we don't know in life, but here is one thing that we do know: God has a plan, and He knows what He is doing. Even if it doesn't make sense to you, you can trust His plan for your life.

Centuries ago, a great architect was secured to design a magnificent church for the king of Spain's magnificent palace, the Escorial. The name of the church is San Lorenzo. When this awesome building was being constructed, the architect designed a huge arch, one larger than any that had ever been built before. That single arch was supposed to support the entire weight of the church's giant roof. The king, however, was worried that the enormous weight of the roof would be too much for that arch. So he insisted that the architect build a column from the floor all the way up to the center of the arch, to help support it. The architect took the king's command to build a center column as a tremendous insult and argued loud and long with the king that this was not necessary, and that his fears were all groundless, but the king insisted, and the column was built. After the building was finished, the king worshipped in peace. He could look at that column and feel secure that the column he had added to the architect's design would hold up that enormous roof.

Many years later, after the king's death, the architect revealed that he had left a quarter-inch space between the top of the column and the arch it was supposed to support!

Even now, though hundreds of years have gone by, that ceiling has not sagged even a quarter of an inch! You can go and visit the Escorial today, and the tour guides will take you to San Lorenzo Church, and they will pass a board between that column and the arch, proving that the great architect's plan was sure. He stands vindicated even after all these centuries!

grace today

God's plan is this way. His plan for our lives is sure and doesn't need our support. We can trust the work that He is doing in our lives, and we can rest in His gracious design. We aren't left in the hands of fate. Lady Luck doesn't control our lives! We are in the hands of a loving God! There is nothing that happens to us which does not dovetail into God's plan for our lives. God has a loving plan, and we can trust Him to engineer our lives!

8 MAY

"And we know that God causes everything to work together for the good of those who love God and are called according to his purpose for them" (Romans 8:28).

It's interesting what Paul *doesn't* say. He doesn't say, "And we hope that all things work together for good to those who love God." Nor does he say, "And we know that some things or most things work together for good!"

But he says: "And we know that *all* things work together for good to those who love God!"

"No verse in the Bible claims more than that, covers more territory, offers more hope and comfort. If what this verse says is so, then every cloud has its silver lining of hope, and every event in our life is capable of producing final and lasting good to our souls."[33]

But look at what Paul is not saying: This promise is for everyone.

This promise has one very important qualification. Paul is not saying that all things work together for good for everyone. He is

saying that all things work together for good *to all those who have responded to the Gospel and put their faith in Christ!*

The literal rendering of the Greek text clarifies this. It reads, "And we know to the ones loving God, all things work together for good..." For some reason the translators took the phrase, "to them that love God" and inserted it at the end of the sentence.

So a lot of times you'll hear people just quote the first part of this verse and say, "Well, all things work together for good." But that's not actually true! When Paul wrote this he put in one very important qualification: "To the ones loving God all things work together for good." If a person is not a child of God, they do not have this assurance. They are in a world where the devil, Satan, desires to work things so that they will not go to heaven!

If you do not know the Lord, chances are that things are not working together for good!

Let's change all that right now. Pray this prayer with me and ask Jesus to come into your life: "Father in Heaven, thank You for loving me and for sending Jesus to die for all the wrong things I have done. I am sorry for what I have done. I want to turn my life over to You. I believe that Jesus died on the cross for me; and that He was buried and rose from the dead. I'm asking that Jesus please come into my life and be my Savior and my Lord."

MAY 9

"And we know that God causes everything to work together for the good of those who love God and are called according to his purpose for them" (Romans 8:28).

grace today

One misconception about this verse is that everything that happens to us will be good.

Look, we need to get this straight. Paul is not saying that everything that happens to us is going to be good! A lot of Christians find themselves spiritually depressed and upset because, somehow, they have the misconception that if they commit their lives completely to the Lord, they have some kind of immunity from trouble, that they will never have problems again.

If you are living with this kind of expectation as a Christian, you're going to experience real disappointment because not everything that happens to you is good! Some things that happen to you may be disastrous!

Being a Christian does not give us some kind of immunity from trouble, pain and suffering.

Christians experience the full gamut of sickness and disease, sorrow, grief, loss, failure and disappointment, just like everyone else!

Look at Jesus' life; His life was completely committed to the life of the Father, and He suffered unjustly. God sends the rain upon the just and the unjust. So even though the same kinds of things happen to all people, the results are not the same.

The hard thing we're going through right now can either drive us away from the Lord or it will drive us closer to the Lord.

"And we know that God causes everything to work together for the good of those who love God and are called according to his purpose for them" (Romans 8:28)

Notice that Paul says he "knows" that God causes all things to work together for good to those who love God.

How do you think he knew this? It wasn't from some institution of higher learning; it was from the "school" of experience! You've taken some of those courses, too, haven't you?

A lot of times we live and believe this *after* the trouble has passed and we can see some purpose in it.

But, Paul lived and believed this in the middle of *all* that he was going through! And knowing this affected how he went through his trials!

Think of what he is saying in the light of the things he had experienced: "I have worked harder, been put in prison more often, been whipped times without number, and faced death again and again. Five different times the Jewish leaders gave me thirty-nine lashes. Three times I was beaten with rods. Once I was stoned. Three times I was shipwrecked. Once I spent a whole night and a day adrift at sea. I have traveled on many long journeys. I have faced danger from rivers and from robbers. I have faced danger from my own people, the Jews, as well as from the Gentiles. I have faced danger in the cities, in the deserts, and on the seas. And I have faced danger from men who claim to be believers but are not. I have worked hard and long, enduring many sleepless nights. I have been hungry and thirsty and have

often gone without food. I have shivered in the cold, without enough clothing to keep me warm. Then, besides all this, I have the daily burden of my concern for all the churches. Who is weak without my feeling that weakness? Who is led astray, and I do not burn with anger?" (2 Corinthians 11:23b-29).

11 MAY

"And we know that God causes everything to work together for the good of those who love God and are called according to his purpose for them" (Romans 8:28).

A lot of times we rejoice *after* we see God's purpose in the pain or suffering revealed.

Too often we think, "What good can possibly come out of this?" We feel sorry for ourselves. "All I'm trying to do is serve You, Lord!"

But why can't we have the faith to rejoice *before* we see God's full purpose? Paul did! Let's hold onto the confidence that God is in control, God is working, and He is working for good in this. So many times we have seen God take a bad situation and turn it into good.

And there are times when we will not know God's purpose, times when we must trust the wisdom of God. "Oh, how great are God's riches and wisdom and knowledge! How impossible it is for us to understand his decisions and his ways! For who can know the Lord's thoughts? Who knows enough to give him advice?" (Romans 11:33-34).

We don't understand why we have to suffer, why we have to hurt. When I come up to these walls where my understanding ceases, I have to fall back on what I do understand:

1. I am God's child.
2. God loves me.
3. God is in control.
4. His plans for me are good.

Because I know this, I know that somehow, some way, even in this terrible thing that is happening, that God is working for my good. Nothing can happen to me that God hasn't allowed to happen. God controls the circumstances around me. If something happens to me, then it is because God has allowed it to happen. There are no accidents.

"...Call on me when you are in trouble, and I will rescue you, and you will give me glory" (Psalm 50:15).

MAY 12

God is in control of your life!

William Cowper, one of the churches' great hymn-writers, had an interesting experience that brought him to Christ.

Apparently his life was such a mess, and he was so full of despair, that he determined to end his life. He decided to take his life by drinking poison. He drank the poison, but he did not die; instead he just got extremely sick. So he decided to buy a gun and shoot himself. But the gun would not go off! Well, he threw the gun away, got a rope, and tried to hang himself, but the rope broke!

In absolute desperation, Cowper hired a carriage in London and instructed the driver to take him to the Thames River. His plan was that he would jump into the river and drown himself. But as he sat down in the carriage, a fog descended on London that was so thick that the cabby got lost and couldn't even find the river!

Cowper went back to his room, and in his despair he noticed a Bible. He picked it up and began to read about a loving Heavenly Father who had a plan and a purpose for the lives of those who would accept His gracious provision of salvation in Jesus Christ.

The verse he read was Romans 8:28: "All things work together for good..." Cowper accepted Christ and in commemoration of this event penned these words:

> God moves in a mysterious way
>   His wonders to perform;
> He plants his footsteps in the sea
>   And rides upon the storm.
>
> You fearful saints, fresh courage take;
>   The clouds you so much dread
> Are big with mercy, and shall break
>   In blessings on your head.
>
> Judge not the Lord by feeble sense
>   But trust him for his grace;
> Behind a frowning providence
>   He hides a smiling face.

His purposes will ripen fast,
   Unfolding every hour;
The bud may have a bitter taste,
   But sweet will be the flower.

Blind unbelief is sure to err,
   And scan his work in vain;
God is his own interpreter,
   And he will make it plain.

"Have mercy on me, O God, because of your unfailing love. Because of your great compassion, blot out the stain of my sins" (Psalm 51:1).

MAY 13

"Have you never heard? Have you never understood? The LORD is the everlasting God, the Creator of all the earth. He never grows weak or weary..." (Isaiah 40:28a).

God is omnipotent. This means that God can do anything!

The angel Gabriel told Mary, the mother of Jesus, that her relative Elizabeth, who had been infertile all her life, had conceived a son in her old age. To an amazed Mary he said, "For nothing will be impossible with God" (Luke 1:37, NASB). To His disciples Jesus said, "The things impossible with men are possible with God" (Luke 18:27; Matthew 19:26; Mark 10:27, NASB).

grace today

God's exercise of His power is effortless! Think about God's power as exercised in creating the world. All God has to do is speak, and His will is accomplished. He created the world out of nothing.

God didn't really say, "Let there be light..." in Genesis 1:3; that implies that there was some kind of room for discussion. But rather the original language says that God said, "Light be!"

The world and the universe that God has created is a demonstration of His mighty power! "But God shows his anger from heaven against all sinful, wicked people who suppress the truth by their wickedness. They know the truth about God because he has made it obvious to them. For ever since the world was created, people have seen the earth and sky. Through everything God made, they can clearly see his invisible qualities—his eternal power and divine nature. So they have no excuse for not knowing God" (Romans 1:18-20).

Whatever God does, whether creating a planet or a butterfly, is effortless.

Think about this: "He creates and sustains all animate and inanimate things without the idea of any labor associated with human activity. He operates unspent."[34]

14 MAY

"Have you never heard? Have you never understood? The LORD is the everlasting God, the Creator of all the earth. He never grows weak or weary..." (Isaiah 40:28a).

Commenting on the Almighty power of God, A. W. Tozer wrote: "Since He has at His command all the power in the universe, the Lord God omnipotent can do anything as easily as anything else. All His acts are done without effort. He expends no energy that must be replenished. His self-sufficiency makes it unnecessary for Him to look outside of Himself for a renewal of strength. All the power required to do all that He wills to do lies in undiminished fullness in His own infinite being."[35]

God never needs to rest. He does not slumber nor sleep (Psalm 121:4). He does not become weary or tired (Isaiah 40:28).

All the power Father in Heaven has is matched by His limitless love for you. Knowing this, living this, will change your life!

"Only fools say in their hearts, 'There is no God.' They are corrupt, and their actions are evil; not one of them does good!" (Psalm 53:1).

MAY 15

"...It is impossible for God to lie" (Hebrews 6:18b).

God is omnipotent. This means that God can do anything. But, this also means that God cannot do everything!

When we say God is omnipotent, God can do anything, we mean that God can do anything that is consistent with His nature and character.

There are some things that God cannot do. These are things that are inconsistent with His character and nature. Through the

Bible, God informs us that:

- He cannot lie – "It is impossible for God to lie" (Hebrews 6:18b). God will never lie to us!
- He cannot be tempted – "Let no one say when he is tempted, 'I am being tempted by God'; for God cannot be tempted by evil, and He Himself does not tempt anyone" (James 1:13, NASB). God will never tempt us, nor can He be tempted by evil.
- He cannot look upon wickedness with favor – "Your eyes are too pure to approve evil, and You can not look on wickedness with favor..." (Habakkuk 1:13a, NASB).
- He cannot deny Himself – "If we are faithless, He remains faithful, for He cannot deny Himself" (2 Timothy 2:13, NASB). He must remain true to His faithful character.
- He cannot desert or forsake His children – " '...I will never leave you nor forsake you' " (Hebrews 13:5b, ESV). God cannot go back on His Word.

"Thank You, Lord, that there are some things You cannot do! I love You and Who You are! In Jesus' Name, Amen!"

16 MAY

"God has spoken plainly, and I have heard it many times: Power, O God, belongs to you" (Psalm 62:11).

God is omnipotent. This means that God has power over everything. God has sent us a clear, understandable picture of His power in His Son, Jesus Christ. Through Jesus Christ we see that God has:

- Power over death – "Then he walked over to the coffin and touched it, and the bearers stopped. 'Young man,' he said,

'I tell you, get up.' Then the dead boy sat up and began to talk! And Jesus gave him back to his mother" (Luke 7:14-15). "Then Jesus shouted, 'Lazarus, come out!' And the dead man came out, his hands and feet bound in graveclothes, his face wrapped in a headcloth. Jesus told them, 'Unwrap him and let him go!' " (John 11:43-44).

- Power over disease – "Jesus reached out and touched him. 'I am willing,' he said. 'Be healed!' And instantly the leprosy disappeared" (Matthew 8:3). "When Jesus arrived at Peter's house, Peter's mother-in-law was sick in bed with a high fever. But when Jesus touched her hand, the fever left her. Then she got up and prepared a meal for him" (Matthew 8:14-15).

- Power over demons – "That evening many demon-possessed people were brought to Jesus. He cast out the evil spirits with a simple command, and he healed all the sick" (Matthew 8:16).

- Power over nature – "...Then he got up and rebuked the wind and waves, and suddenly there was a great calm. The disciples were amazed. 'Who is this man?' they asked. 'Even the winds and waves obey him!' " (Matthew 8:26b-27).

Nothing is too difficult for God!

"For those who are believers, the doctrine of God's omnipotence is a vehicle to a profound trust. Believing in God's omnipotence means that we must also believe in his omnicompetence."[36]

"Give your burdens to the LORD, and he will take care of you. He will not permit the godly to slip and fall" (Psalm 55:22).

17 MAY

"God has spoken plainly, and I have heard it many times: Power, O God, belongs to you" (Psalm 62:11).

Remember, nothing is too difficult for God!

I read the story of a South American company that purchased a very nice printing press from a firm in the United States. After the press had been shipped and was assembled in South America, the workers couldn't get it to work properly.

After trying repeatedly to get it to work, the company finally wired a message to the manufacturer, asking for them to send a representative immediately to fix the press.

The U.S. firm understood how upset the South American company was, so they sent the person who had designed the press. But when he arrived, the purchasers were skeptical and cabled the manufacturer: "Your man is too young; send a more experienced person."

The reply came back: "He made the machine. He can fix it."

How much more true is this of God! What is the problem facing you? Ask yourself, "Is this problem too big for God?" God can make a way when there doesn't seem to be a way.

- He parts the sea.
- He brings water out of a rock.
- He provides manna in the desert.

Abraham and Sarah were facing an impossible situation (Genesis 18:14), but God, by His mighty power, supplied their

need, because, "...what God had promised, He was able also to perform" (Romans 4:21b, NASB).

Are you facing an impossible situation? What do these verses say to you?

May 18

"And we know that God causes everything to work together for the good of those who love God and are called according to his purpose for them" (Romans 8:28).

"Well, if God is all-powerful, why do bad things happen?" "Why doesn't God work to heal every sick person and part Red Seas and always miraculously supply again?"

People have honestly struggled with this for years. Rabbi Rubenstein, a leading Jewish theologian who lived through the Holocaust, concluded God was absent. Another rabbi, Harold S. Kushner, in his book, *When Bad Things Happen to Good People,* suggests that God must be helpless to stop the tragedies that come into our lives.

But the Scripture is still true, "...power belongs to God" (Psalm 62:11b). What we need to understand is that God's power serves His purposes, not ours.

Phillips Brooks said, "Faith says not, 'I see that it is good for me, so God must have sent it,' but, 'God sent it, and so it must be good for me.' "[37]

But, we also need to understand that God's Power is forever linked to His love!

Grace today

The historian Lord Acton wrote, "O, it is excellent to have a giant's strength. But it is tyrannous to use it like a giant."[38]

19 MAY

"You chart the path ahead of me and tell me where to stop and rest. Every moment you know where I am" (Psalm 139:3, TLB).

It takes faith and patience to not walk our own way but instead to take all our cues from the Lord. It goes without saying that this is also the wisest way to live. God has your life charted out, not like some kind of astrological prognostication, but plans of love, like a father has with a child.

Here's a verse to claim, perhaps it will become the verse you live by for the rest of this year: "For since the world began, no ear has heard, and no eye has seen a God like you, who works for those who wait for him!" (Isaiah 64:4).

"For from days of old they have not heard or perceived by ear, nor has the eye seen a God besides You, who acts in behalf of the one who waits for Him" (Isaiah 64:4, NASB).

20 MAY

"Oh, what a wonderful God we have! How great are his wisdom and knowledge and riches! How impossible it is for us to understand his decisions and his methods!" (Romans 11:33, TLB).

God is omniscient. That is, God knows everything or is all-knowing.

He has complete and infinite knowledge! One theologian put it this way: "He knows all things both actual and possible; past, present, and future; completely, perfectly, simultaneously, and eternally."

God does not learn. He has never learned, and He cannot learn! Because He has perfect knowledge, He never has to learn anything! If He ever had to learn anything, He would be less than perfect and would not be God. God's complete knowledge is an innate knowledge that is complete and entire all the time. He had it before anything existed (archetypal knowledge), and it is not the result of observation or learning.

A. W. Tozer gave us such a classic statement on God's omniscience in his book, *The Knowledge of the Holy.* In it he said, "God knows instantly and effortlessly all matter and all matters, all mind and every mind, all spirit and all spirits, all being and every being, all creaturehood and all creatures, every plurality and all pluralities, all law and every law, all relations, all causes, all thoughts, all mysteries, all enigmas, all feeling, all desires, every unuttered secret, all thrones and dominions, all personalities, all things visible and invisible in heaven and in earth, motion, space, time, life, death, good, evil, heaven, and hell."[39]

You could never give God a surprise party! Our all-knowing God knows all things!

21 MAY

"For who can know the LORD's thoughts? Who knows enough to give him advice?" (Romans 11:34).

Though Father knows all about you, He still loves you and accepts you!

It's not like God gets a surprise when He gets us! He's not ordering us sight unseen over the web.

Marriage: it's always a surprise, no matter how well you think you know the person you are marrying!

God is never surprised! He never sits in heaven saying, "I can't believe he did that!"

Most of us fear being known, and we put up walls in our lives because we feel that if people really knew us, they would not like us. So we live to try to gain, or keep, or not lose people's love and acceptance. Approval is so important to us!

God's knowledge is perfect and complete. This means He knows us perfectly and completely! And even though God knows us like this, He still loves us and accepts us!

22 MAY

"O LORD, you have examined my heart and know everything about me" (Psalm 139:1).

Though Father in Heaven knows all about us, He still loves us!

Let's look at Psalm 139:2-4 (TLB):

- Verse 2a – "You know when I sit or stand." The Lord's knowledge extends to every intimate detail of our lives—more detail than we could/would even imagine: "Are not two sparrows sold for a cent? And yet not one of them will fall to the ground apart from your Father. But the very hairs of your head are all numbered" (Matthew 10:29-30, NASB).
- Verse 2b – "When far away you know my every thought." The prophet Ezekiel said, "Then the Spirit of the LORD came upon me, and he told me to say, '...for I know every thought that comes into your minds...' " (Ezekiel 11:5).
- Verse 3a – "You chart the path ahead of me and tell me where to stop and rest."
- Verse 3b – "Every moment you know where I am." A term that refers to our whole manner of life and everything that pertains to it. Job said, "But He knows the way I take; when He has tried me, I shall come forth as gold" (Job 23:10, NASB). "Does He not see my ways, and number all my steps?" (Job 31:4, NASB). Psalm 1:6 says: "For the LORD knows the way of the righteous, but the way of the wicked will perish" (NASB).
- Verse 4 – "You know what I am going to say before I even say it."

MAY 23

"Don't worry about the wicked or envy those who do wrong. For like grass, they soon fade away. Like spring flowers, they soon wither" (Psalm 37:1-2).

Grace today

Sometimes we need to step back and get a bigger picture. The wicked are not getting away with anything in the long term, actually anything they gain they will ultimately lose.

You, however, have eternal life with the Lord Jesus! You have been given everything. Your joy will never end.

Here's the perspective: Grass and flowers or eternal glory!

I'm praying the Lord gives you a *big* picture day!

24 MAY

Do you ever worry about your children? "What's going to happen to them?" "How are they going to get through this dangerous world?" Well, the Bible tells us that our faithful Father is going to continue to take care of them. Psalm 119:90 says: "Your faithfulness extends to every generation, as enduring as the earth you created."

God is faithful in what He says. Our Living God would never lie to you or lead you astray. The Bible testifies to this.

"God is not a man, so he does not lie. He is not a human, so he does not change his mind. Has he ever spoken and failed to act? Has he ever promised and not carried it through?" (Numbers 23:19).

God is the "...God, who cannot lie..." (Titus 1:2, NASB).
The Book of Hebrews 6:18 says that "...it is impossible for God to lie..."

"If we are faithless, He remains faithful, for He cannot deny Himself" (2 Timothy 2:13, NASB).

Having a faithful God is such a blessing to us. God will never deceive you nor betray you. He is always there for you and your family. You are His beloved child!

MAY 25

Have you been struggling with temptation lately? Here are some things I think will encourage you.

One man said, "My temptation has become my strength, for to the very fight with it I owe my force." Remember, if you were not saved, you wouldn't have this struggle. You didn't fight temptation before you were saved; usually you just gave into it! Struggling is a sign of life! Keep in mind the daily battles you are having are part of a much larger picture. Jesus is coming back soon. He has won the war! You do have His victory.

"Be strong! Be courageous! Do not be afraid of them! For the Lord your God will be with you. He will neither fail you nor forsake you" (Deuteronomy 31:6, TLB).

Martin Luther said, "My temptations have been my masters in divinity."

"A final word: Be strong in the Lord and in his mighty power" (Ephesians 6:10).

26 MAY

Corrie ten Boom shared a special story about God's protection:

Many people came to know and trust the Lord during World War II. One was an Englishman who was held in a German prison camp for a long period of time.

One day he read Psalm 91: "He who dwells in the shelter of the Most High will abide in the shadow of the Almighty. I will say to the LORD, 'My refuge and my fortress, my God, in whom I trust!' ...For you have made the LORD, my refuge, even the Most High, your dwelling place. No evil will befall you, nor will any plague come near your tent. For He will give His angels charge concerning you, to guard you in all your ways" (Psalm 91:1-2, 9-11, NASB).

"Father in Heaven," he prayed, "I see all these yet I also have to die here? I am still young and I very much want to work in Your kingdom here on earth."

He received this answer: "Rely on what you have just read and go home!"

Trusting in the Lord, he got up and walked into the corridor toward the gate. A guard called out, "Prisoner, where are you going?"

"I am under the protection of the Most High," he replied. The guard came to attention and let him pass, for Adolf Hitler was known as "the Most High."

He came to the gate, where a group of guards stood. They

commanded him to stop and asked where he was going. "I am under the protection of the Most High." All the guards stood at attention as he walked out the gate.

The English officer made his way through the German countryside and eventually reached England, where he told how he had made his escape.

He was the only one to come out of that prison alive.[40]

"Never be afraid to trust an unknown future to a known God" (Corrie ten Boom).

MAY 27

Look at what God says of Himself in Malachi 3:6: "I am the LORD, and I do not change..."

So many things in our life change so fast! Change can happen quickly. Someone has said, "The president of today is the postage stamp of tomorrow." Just think for a moment about all the change around us:

- Changes in technology – make it difficult for us to keep up and stay "state of the art."
- Changes in vocation – are not uncommon anymore. Who works in the precise area of their degree ten years after graduating from college anymore?
- Changes at work – can cause real insecurity. You see yourself trying to keep up in a market where "younger is better" and twenty-somethings have the stress on them that people in mid-career used to carry.
- Changes in the financial world – are unsettling. People

run ahead of debt, but how long can they run that kind of marathon?

Someone has said, "The only thing you can count on in this life is change." But, you know what? There's one more thing you can count on: God never changes!

"Jesus Christ is the same yesterday, today, and forever" (Hebrews 13:8).

Not all change is bad! I'm glad for some of the huge changes that occurred in the last century. You may have had a grandparent who actually had horse-drawn carriages instead of cars! They cooked over wood stoves and didn't have any electricity or electric appliances. They raised families without microwaves, did homework or business without computers and the Internet! I wouldn't want to go back to those days, would you? What would happen if we had to live without:

- microwaves
- cell phones
- antibiotics
- cars
- air conditioning

The Bible tells us that God is unchanging or immutable, which means He does not mutate or change.

Obviously, we change, we grow, we mature, we grow wiser. Our hair color changes or it falls out, we lose weight or gain weight, we can be moody or joy-filled, but God never changes.

A. W. Tozer wrote: "The immutability [unchangeableness] of God appears in its most perfect beauty when viewed against the

mutability [changeability] of men. In God no change is possible; in men change is impossible to escape. Neither the man is fixed nor his world, and he and it are in constant flux."[41]

MAY 28

Look at what God says of Himself in Malachi 3:6: "I am the LORD, and I do not change..."

Change can be sad and difficult; you know that all too well. Sometimes we experience the heartbreak of changes in relationships. Even the most sacred relationships sometimes change. Couples who fell in love and were sure it would never end, find themselves consulting with attorneys and wondering how it all changed.

You may be experiencing a change in a friendship. People change, people move away physically or emotionally, and you are left alone.

Moms and Dads who once held a precious little baby and looked lovingly into those little eyes, fifteen to eighteen years later can't figure out what's going on behind those eyes anymore, if they can even get their child to look at them. What changed?

"Why did things have to change?" — you think as you sit in the nursing home with an aging parent. You want to remember them as that young Mom or Dad who used to run around the house and play hide-and-go-seek with you, but now they can't even get around without a walker. Life has changed.

grace today

As a result, many of us feel lonely and isolated today even though we are surrounded with others and are busier than ever. What's changed?

Change makes life distressing at times and uncertain at all times.

Where can we turn for stability, for security? We can turn to God!

Your loving Father in Heaven never changes! God is unchangeable! He will never leave you! Hold onto this:

"...For He [God] Himself has said, I will not in any way fail you nor give you up nor leave you without support. [I will] not, [I will] not, [I will] not in any degree leave you helpless nor forsake nor let [you] down (relax My hold on you)! [Assuredly not!] So we take comfort and are encouraged and confidently and boldly say, The Lord is my Helper; I will not be seized with alarm [I will not fear or dread or be terrified]. What can man do to me?" (Hebrews 13:5b-6, AMP).

29 MAY

"Jesus Christ is the same yesterday, today, and forever" (Hebrews 13:8).

There is an inward consistency in the nature of God.

Pastor A. W. Pink, in his book, *The Attributes of God,* wrote: "[God] cannot change for the better, for He is already perfect; and being perfect, he cannot change for the worse. Altogether unaffected by anything outside Himself, improvement or deterioration is impossible. He is perpetually the same."[42]

We can be sure that God will never change. Look at James 1:17, "Every good thing given and every perfect gift is from above, coming down from the Father of lights, with whom there is no variation, or shifting shadow" (NASB).

Look at what this means. Our Father is always good and has no dark side! When we became His children, we became a child of the light!

"For you are all children of the light and of the day; we don't belong to darkness and night. So be on your guard, not asleep like the others. Stay alert and be clearheaded. Night is the time when people sleep and drinkers get drunk. But let us who live in the light be clearheaded, protected by the armor of faith and love, and wearing as our helmet the confidence of our salvation. For God chose to save us through our Lord Jesus Christ, not to pour out his anger on us. Christ died for us so that, whether we are dead or alive when he returns, we can live with him forever. So encourage each other and build each other up, just as you are already doing" (1 Thessalonians 5:5-11).

MAY 30

"Trust in the LORD always, for the LORD GOD is the eternal Rock" (Isaiah 26:4).

Because God does not change:
- God can be trusted – You can put your trust in God. You can know that no matter what happens, if you come to Him by faith through Jesus Christ, He will be your friend forever.

grace today

- His character will never change – Who He is, how He acts and reacts. He is holy, He is unlike anyone you could ever know. He is righteous, what is right is right, that will never change. He is loving! He is forgiving! He is merciful, not giving us what we deserve! He is gracious, giving us what we don't deserve!
- We can count on Him to always be there for us! – "Make sure that your character is free from the love of money, being content with what you have; for He Himself has said, 'I WILL NEVER DESERT YOU, NOR WILL I EVER FORSAKE YOU' " (Hebrews 13:5, NASB).

31 MAY

"That is why the LORD says, 'Turn to me now, while there is time. Give me your hearts. Come with fasting, weeping, and mourning. Don't tear your clothing in your grief, but tear your hearts instead.' Return to the LORD your God, for he is merciful and compassionate, slow to get angry and filled with unfailing love. He is eager to relent and not punish" (Joel 2:12-13).

God's patience is different than ours. For one thing, it's perfect and it's also different in that it's directed, not towards time-bound events, but towards people.

God never has to be patient with events because He controls them. His patience is always exercised towards us, towards people.

The Apostle Peter wrote, "The Lord... he is being patient for your sake. He does not want anyone to be destroyed, but wants everyone to repent" (2 Peter 3:9).

God has been accused of being too patient with people. This was the prodigal prophet Jonah's complaint against God. He complained, "...I knew that you are a merciful and compassionate God, slow to get angry and filled with unfailing love. You are eager to turn back from destroying people" (Jonah 4:2b).

We may complain about God's patience towards other people, but we'd never complain when God shows us great patience!

Here's the application: "Always be humble and gentle. Be patient with each other, making allowance for each other's faults because of your love" (Ephesians 4:2-3). I know we're going to have plenty of opportunities to apply this text today!

"The LORD is slow to get angry, but his power is great, and he never lets the guilty go unpunished" (Nahum 1:3a).

There is a difference between God's mercy and God's long-suffering or patience.

God's mercy has more to do with the results of our sin, sin's consequences.

God's long-suffering or patience has to do with the sin itself. God is patiently bearing with our sins waiting for us to repent, temporarily withholding the judgment and wrath that we deserve.

God, in patience, may be withholding His wrath right now, but ultimately His wrath will be poured out on sin. For those who refuse to turn to the Lord and turn away from their sins, a day of reckoning is coming:

> "But because you are stubborn and refuse to turn from your sin, you are storing up terrible punishment for yourself. For a day of anger is coming, when God's righteous judgment will be revealed" (Romans 2:5).

A day of judgment is coming when God's wrath will be revealed:

> "God overlooked people's ignorance about these things in earlier times, but now he commands everyone everywhere to repent of their sins and turn to him. For he has set a day for judging the world with justice by the man he has appointed, and he proved to everyone who this is by raising him from the dead" (Acts 17:30-31).

2 June

"The LORD is slow to get angry, but his power is great, and he never lets the guilty go unpunished" (Nahum 1:3a).

I read about a little farming community where most of the farmers were godly men. They would spend Sunday in fellowship in church and with believers instead of working in their fields; but there was one notable exception: there was one man who claimed to be an atheist. He'd often make fun of his neighbors' religious habits and say, "Hands that work are better than hands that pray."

Part of his land was right next to the church; so just to be ornery, he would make a point of driving his tractor by the church during the worship services.

One year his land produced more than anyone else's in the county, and he boasted about it in a letter to the editor that was published in the local newspaper. In it he boasted of what a man could do without God. The editor printed the man's letter and then added this terse comment: "God doesn't settle all His accounts in the month of October."

Don't make the mistake of misinterpreting or misunderstanding the patience and longsuffering of the Lord in your life. The Lord is patient because He doesn't want anyone to perish, but people who abuse the patience of God will ultimately ruin their lives.

There's a hefty warning in Proverbs 29:1, "A man who hardens his neck after much reproof will suddenly be broken beyond remedy" (NASB).

"For God is Spirit, so those who worship him must worship in spirit and in truth" (John 4:24).

"But sanctify Christ as Lord in your hearts, always being ready to make a defense to everyone who asks you to give an account for the hope that is in you..." (1 Peter 3:15a, NASB).

Worship is not merely meant to be our weekly emotional fix. We do not come to worship God because we get something, but because He is worthy of our worship.

Remember Asaph in Psalm 73? He was troubled, discouraged, and weak. He had hard questions about life and no answers in sight; that is... "until [he] came into the sanctuary of God" (Psalm 73:17, NASB).

He did not come to worship God to "forget his problems" as so many do. He came to find a solution! And He did!

Dr. Martyn Lloyd-Jones in his book, *Faith on Trial,* comments on Asaph's experience and makes some wonderful applications for us today:

> What happened to this man [Asaph] was not that he went to the temple—into the church, so to speak—and that listening to the strains of beautiful music coming from the organ, and looking at the stained-glass windows and the beautiful lighting, he gradually began to feel a little bit better and forgot his troubles for the time being. No! It was something rational—'then understood I their end'—it was a matter of understanding.

grace today

True religion was never meant just to produce some general effect. The Bible is a revelation of God's ways with respect to man. It is meant to give 'understanding.' If our practice of religion does not give us understanding, then it is something that may well do us harm and we should be better without it.

Let us never forget that the message of the Bible is addressed primarily to the mind, to the understanding. There is nothing about the gospel that is more satisfying than this. It does not merely give me an experience; it enables me to understand life. I have knowledge; I have understanding; I know. I can 'give a reason' for the hope that is in me.[43]

4 JUNE

"Therefore I urge you, brethren, by the mercies of God, to present your bodies a living and holy sacrifice, acceptable to God, which is your spiritual service of worship" (Romans 12:1, NASB).

When God saved us, He saved not only our souls and spirits, He saved our bodies. The Bible teaches that real worship involves offering our bodies to God.

God says that our bodies are His temples.

1 Corinthians 6:19-20: "Don't you know that your body is the temple of the Holy Spirit, who lives in you and was given to you by God? You do not belong to yourself, for God bought you with a high price. So you must honor God with your body."

We are to live in such a way that Christ is "exalted in our bodies." See Philippians 1:20.

Romans 6:13: "Do not let any part of your body become an instrument of evil to serve sin. Instead, give yourselves completely to God, for you were dead, but now you have new life. So use your whole body as an instrument to do what is right for the glory of God."

Richard J. Foster said, "If worship does not change us, it has not been worship. To stand before the Holy One of eternity is to change. Worship begins in holy expectancy; it ends in holy obedience."

May the Lord bless you with a sense of His presence and give you His strong comfort and peace!

JUNE 5

"Therefore I urge you, brethren, by the mercies of God, to present your bodies a living and holy sacrifice, acceptable to God, which is your spiritual service of worship" (Romans 12:1, NASB).

Are you orthodox? The term "orthodox" means "right praise!" Are you orthodox? Are you offering God the "right praise?"

Are you worshipping God with all that you are? Deuteronomy 6:5 commands, "And you must love the LORD your God with all your heart, all your soul, and all your strength."

One person has called worship, "the response of the creature to the Eternal."[44]

grace today

Whenever people have seen God for Who He really is, it has shattered their pride, and has changed them!

Think of the lost, they hate Jesus, but they will have to bow and say that He is Lord, not because some angel is behind them forcing them to, but because merely standing in His presence they will *have* to!

Bishop Hadley Moule said that he would rather tone down a fanatic than raise a corpse!

Think about how we can more expressively and appropriately worship our mighty God and Savior.

6 JUNE

"You must fear the LORD your God and worship him and cling to him..." (Deuteronomy 10:20a).

A life of real, extreme worship involves offering God more than praise, offerings of money and song. It also involves washing our hands!

Look at what David says Psalm 24:3-4: "Who may ascend into the hill of the LORD? And who may stand in His holy place? He who has clean hands and a pure heart, who has not lifted up his soul to falsehood and has not sworn deceitfully" (NASB).

"Did you wash your hands?" I think I'd be a millionaire if I got a dollar for every time I asked my three children that question. How about you?

After shaking thousands of hands before and after each service at Calvary, I always go and wash my hands. It's the healthy thing to do! Most colds and flues are passed through the hands. I often joke with those around me that I need to go and "wash off the fellowship!" On Saturdays and Sundays I may wash my hands dozens of times.

Keep your hands clean. Your hands are the quickest way for you to pick up disease. The Lord knows that and that's why He uses this analogy.

That's what we need to do with our contact with the world. Realize that what the world has is contagious. It won't kill us anymore, but it can make us really sick. We need to wash up and stay clean.

Here are two promises of cleansing for you:
- Psalm 51:7 – "Purify me from my sins, and I will be clean; wash me, and I will be whiter than snow."
- 1 John 1:8-9 – "If we say that we have no sin, we are only fooling ourselves and refusing to accept the truth. But if we confess our sins to him, he can be depended on to forgive us and to cleanse us from every wrong" (TLB).

JUNE 7

"O God, we meditate on your unfailing love as we worship in your Temple. As your name deserves, O God, you will be praised to the ends of the earth..." (Psalm 48:9-10).

grace today

How is our Christian worship different from religious worship?

Religion can be defined as man's attempts to reach to God. Christianity is defined by the fact that God has reached down to us and brought us to Himself through the death and resurrection of our Lord Jesus Christ.

Sammy Tippet states the difference between Christian worship and religious worship very well in His book, *Worthy of Worship:*

> Herein lies the great difference between religious worship and true Christian worship:
>
> Religious worship originates in the flesh, or in the outer man. Christian worship originates in the Spirit, or in the innermost man.
>
> Religious worship is based on human performance. Christian worship is a work of the grace of God in the heart of man.
>
> Religious worship attempts to build an inward relationship with God by outward works. Christian worship is a result of an inward relationship with God where the Spirit of God freely flows outward, producing works of God's righteousness.
>
> Religious worship honors the worshiper. Christian worship honors the One worshiped.
>
> Religious worship compares itself to the worship of others. Christian worship sees only the glory of Jesus.[45]

"Then Jesus said to His disciples, 'If anyone wishes to come after Me, he must deny himself, and take up his cross and follow Me' " (Matthew 16:24, NASB).

"Deny yourself?" Is this cruel? No, this is crucial. Jesus says, "his" cross. There is a cross for every believer, a cross that Jesus wants us to carry. The cross is something that comes to you, not something redemptive, for Jesus died on the redemptive cross for you. The cross that Jesus is talking about is the experience of laying down your life, perhaps your will, your desires, your attitudes, going your own way. There is always a death with a cross. A death to our own way, but when Jesus gives us a cross, He always gives a resurrection! The sooner we die to "my image," "my reputation," "my will," etc., the sooner we will experience resurrection life!

Paul experienced this life. He said, "that I may know Him and the power of His resurrection and the fellowship of His sufferings, being conformed to His death; in order that I may attain to the resurrection from the dead" (Philippians 3:10-11, NASB).

Look at the power at work in your life!

"I also pray that you will understand the incredible greatness of God's power for us who believe him. This is the same mighty power that raised Christ from the dead and seated him in the place of honor at God's right hand in the heavenly realms. Now he is far above any ruler or authority or power or leader or anything else—not only in this world but also in the world to come. God has put all things under the authority of Christ and

has made him head over all things for the benefit of the church. And the church is his body; it is made full and complete by Christ, who fills all things everywhere with himself" (Ephesians 1:19-23).

9 JUNE

"Simon, Simon, Satan has asked to sift each of you like wheat. But I have pleaded in prayer for you, Simon, that your faith should not fail. So when you have repented and turned to me again, strengthen your brothers" (Luke 22:31-32).

Satan desired to sift Peter like wheat. Peter was being groomed to be a leader in the New Testament church. That made him a target.

Satan is targeting you. He wants to discredit and attack you, and the bigger and larger the work and more successfully the Lord uses you, the larger the attacks become.

It's sort of terrifying to know that you are in the crosshairs of the enemy of your soul. But Jesus prayed for Peter, "...I have pleaded in prayer for you... that your faith should not fail..."

The Lord doesn't pray for a smooth path, but He prays that we might endure the affliction. True growth comes through affliction. There is a depth of fellowship that only comes from suffering. There's a depth of suffering that is the only way to find fellowship; it stimulates tremendous spiritual growth. This is suffering according to the will of God. Peter, later writing under the inspiration of the Holy Spirit, would say, "Therefore, those also who suffer according to the will of God shall entrust their

souls to a faithful Creator in doing what is right" (1 Peter 4:19, NASB).

Right now, as you read this, Jesus is praying for you. You're not on your own! He's on your side!

To think of the Lord praying for you is a wonderful thought. I know when people say, "I'm praying for you," it always feels so great, but here Jesus says *He's* praying for you! It just doesn't get any better than that!

He is praying five prayers for you. The real Lord's Prayer is recorded in John 17; Jesus prays:

- That we might be one in Him (verses 11b, 21-23).
- That Father would be glorified in us (verse 5).
- That we might be with Him in glory (verse 24).
- That we might be kept safe (verse 12).
- That we would be sanctified (verses 17-19).

Jesus is praying these prayers for you. He said, "I do not ask on behalf of these alone, but for those also who believe in Me through their word" (verse 20).

Remember, all through this day Jesus is praying for you.

June 10

"Simon, Simon, Satan has asked to sift each of you like wheat. But I have pleaded in prayer for you, Simon, that your faith should not fail. So when you have repented and turned to me again, strengthen your brothers" (Luke 22:31-32).

grace today

God is for us! Greater is He that is in us than he that is in the world. The Book of Hebrews tells us that Jesus "...is able to save completely those who come to God through him, because he always lives to intercede for them" (Hebrews 7:25, NIV).

There were steps that led to Peter's denial of the Lord. They are the same steps that lead us into big trouble. Here are some of the things that led to his fall:

- His self-confidence – Peter was convinced that though the other disciples might deny the Lord, he never would.
- Arguing with Jesus – Need I say more?
- Sleeping when he should have been praying.
- He tried to fight in the flesh.
- He followed Jesus from far off.
- He was warming his hands at the enemy's fire. He was becoming comfortable around worldly things, getting closer and closer to them.

Retracing Peter's steps is definitely learning things the hard way. It's much better to learn the lesson of absolute reliance on Jesus and not your own strength. I believe, don't you, that many times God allows us to fail so that we learn to be dependent upon Him?

If I have followed in Peter's steps, I can learn the lesson that "apart from Jesus, I can do nothing." Peter learned to be dependent and went on to be mightily used by God!

11 JUNE

"...And who is adequate for such a task as this?" (2 Corinthians 2:16b).

What do you think Peter, James and John thought when Jesus said, "You are the light of the world," or "You are the salt of the earth," or "Go into the whole world and preach the Gospel"? They were simple Galileans. Who is adequate for such a task as this?

Think about this: the first word Jesus gave to His disciples wasn't, "Go," it was "Wait" (Acts 1:4, NASB).

One of the problems today is that many of those who are going out to serve the Lord are not first waiting. Before we try to do something *for* the Lord, we must first receive the Holy Spirit's power *from* the Lord.

The only way to have victory in the Christian life is to have the full power of the Holy Spirit. Jesus wants to pour out His Spirit on you (Luke 24:49; Acts 1:5, 8).

Jesus put it so simply: "You fathers—if your children ask for a fish, do you give them a snake instead? Or if they ask for an egg, do you give them a scorpion? Of course not! So if you sinful people know how to give good gifts to your children, how much more will your heavenly Father give the Holy Spirit to those who ask him" (Luke 11:11-13).

The only way we can be adequate to serve the Lord is to have the Lord's special power.

"Heavenly Father, please give me the power of the Holy Spirit. Cleanse my life and fill me with His power. I believe Your promise and receive from You right now. In Jesus' Name, Amen."

12 JUNE

"...For I know the one in whom I trust, and I am sure that he is able to guard what I have entrusted to him until the day of his return" (2 Timothy 1:12b).

Paul lived his life in tremendous assurance and peace. He trusted God and lived as one who knew that God was absolutely in control of everything that happened to him.

Let's look at verse 8: "So never be ashamed to tell others about our Lord. And don't be ashamed of me, either, even though I'm in prison for him. With the strength God gives you, be ready to suffer with me for the sake of the Good News" (2 Timothy 1:8).

Paul didn't consider himself to be a prisoner of Rome! He considered himself to be "In prison for him," "the Lord's prisoner!" (NASB).

Paul gives us several reasons why we can face uncertain times having the assurance of salvation.

We are saved! 2 Timothy 1:9 says, "For God saved us..." The Greek word "saved" used here is in the aorist tense, which means, "He has saved us in a point of time." In other words, our salvation is an accomplished thing!

This should encourage us to continue on in suffering for the Lord, knowing that we are saved and accepted right now "in Christ Jesus!" We have eternal life. We don't have to live in uncertainty of that anymore.

"...for I know the one in whom I trust, and I am sure that he is able to guard what I have entrusted to him until the day of his return" (2 Timothy 1:12b).

We can face the future with certainty because Jesus has abolished death!

2 Timothy 1:10b says, "...our Savior Christ Jesus, who abolished death and brought life and immortality to light through the gospel" (NASB).

True believers in Jesus can say with absolute assurance, "I shall never die!"

Jesus has abolished death! Jesus has broken the power of death!

Look at what Jesus said to Martha in John 11:25-26: "Jesus said to her, 'I am the resurrection and the life; he who believes in Me will live even if he dies, and everyone who lives and believes in Me will never die. Do you believe this?' " (NASB).

Look at John 8:51, "Truly, truly, I say to you, if anyone keeps My word he will never see death" (NASB).

I read the moving story of D. L. Moody's last days and of his confidence in Christ as he faced death.

On a hot August Sunday in 1899, D.L. Moody preached in New York City and said, "Someday, you will read in the papers that Moody is dead. Don't believe a word of it. At

that moment, I shall be more alive than I am now... I was born of the flesh in 1837. I was born of the Spirit in 1855. That which is born of the flesh may die. That which is born of the Spirit shall live forever."

Moody didn't realize that by December 22nd, he would be dead. He became ill during meetings in November in Kansas City. He had to go home and have R. A. Torrey finish them for him.

Thursday, December 21st, he told his family, "I'm not discouraged. I want to live as long as I am useful, but when my work is done I want to be up and off."

The next day, Moody awakened after a restless night. In careful, measured words he said, "Earth recedes, heaven opens before me!" His son, Will, thought that his father was dreaming. "No, this is no dream, Will. It is beautiful. It is like a trance. If this is death, it is sweet. There is no valley here. God is calling me, and I must go."

A little while later he said, "This is my triumph; this is my coronation day." After speaking these words, he quietly moved into the presence of Christ.[46]

Look at John 8:51-52, " 'Truly, truly, I say to you, if anyone keeps My word he will never see death.' The Jews said to Him, 'Now we know that You have a demon. Abraham died, and the prophets also; and you say, "If anyone keeps My word, he will never taste of death" ' " (NASB).

"For to me, to live is Christ and to die is gain" (Philippians 1:21, NASB).

I read about a woman who had been diagnosed with a terminal illness and had been given three months to live. So as she was getting her things "in order," she contacted her pastor and had him come to her house to discuss certain aspects of her final wishes.

She told him which songs she wanted sung at the service, what Scriptures she would like read, and she even chose the clothes she wanted to be buried in. The woman also requested to be buried with her Bible.

Everything was in order, and the pastor was about to leave when the woman suddenly remembered something very important to her. "There's one more thing," she said excitedly.

"What's that?" he replied. "This is very important, I want to be buried with a fork in my right hand!"

The pastor stood looking at the woman, not knowing quite what to say. "That's surprises you, doesn't it?" the woman asked.

"Well, to be honest, I'm puzzled by the request," said the pastor. The woman explained, "In all my years of attending church socials and potluck dinners, I always remember that when the dishes of the main course were being cleared, someone would inevitably lean over and say, 'keep your fork.' It was my favorite part because I knew that something better was coming... like

velvety chocolate cake or deep-dish apple pie. Something wonderful and with substance!"

"So I just want people to see me there in that casket with a fork in my hand, and I want them to wonder, 'What's with the fork?' Then I want you to tell them: 'Keep your fork... the best is yet to come!' "

"For to me, to live is Christ and to die is gain. But if I am to live on in the flesh, this will mean fruitful labor for me; and I do not know which to choose. But I am hard-pressed from both directions, having the desire to depart and be with Christ, for that is very much better" (Philippians 1:21-23, NASB).

"That is why we never give up. Though our bodies are dying, our spirits are being renewed every day. For our present troubles are small and won't last very long. Yet they produce for us a glory that vastly outweighs them and will last forever! So we don't look at the troubles we can see now; rather, we fix our gaze on things that cannot be seen. For the things we see now will soon be gone, but the things we cannot see will last forever... So we are always confident, even though we know that as long as we live in these bodies we are not at home with the Lord. For we live by believing and not by seeing. Yes, we are fully confident, and we would rather be away from these earthly bodies, for then we will be at home with the Lord" (2 Corinthians 4:16-18; 5:6-8).

15 JUNE

"When he sits on the throne as king, he must copy for himself this body of instruction on a scroll in the presence of the Levitical

priests. He must always keep that copy with him and read it daily as long as he lives. That way he will learn to fear the LORD his God by obeying all the terms of these instructions and decrees. This regular reading will prevent him from becoming proud and acting as if he is above his fellow citizens. It will also prevent him from turning away from these commands in the smallest way. And it will ensure that he and his descendants will reign for many generations in Israel" (Deuteronomy 17:18-20).

Israel's kings were to immerse themselves in the Word of God. They were to:
- Copy the Word.
- Consult it daily (read it every day).
- Carry it with them (always keep it near).

I'd like to encourage you to try living like a king! Take a portion of the Word of God and copy it, type it out or write it out by hand. Start with a short book like Jude or Second or Third John. You'll be amazed at how much you get out of it. You'll see things you've never seen before. It's like the difference between driving through a neighborhood at thirty-five miles per hour and walking through it and seeing all the details!

Then get a small New Testament or New Testament portion, like the Gospel of John, and carry it with you. Read it when you have time and consult it daily. You can also load the Scriptures onto your PDA or your iPod.

Hey! You're starting to look like a king already!

16 JUNE

"The LORD said to Moses, 'Give Aaron the following
instructions: When you set up the seven lamps in the lampstand,
place them so their light shines forward in front of the
lampstand.' So Aaron did this. He set up the seven lamps so they
reflected their light forward, just as the LORD had commanded
Moses" (Numbers 8:1-3).

The light of the lampstand in the tabernacle was to shine
forward. We are to shine as lights in this world, forwarding the
light of Jesus into the darkness all around us.

Is your life shining in the right direction?

17 JUNE

"For God loved the world so much that he gave his one and only
Son, so that everyone who believes in him will not perish but
have eternal life" (John 3:16).

The Bible contains a love story, the story of God's love for you
and me.

What is God's love like? God's love is passionate.

"God told them, 'I've never quit loving you and never will.
Expect love, love, and more love!' " (Jeremiah 31:3b, MSG).

God's love is also personal.

God loves you as if you were the only person on earth. He
knows you and cares for you.

I want to share with you the verse the Lord used to tell me how much He personally loved me. I was a depressed teenager, desperate to know if the Lord loved me. I had just thrown my Bible across the room. I was mad at God and angry with life. I cried out to God, "You'd better tell me You love me or I'll never have anything to do with You the rest of my life!" Something compelled me to pick up the Bible, and it opened to this passage; it's the only place in the Bible where God says, "I love you!"

Look at what the Lord, in His great grace and mercy, showed me:

> "But now, ...the one who formed you says, 'Do not be afraid, for I have ransomed you. I have called you by name; you are mine. When you go through deep waters, I will be with you. When you go through rivers of difficulty, you will not drown. When you walk through the fire of oppression, you will not be burned up; the flames will not consume you. For I am the LORD, your God, the Holy One of Israel, your Savior... you are precious to me. You are honored, and I love you' " (Isaiah 43:1-4).

God is loving and God is good!

JUNE 18

No one will love you the way the Lord loves you!

David expresses God's unique love: "O LORD, you have examined my heart and know everything about me... You know what I am going to say even before I say it, LORD... How precious are your thoughts about me, O God! They cannot be

numbered! I can't even count them; they outnumber the grains of sand! And when I wake up, you are still with me!" (Psalm 139:1, 4, 17-18).

Human love is generally conditional! But God's love is absolutely perfect; He loves His children unconditionally!

Just think about how much God loves you: "Yet Jerusalem says, 'The LORD has deserted us; the Lord has forgotten us.' 'Never! Can a mother forget her nursing child? Can she feel no love for the child she has borne? But even if that were possible, I would not forget you! See, I have written your name on the palms of my hands...' " (Isaiah 49:14-16a).

Your name is written on the hands of the LORD!

Everything in the world is revolving around God's plan, and we are at the center of God's plan!

19 JUNE

God's love is persevering. We have Jesus' own promise that His love for us will keep us close to Him!

"And this is the will of God, that I should not lose even one of all those he has given me, but that I should raise them up at the last day" (John 6:39).

"And I am certain that God, who began the good work within you, will continue his work until it is finally finished on the day when Christ Jesus returns" (Philippians 1:6).

There are three things you can always count on:
1. God loves you.
2. God has a plan.
3. God is in control.

God cares for us. Everything in the world is revolving around God's plan, and we are at the center of His plan.

JUNE 20

QUESTION: "Who's the greatest giver of all time?"

ANSWER: "Jesus!"

"You know the generous grace of our Lord Jesus Christ. Though he was rich, yet for your sakes he became poor, so that by his poverty he could make you rich" (2 Corinthians 8:9).

Do we really understand His love and His grace? Are we living like people who understand His grace?

Let's spend some time looking at His grace. We see it best as we look at His giving. We see the Greatest Giver of all time!

Jesus gave freely; His motivation was His love for us. No one had to coerce Him into giving to us because He delights to give to us. Jesus said, "If you then, being evil know how to give good gifts to your children, how much more... your Heavenly Father..." (Luke 11:13, NASB).

Jesus left us a model for giving. He gave freely; His motivation was love.

grace today

Think about it: Do I give to God? Why do I give? What is my deep-seated motivation for giving to God?

"You know the generous grace of our Lord Jesus Christ. Though he was rich, yet for your sakes he became poor, so that by his poverty he could make you rich" (2 Corinthians 8:9).

He gave sacrificially. This Scripture says, "Though he was rich, yet for your sakes he became poor..." Love led Him to give all that He was and all that He had.

Think of who He was and what He had. He was:

> God....................yet He humbled Himself and became a man.
> Lord of angels....yet He became a little lower than the angels.
> All-powerful...yet He became weak.
> Lord of lords..yet He became a servant.
> Loved...yet He became despised.
> Honored........................yet He took on Himself all our shame.
> Forever blessed............................yet He became a curse for us.
> One with the Father....yet He separated from God on the cross.
> The Lord of life............yet He became obedient even to death.

Though He was rich, He became poor! He had to borrow a room for His last supper with His disciples.

When He died, His disciples had to borrow a tomb in which to place Him. Jesus is *the* example of sacrificial giving.

Think about it:
- What is my attitude about giving?
- Is giving to God my priority?
- Besides my money, what else can I offer to God?
- What is the hardest thing for me to give to God?

"Therefore, go and make disciples of all the nations..." (Matthew 28:19a).

Recently I was reading D. L. Moody's book, *Secret Power*, and came upon something that surprised me. He said, "At least nine-tenths of church members never think of speaking for Christ. If they see a man, perhaps a near relative, going rapidly down to ruin, they never think of speaking to him about his sinful course and of seeking to win him to Christ."[47]

The thing that surprised me about this was that I thought the problem of Christians not sharing their faith was a new problem, but I was wrong, Moody struggled with it over one hundred years ago!

Share your faith with someone. Think about what would happen if we all shared Jesus with someone in the next few weeks.

The multiplication of disciples:
- If we add 1+1=2, then 2+2=4, 4+4=8, 8+8=16, 16+16=32. This is the result of addition.
- If we take 1+1=2, and then multiply 2x2=4. Then 4x4=16, then 16x16=256, and 256x256=65,536 we're getting the results of multiplication! 65,536x65,536=4,294,967,296!

Let's start sharing and asking God to multiply His work in these last days!

It's been suggested that by discipling one person a year, in six years all six billion people on earth could potentially be reached for Christ!

grace today

22 JUNE

Here are some helpful ways to pray for your children or grandchildren. Pray this psalm for their protection:

> "The LORD himself watches over you! The LORD stands beside you as your protective shade. The sun will not harm you by day, nor the moon at night. The LORD keeps you from all harm and watches over your life. The LORD keeps watch over you as you come and go, both now and forever" (Psalm 121:5-8).

Claim this promise for your children:

> "Teach a child to choose the right path, and when he is older, he will remain upon it" (Proverbs 22:6, TLB).

Here's a grace/parenting prayer:

> "Lord, I can't. You never said I could. But You can. You always said You would. In Jesus' Name, Amen!"

23 JUNE

"I have hidden your word in my heart, that I might not sin against you" (Psalm 119:11).

Study is an act of praise because the better God is known, the more He is loved and adored.

"I honor and love your commands. I meditate on your decrees" (Psalm 119:48).

Meditation leads us to know God from "the inside out" — knowing who God is and not just knowing about God.

May the strong grace of Jesus keep you encouraged today!

JUNE 24

"You know the generous grace of our Lord Jesus Christ. Though he was rich, yet for your sakes he became poor, so that by his poverty he could make you rich" (2 Corinthians 8:9).

Jesus doesn't just care about your eternity; He has made provision for you for today! Take some time and look at how Jesus has expressed His love towards you:

> JESUS' Love thought of you!
> Love sought you!
> Love found you!
> Love carried you!
> Love accepted you!
> Love seated you!
> Love covered you!
> Love restored you!
> Love provided for your whole life!

Walk and work and live in the strength of His love!

grace today

25 June

The great evangelist D. L. Moody illustrates today's text:

> Now there are two ways of digging a well. When I was a boy, I lived on a farm in New England. I remember there was a well with an old wooden pump, and I used to have to pump the water from that well in order to have water for the laundry and for the cattle. I had to pump and pump and pump until my arm got tired, many a time.
>
> But there is a better way now. When a well is dug, the men don't dig down a few feet and brick up the hole and put the pump in. No, they go down through the clay and the sand and the rock and on down until they strike what they call a lower stream and then it becomes an artesian well, which needs no labor because the waters rises spontaneously from the depths below.
>
> Now, I think God wants all His children to be a sort of artesian well: not to keep pumping, but to flow right out… What is the trouble? The living water is not there, they are just pumping, when there is not water in the well! You can't get water out of a dry well; you need to have something in the well, or you can't get anything out.
>
> Now, when the Spirit of God is on us for service, resting upon us, we are anointed, and then we can do great things. "I will pour water upon him that is thirsty" (Isa. 44:3), says God.[48]

" 'If anyone is thirsty, let him come to me and drink. For the Scriptures declare that rivers of living water shall flow from the inmost being of anyone who believes in me.' (He was speaking of the Holy Spirit, who would be given to everyone believing in him; but the Spirit had not yet been given, because Jesus had not yet returned to his glory in heaven)" (John 7:37b-39, TLB).

JUNE 26

"Then Jesus suggested, 'Let's get away from the crowds for a while and rest'... " (Mark 6:31a, TLB).

Craig Brian Larson wisely shares, "Work and rest are both spiritual disciplines, dependent upon rhythm and balance, issuing in increasing knowledge of the Father... Being involved in spiritual work, I must breathe the Spirit, think and pray in the Spirit. Indeed, spirituality becomes my requisite skill."[49]

It's hard work to rest! It's something you've got to determine to do because it's God's will for you. Let me share one more insight from Larson with you:

"The discipline of rest shows that God has set boundaries on my life: the limitations of time and energy... While work teaches me what I can do, rest teaches me what I cannot do."[50]

Plan some time to rest. Draw near to the Lord during this time. It's interesting that the word for rest is "Sabbath." Look at who is in the middle of spiritual rest: "sABBAth!"

grace today

27 JUNE

"And He said to them, 'Come away by yourselves to a secluded place and rest a while...'" (Mark 6:31, NASB).

How do we come to Jesus? How do we get away?

Just as you are: weary, worn out, discouraged and distracted. Jesus never rejects anyone who comes to Him! No one is ever turned away!

It's significant that Jesus says, "Come... by yourselves," Jesus is interested in you—just you! He has not forgotten you. Jesus has something just for you! You need this time of rest for your spiritual strengthening.

Listen to what Jesus says: "Are you tired? Worn out? Burned out on religion? Come to me. Get away with me and you'll recover your life. I'll show you how to take a real rest. Walk with me and work with me—watch how I do it. Learn the unforced rhythms of grace. I won't lay anything heavy or ill-fitting on you. Keep company with me and you'll learn to live freely and lightly" (Matthew 11:28-30, MSG).

Psalm 122, verse 1, "I was glad when they said to me, 'Let us go to the house of the LORD.'"

"And He said to them, 'Come away by yourselves to a secluded place and rest a while...'" (Mark 6:31, NASB).

Jesus told His disciples to "Come... to a secluded place..." The Greek word for secluded means "a deserted place," "an uninhabited place," a quiet place away from the hustle and

bustle. Jesus wants to take you to a place of quiet each day and He wants to fellowship with you there.

It is not a waste of time to fellowship with God. Too often we miss out on blessings by not spending time with the Lord. It's also important to understand that you can't do anything really significant *for* God without having spent time *with* God. The greater things are the outflow of communion with Him.

June 28

"Be at rest once more, O my soul, for the LORD has been good to you" (Psalm 116:7, NIV).

Soul-rest is what we crave.

Psalm 116:7-9 reads, "Be at rest once more, O my soul, for the LORD has been good to you. For you, O LORD, have delivered my soul from death, my eyes from tears, my feet from stumbling, that I may walk before the LORD in the land of the living" (NIV).

It's been said, "We must know how to put occupation aside, which does not mean that we must be idle. In an inaction, which is meditative and attentive, the wrinkles of the soul are smoothed away. The soul itself spreads, unfolds, and springs afresh; and, like the trodden grass of the roadside or the bruised leaf of a plant, repairs its injuries, becomes new, spontaneous, true and original."

May the strong grace of Jesus encourage you today!

grace today

29 JUNE

"Your words were found, and I ate them, And Your word was to me the joy and rejoicing of my heart..." (Jeremiah 15:16, NKJV).

Here's a fresh way to approach your Bible reading. First, take your Bible and choose a book to study. When you have done that; read a chapter, and after you have read it ask these four questions:

1. "What is the most beautiful verse to me?"
2. Now look through the passage again and ask, "Is there a promise for me to claim in this section?"
3. Next ask, "Is there a warning for me?"
4. The last question to ask is, "Did a prayer come into my heart while I was reading this passage?"[51]

Pray the Scripture to the Lord.

To get more out of your Bible, read it with your ears open.

30 JUNE

"Haughtiness goes before destruction; humility precedes honor" (Proverbs 18:12).

You can never be too small for God to use, but you can be too big. The way up is down. As the Scriptures say, "...God opposes the proud but favors the humble" (James 4:6b).

Peter had learned quite a lesson on humility. His words are wise: "So humble yourselves under the mighty power of God, and at the right time he will lift you up in honor" (1 Peter 5:6).

The Amplified Version translates this well, "Therefore humble yourselves [demote, lower yourselves in your own estimation] under the mighty hand of God, that in due time He may exalt you."

God will use humble-hearted men and women. "Fear of the LORD teaches wisdom; humility precedes honor" (Proverbs 15:33).

St. Augustine of Hippo (354-430) shared some great insight on humility. He said, "Do you wish to be great? Then begin by being humble. Do you desire to construct a vast and lofty fabric? Think first about the foundations of humility. The higher your structure is to be, the deeper must be its foundation."

"…Godliness accompanied with contentment (that contentment which is a sense of inward sufficiency) is great and abundant gain. For we brought nothing into the world, and obviously we cannot take anything out of the world; but if we have food and clothing, with these we shall be content (satisfied)" (1 Timothy 6:6-8, AMP).

Keys to contentment:
- I am satisfied with what I have (see Philippians 4:11).
- I have so much. Discontentment is always looking at what we don't have and leads to jealousy and sin. It's like the story of King Ahab and Naboth (see 1 Kings 21).
- I want to remember that comparison is very selective. Stop looking at the other person (see 2 Corinthians 10:12-13).
- My race is my race (see Hebrews 12:1). If I get my eyes on other runners, I may stumble and not finish my race in good time, or at all.

Often trouble brings with it a sense of loneliness. Sometimes the loneliness is there because we know that, due to the nature of our circumstances, we can't share what we're going through with anyone. Is that the way you're feeling right now?

David expresses that kind of anguish: "Turn to me and have mercy, for I am alone and in deep distress" (Psalm 25:16).

Trouble isolates us! Here's something that will help you with the feelings of isolation: the biblical truth of Jesus' presence.

grace today

Remember, Jesus is always near. You can share everything with Him; you're never alone.

It also really helps to share your burden with another caring Christian brother or sister in Christ that you can really trust. The Apostle Paul encourages us to do this: "Share each other's burdens, and in this way obey the law of Christ" (Galatians 6:2).

Ecclesiastes 4:9-12 says, "Two people are better off than one, for they can help each other succeed. If one person falls, the other can reach out and help. But someone who falls alone is in real trouble. Likewise, two people lying close together can keep each other warm. But how can one be warm alone? A person standing alone can be attacked and defeated, but two can stand back-to-back and conquer. Three are even better, for a triple-braided cord is not easily broken."

I pray that you have a conscious sense of Jesus' presence in your life today!

3 July

It's important to remember that trouble seems to magnify and exaggerate reality.

David experienced this happening to him. In Psalm 25:17 he shares: "My problems go from bad to worse..." "The troubles of my heart are enlarged..." (NASB).

When we're in trouble, everything that is bothering us seems to become larger than life. It's as if Satan moves in with a magnifying glass and some smoke and mirrors, making what is

in reality only a dinky mouse look like a dangerous monster!

He works much like the Wizard of Oz! Fear, intimidation and appearance is everything to the enemy of our souls!

So if mice are beginning to look like monsters to you, you know what really helps? Getting God's view! Putting things into perspective, which is nothing more than appropriating the biblical truths of God's omnipotence and sovereignty!

JULY 4

This isn't your ordinary devotional, but today isn't an ordinary day!

I know that the founding fathers of the United States of America would not understand the anti-Christian bias and prejudice towards Christianity that is rapidly growing in America. That wouldn't be the America they sacrificed everything to found. Listen to Patrick Henry's last words:

> I have now disposed of all my property to my family. There is one thing more I wish I could give them and that is faith in Jesus Christ. If they had that, and I had not given them one shilling, they would have been rich; and if they had not that, and I had given them all the world, they would be poor indeed.

The Christian faith is revealed in every one of the original thirteen Colonies—seen in the people who founded them and in their charters and constitutions.[52]

Let's take a look at the Declaration of Independence. I want to share with you some research that you'll never hear in an American History class:

> Our Declaration of Independence is a Christian document: The events leading to the signing reveal the providence of God; the ideas contained in the Declaration are biblical; the wording reveals our founders reliance upon God — "they are endowed by their Creator with certain inalienable rights;" "Appealing to the Supreme Judge of the World, for the rectitude of our intentions;" "with a firm reliance on the protection of divine Providence."[53]

It is not commonly known today that the people involved in passing the Declaration had very solid faith in God. After signing, Samuel Adams said:

> We have this day restored the Sovereign to Whom alone men ought to be obedient. He reigns in heaven and... from the rising to the setting sun, may His kingdom come.[54]

John Hancock, the President of the Continental Congress, who boldly wrote his signature large enough so that the King could read it "without his spectacles on," said, "Let us humbly commit our righteous cause to the great Lord of the Universe... Let us joyfully leave our concerns in the hands of Him who raises up and puts down the empires and kingdoms of the earth as He pleases."[55]

Let me share one more piece of information with you. They understood that the birth of America marked the establishment of the first truly Christian nation in history — Christian, not

because all who founded it were Christians, but because it was founded upon Christian principles. J. Wingate Thornton relates how our sixth President, John Quincy Adams, stated that "the highest glory of the American Revolution... was this: it connected in one indissoluble bond, the principles of civil government with the principles of Christianity."[56]

"Blessed is the nation whose God is the LORD, the people whom He has chosen for His own inheritance" (Psalm 33:12, NASB).

Take time to pray for your country and for God's hand to move on your President (or Prime Minister), and Senate, Courts, and Congress (or Parliament). In these last days, let's all pray that the Gospel goes forward to every nation!

"You can be sure of this: The LORD set apart the godly for himself. The LORD will answer when I call to him" (Psalm 4:3).

JULY 5

There are times when our troubles can seem to block out hope. Is that happening to you? One time, when my daughter Emily was very young, she lost sight of me at a store. She panicked and began to cry. I think she lost hope of ever finding her daddy! But was it all over? No way! I heard her cries and I was right there!

Asaph, the psalmist, experienced temporarily losing sight of hope. In Psalm 77 Asaph says, "I am so troubled that I cannot speak" (verse 4b, ESV). (Note this whole Psalm; it probably speaks the way you are feeling if you are depressed, yet it ends with hope!)

grace today

Today we'd say Asaph was "down" or was depressed. He temporarily lost sight of hope! But that's not the end!

The reality is that prolonged exposure to trouble can make you susceptible to depression. It can appear that there's no light at the end of the tunnel.

In Psalm 142:4 at a low moment David said, "I look for someone to come and help me, but no one gives me a passing thought! No one will help me; no one cares a bit what happens to me."

In times like these hold onto God's promises!

Here are some precious promises for you to hold onto:
- "For I have given rest to the weary and joy to the sorrowing" (Jeremiah 31:25).
- "Long ago the LORD said to Israel: 'I have loved you, my people, with an everlasting love. With unfailing love I have drawn you to myself' " (Jeremiah 31:3).
- "I—yes, I alone—will blot out your sins for my own sake and will never think of them again" (Isaiah 43:25).
- "You will keep in perfect peace all who trust in you, all whose thoughts are fixed on you! Trust in the LORD always, for the LORD GOD is the eternal Rock" (Isaiah 26:3-4).
- "Let my soul be at rest again, for the LORD has been good to me. He has saved me from death, my eyes from tears, my feet from stumbling. And so I walk in the LORD's presence as I live here on earth!" (Psalm 116:7-9).

I love going up high, don't you! I like being on the tops of mountains. I've climbed some of the highest peaks in Arizona and Northern California. I've been to the top of Pike's Peak in Colorado, and enjoyed the breath-taking beauty of the Bear Tooth Mountains in Montana. But, to get to the top of the mountain, you usually have to start in the valley. This really resembles our life in Christ.

Valley times are low times. Between every high, mountaintop experience we have with the Lord, there will usually be low times, trouble-times. The low times punctuate our lives and give us an appreciation for the mountaintop experiences we have with the Lord.

We have no trouble believing that God is the LORD of the mountaintop! We must also believe that God is LORD of the valley times. With this in mind, there is a promise from the Lord that I want to share with you that will be a huge encouragement to you. God says: "I will... transform the Valley of Trouble into a gateway of hope..." (Hosea 2:15a).

Eugene Peterson paraphrases it: "I'll turn Heartbreak Valley into Acres of Hope" (MSG).

Trust that God is able to make the valley of trouble a door of hope!

May the strong grace of Jesus turn your heartbreak into hope.

grace today

7 JULY

One of the first things people say when they step into trouble is, "Why me?" "Why did I lose my job?" "Why did my loved one have to die?" "Why am I still so sick?" "Why are bad people getting ahead?" "Why do our enemies win?" "Why?... Why?... Why?"

We usually react to trouble by asking, "Why?"

But asking, "Why?" never helps, and frankly, it's a question that's never answered in the Bible. I've found that rather than asking, "Why Lord?" it's much more helpful to ask "What Lord?"

- "What do You want me to do?"
- "What place might You be moving me to?"
- "What work are You doing in my life through this trouble?"

Child of God, know this: God is not allowing anything in your life to destroy you! In Jeremiah 29:11 God says, " 'For I know the plans I have for you,' says the LORD. 'They are plans for good and not for disaster, to give you a future and a hope.' "

8 JULY

We're called to give thanks *during* the trial!

People who are unthankful actually become prisoners of their circumstances. People who are thankful to God seem to be liberated, even when in an imprisoning situation.

Learn to give thanks *before* you see the end. Give thanks in the

darkness. Give thanks in faith! This is living in faith! This is walking in faith!

Isaiah 50:10 says, "Who is among you that fears the LORD, that obeys the voice of His servant, that walks in darkness and has no light? Let him trust in the name of the LORD and rely on his God" (NASB).

The Bible is teaching us to trust God in everything!

This is the Principle of Psalm 84:11. Let's look at it: "For the LORD God is a sun and shield; The LORD gives grace and glory; No good thing does He withhold from those who walk uprightly. O LORD of hosts, How blessed is the man who trusts in You!" (NASB).

JULY 9

"Instruct the wise, and they will be even wiser. Teach the righteous, and they will learn even more" (Proverbs 9:9).

Wouldn't it be neat to have the "gift" of hindsight? I think I'd live life quite a bit more relaxed, and I'd definitely trust the Lord much more! But that wouldn't be a life of faith anymore, would it?

Years ago, when Chuck Swindoll was saying goodbye to his congregation of twenty three years at First Evangelical Free Church of Fullerton, California, he shared a number of truths he had learned over the years. Here are a few of them:

- I've learned that I should tell people how I feel about them now, not later.

grace today

- I've learned that things I'm not even aware of are being noticed and remembered.
- I've learned that being real is a lot better than looking pious.
- I've learned that when you "fit," most things flow... they don't have to be forced.
- I've learned that it doesn't pay to talk someone into or out of a big decision.
- I've learned that days of maintenance are far more in number than days of magnificence.
- I've learned that some people aren't going to change, no matter what.
- I've learned that I seldom felt badly for things I did not say.
- I've learned that perception overshadows reality.
- I've learned that time spent with my family is a good investment.
- I've learned that grace is worth the risk.
- I've learned to stop saying "never" or "always" when it comes to the future.
- I've learned that thinking theologically pays off, big time.
- I've learned that some things are worth the sweat.
- I've learned that you can't beat fun.
- Finally, I've learned to give credit where credit is due.[57]

10 JULY

I saw Deuteronomy 6 in William Tyndale's first edition of the English Bible. The English is old, but the way he translated it is fascinating. It reads: "And these wordes which I command thee this day shall be in thyne heart and thou shalt write them on thy children and shalt talk of them. When thou are at home on thine

house and as thou walketh up the way..." (Deuteronomy 6:6-7, Tyndale's Bible).

Note that it says that "...these wordes [words] ...shall be in thyne [your] heart and thou shalt write them on thy children..."

I see two things here:
- We can't give our kids what we don't have ourselves.
- We "write" the truth on our kids. How do we do that? We are writing every day by the way we live, talk and relate.

"My father's greatest impact on my life was his consistency," recalls Billy Graham's son, Franklin. "The man you saw on TV was the same man we saw at home. Spiritually, that had a huge impact on us. My father always led devotions at home. He would open the Bible and read four or five verses, then we'd pray as a family, on our knees, always on our knees. I follow his example with my own family."[58]

JULY 11

"Therefore I, a prisoner for serving the Lord, beg you to lead a life worthy of your calling, for you have been called by God" (Ephesians 4:1).

Years ago, a friend shared with me a tract that has a powerful message. I know that it will speak to you. It's titled, "Others May, You Cannot."

> If God has called you to be really like Jesus in all your spirit, He will draw you into a life of crucifixion and humility, and put on you such demands of obedience, that He will not

allow you to follow other Christians, and in many ways He will seem to let other good people do things which He will not let you do.

Other Christians and ministers who seem very religious and useful may push themselves, pull wires, and work schemes to carry out their plans, but you cannot do it; and if you attempt it, you will meet with such failure and rebuke from the Lord as to make you sorely penitent.

Others can brag on themselves, on their work, on their success, on their writings, but the Holy Spirit will not allow you to do any such thing, and if you begin it, He will lead you into some deep mortification that will make you despise yourself and all your good works. (To be continued...)

12 JULY

"Therefore I, a prisoner for serving the Lord, beg you to lead a life worthy of your calling, for you have been called by God" (Ephesians 4:1).

"Others May, You Cannot" (Continued...)

Others will be allowed to succeed in making money, or having a legacy left to them, or in having luxuries, but it is likely God will keep you poor, because He wants you to have something far better than gold, and that is a helpless dependence on Him, that He may have the privilege of supplying your needs day by day out of an unseen treasury.

The Lord will let others be honored, and put forward,

and keep you hid away in obscurity, because He wants to produce some choice, fragrant fruit for His coming glory, which can only be produced in the shade. (To be continued...)

JULY 13

"...You learned Christ! My assumption is that you have paid careful attention to him, been well instructed in the truth precisely as we have it in Jesus. Since, then, we do not have the excuse of ignorance, everything—and I do mean everything—connected with that old way of life has to go. It's rotten through and through. Get rid of it! And then take on an entirely new way of life—a God-fashioned life, a life renewed from the inside and working itself into your conduct as God accurately reproduces his character in you" (Ephesians 4:20b-23, MSG).

"Others May, You Cannot" (Conclusion.)

God will let others be great, but keep you small. He will let others do a work for Him, and get the credit for it, but He will make you work and toil on without knowing how much you are doing; and then to make your work still more precious, He will let others get the credit for the work which you have done, and this will make your reward ten times greater when Jesus comes. The Holy Spirit will put a strict watch over you, with a jealous love, and will rebuke you for little words and feelings or for wasting your time, which other Christians never seem distressed over. So make up your mind that God is an infinite Sovereign, and has a right to do as He pleases with His own, and He will not explain to you a thousand things which may puzzle your reason in

His dealings with you. God will take you at your word; and if you absolutely sell yourself to be His slave, He will wrap you up in a jealous love, and let other people say and do many things that you cannot do or say. Settle it forever, that you are to deal directly with the Holy Spirit, and that He is to have the privilege of tying your tongue, or chaining your hand, or closing your eyes, in ways that others are not dealt with. Now when you are so possessed with the living God that you are, in your secret heart, pleased and delighted over this peculiar, personal, private, jealous guardianship and management of the Holy Spirit over your life, you will have found the vestibule of heaven.[59]

14 JULY

Job *chose* his response to very hard times of trial in his life. Despite his grief and his loss, Job declares his trust in the Lord. He holds onto who he knows God is with every ounce of strength that is left in him: "Though He slay me, I will hope in Him..." (Job 13:15a, NASB).

We all experience those times in our walk with the Lord where "Maturity" is spelled "T R U S T."

One of the marks of Christian maturity is having and demonstrating a genuinely thankful heart to God for every circumstance that He allows, and trusting that He will bring blessing out of our sufferings.

We trust the infinite wisdom of God and we give thanks, though we don't always understand why God is allowing what He allows in our lives.

There are lots of times when God's hand and purpose can't be readily seen in situations.

Nineteenth century pastor and Bible teacher, Charles Spurgeon, expressed it so well when he said, "When we cannot trace God's hand, we can trust God's heart."

A big piece of maturing as a Christian means learning to trust God and being thankful to God for every circumstance that God sovereignly allows to enter our lives.

We know that there's no such thing as fate, or chance, or luck. We believe the hand of God works for us in every situation (see Romans 8:28).

JULY 15

"Singing psalms and hymns and spiritual songs among yourselves, and making music to the Lord in your hearts. And give thanks for everything to God the Father in the name of our Lord Jesus Christ" (Ephesians 5:19-20).

Hymns are a part of the treasury of the Church. They teach truth while they lead worship. They are great ways of popularizing the great teaching of Scripture. Hymns don't have to sound old to be hymns. Some hymns are very new. It's the content that makes a hymn.

I want to share with you a hymn written by the daughter of an Irish pastor. I know the Lord will bless you while you read and meditate on the words.

BEFORE THE THRONE OF GOD ABOVE

Before the throne of God above
I have a strong, a perfect plea:
A great High Priest, whose name is Love,
Who ever lives and pleads for me.

My name is graven on His hands,
My name is written on His heart;
I know that while in heaven He stands,
No tongue can bid me thence depart.

When Satan tempts me to despair,
And tells me of the guilt within,
Upward I look, and see Him there
Who made an end of all my sin.

Because the sinless Savior died,
My sinful soul is counted free;
For God, the Just, is satisfied
To look on Him and pardon me.

Behold Him there! The risen Lamb!
My perfect, spotless Righteousness,
The great unchangeable I AM,
The King of glory and of grace!

One with Himself, I cannot die;
My soul is purchased by His blood;
My life is hid with Christ on high,
With Christ, my Savior and my God.[60]

"Let the word of Christ dwell in you richly, teaching and admonishing one another in all wisdom, singing psalms and

hymns and spiritual songs, with thankfulness in your hearts to God" (Colossians 3:16, ESV).

JULY 16

"Praise the LORD, for he has shown me the wonders of his unfailing love. He kept me safe when my city was under attack" (Psalm 31:21).

In 1895, Andrew Murray was in England suffering from a terrible, painful back, the result of an injury he had incurred years before.

One morning while he was eating breakfast in his room, his hostess told him of a woman downstairs who was in great trouble and wanted to know if he had any advice for her.

Murray handed her a paper he had been writing on and said, "Give her this advice I'm writing down for myself. It may be that she'll find it helpful." This is what was written and it says it all.

In times of trouble, say:
- "He brought me here. It is by His will I am in this strait place, in that I will rest."
- "He will keep me here in His love, and give me grace in this trial to behave as His child."
- "He will make the trial a blessing, teaching me lessons He intends me to learn, and working in the grace He means to bestow."
- "In His good time He can bring me out again. How and when, He knows."

Therefore, we can say, "I AM HERE..."
1. "By God's appointment."
2. "In His keeping."
3. "Under His training."
4. "For His time."

17 JULY

"But Moses said to God, 'Who am I that I should go to Pharaoh and bring the children of Israel out of Egypt?' " (Exodus 3:11, ESV).

Moses was humble. He didn't think that He was God's gift to the world! And so he wasn't going to be the kind of person that would rob God of His glory.

He would be a common container into which God could pour the riches of His grace!

Here's a Kingdom Rule: If you think you're a somebody, you're really a nobody. But if you think you're nothing, God can make you into something!

True humility comes from a conscious sense of Who God is and a realistic view of who you are!

I'm not saying that God can't use proud people, but He may not use them more than once! He wants to use people who will give Him the glory!

"God answered, 'I will be with you...' " (Exodus 3:12a).

"But Moses protested again, 'What if they won't believe me or listen to me? What if they say, "The LORD never appeared to you"?' " (Exodus 4:1).

Moses didn't have to go out and get something he didn't have. God used what He had in His hand, his staff, and used it in an extraordinary way! God used a foolish thing like Moses' staff to confound all the wisdom of Egypt.

When Moses worried about results, again God referred him to that staff in his hand. God was saying, "There will be many who will believe when they see what I am doing through you. My power flowing through your life will have an effect on them."

Throughout holy history we see God using the foolish things of the world:

Maybe all you have is a small handful of rocks in your pocket, but God can use them to destroy the enemy. Isn't that what He did with David when he fought against Goliath?

All Elijah had was his cloak, his mantle, but God used it to part the Jordan River.

All Jesus' disciples could come up with were five little loaves of bread and a few fish to feed way over five thousand people, and look at what the Lord did with their little foolish offering. He showed His power and His glory by choosing to use a foolish thing.

grace today

Are you feeling afraid to step out and do what God calls you to do for fear of failing, or fear of looking like a failure? Don't be discouraged from stepping out on the adventure God is calling you to! All you're responsible to be is obedient. The results are God's department!

19 JULY

"So let's not get tired of doing what is good. At just the right time we will reap a harvest of blessing if we don't give up" (Galatians 6:9).

Just when you think *your* marriage has problems...

> Samuel and Susanna Wesley had a terrible marriage! One time Samuel went on and on praying for King William of Orange. At last he was done, and the children could add their "Amens" to the end of his prayer. But there was no "Amen" from his wife, Susanna. She lifted her head only to meet her husband's accusing gaze.
>
> "Why do you not say 'Amen' and thus honor your king and obey Scripture?" Samuel asked. Samuel knew why. The children knew why.
>
> "Because he is not my king," Susanna answered, in a determined voice. "He is a usurper. The throne belongs to the House of Stuart, not William of Orange." "Sukey, if that be the case," Samuel replied, "we must part, for if we have two kings, we must have two beds."

Susanna replied, "Since I'm willing to let you quietly enjoy your opinions, you ought not to deprive me of my little liberty of conscience." It had started again! They had a terrible time getting along! Their marriage was not good.

Later that evening Samuel called her into his study and knelt before her. He closed his eyes and began to pray. "O God, I pray that thou wouldst send down divine vengeance on me and my offspring if ever again I touch this woman or come into bed with her before she entreats both thee and me for pardon."

He looked up, expecting an apology, but Susanna held her ground and Samuel walked out of the house and went to London. It's recorded that she thought, "Will this be the end of our marriage?"

Susanna wrote to a close friend about her problems. "I am more easy in the thoughts of parting because I think we are not likely to live happily together. Are we the same two people who couldn't endure the separation of Samuel's naval chaplaincy before we married? Now it seems we cannot endure one another's nearness."

God can use people who have problems.

But despite repeated marital problems Susanna raised her ten children who survived infancy to love the Lord. Two of them today are remembered as the founders of the Methodist Church, John and Charles Wesley.[61]

20 JULY

Jesus says: "Peace I leave with you; My peace I give to you; not as the world gives, do I give to you. Do not let not your heart be troubled, nor let it be fearful" (John 14:27, NASB).

"These things I have spoken to you, so that in Me you may have peace. In the world you have tribulation, but take courage; I have overcome the world" (John 16:33, NASB).

Following Jesus and relying on Him will not grant us immunity from life's storms, but it makes them purposeful.

When we read the news about a vicious tornado or hurricane killing thousands of people and causing billions of dollars of damage, we kind of get the idea that these storms are bad. I've thought, "I wish there would never be another hurricane again." How many people do you think pray that way?

But something I was reading recently caused me to reevaluate the way I think about storms, and even the horrific power of hurricanes in particular!

Apparently, hurricanes in general serve a good purpose. It doesn't mean that the damage and the death associated with them can be discounted, but they actually serve a life-giving purpose!

"Hurricanes are an effect and cause of life-essential balances on earth," says Hugh Ross.

> Advanced life requires a rotation period no slower than about 24 hours. A slower rotation rate would result in deadly

differences between day and night temperatures. A rotation rate of 24 hours, however, yields surface wind velocities that will, on occasion, stir up hurricanes and tornadoes. So in this case, such storms represent the necessary effect of Earth's life-sustaining spin rate.

Fresh-off-the-press studies done in the vicinity of Bermuda demonstrate that hurricanes also play a vital role in sustaining the right range of temperatures for life. On the one hand, they counterbalance the ocean's tendency to leach carbon dioxide from the atmosphere. This leaching, if unchecked, would result in a catastrophic cooling of the planet. On the other hand, hurricanes prevent the oceans from trapping too much of the sun's heat. They help circulate greenhouse gases globally as they shade the ocean (reflecting solar radiation) locally, preventing heat from building up too dramatically for the safety of certain sea creatures. During the summer of 1995, three hurricanes over the Sargasso Sea increased the flow of carbon dioxide from the water to the atmosphere by more than fifty percent. At the same time, each hurricane cooled the sea water (near the surface) by 7 degrees F (4 degrees C) for two to three weeks at a time.

Meteorologists affirm that too many or too few hurricanes would spell disaster for advanced life on Earth. The fact that their frequency and intensity fall into precisely the right range for life support provides one more piece of evidence that God carefully designed Earth with the necessities of life in mind.[62]

grace today

21 JULY

I read about an old missionary couple who were finally going home after working in Africa for years, returning to New York City to retire. They had no pension; their health was broken; they were defeated, discourage, and afraid. They discovered they were booked on the same ship as President Teddy Roosevelt, who was returning from one of his big-game hunting expeditions.

No one paid attention to them. They watched the fanfare that accompanied the President's entourage, with passengers trying to catch a glimpse of the great man.

As the ship moved across the ocean, the old missionary said to his wife, "Something is wrong. Why should we have given our lives in faithful service for God in Africa all these many years and have no one care a thing about us? Here this man comes back form a hunting trip and everybody makes much over him, but nobody gives two hoots about us."

"Dear, you shouldn't feel that way," his wife said.

"I can't help it; it doesn't seem right."

When the ship docked in New York, a band was waiting to greet the President. The mayor and other dignitaries were there. The papers were full of the President's arrival, but no one noticed this missionary couple. They slipped off the ship and found a cheap apartment on the east side, hoping the next day to see what they could do to make a living in the city.

That night the man's spirit broke. He said to his wife, "I can't take this; God is not treating us fairly."

His wife replied, "Why don't you go in the bedroom and tell that to the Lord?"

A short time later he came out from the bedroom, but now his face was completely different. His wife asked, "Dear, what happened?"

"The Lord settled it with me," he said. "I told Him how bitter I was that the President should receive this tremendous homecoming, when no one met us as we returned home. And when I finished, it seemed as though the Lord put His hand on my shoulder and simply said, 'But you're not home yet!' "[63]

We're going home soon!

"Let us not lose heart in doing good, for in due time we will reap if we do not grow weary" (Galatians 6:9, NASB).

JULY 22

"When everything is ready, I will come and get you, so that you will always be with me where I am" (John 14:3).

Amazingly, both the Old and New Testaments are full of promises about the return of Jesus Christ. Over 1,800 references appear in the Old Testament, and 17 Old Testament books give prominence to this theme.

Of the 260 chapters in the New Testament, there are more than 300 references to the Lord's return—1 in every 30 verses!

Jesus promised His followers that He would return. "In my Father's house are many rooms. If it were not so, would I have

told you that I go to prepare a place for you? And if I go and prepare a place for you, I will come again and will take you to myself, that where I am you may be also" (John 14:2-3, ESV).

Angels promised Jesus' followers that He would return; Acts 1:10-11 records this: "As they strained to see him rising into heaven, two white-robed men suddenly stood among them. 'Men of Galilee,' they said, 'why are you standing here staring into heaven? Jesus has been taken from you into heaven, but someday he will return from heaven in the same way you saw him go!' "

Jesus is coming back for us very soon! The signs He spoke of are all around us! How does the hope of Jesus' soon return affect the stress or trouble you face today?

I pray that the strong grace of our Lord Jesus encourages your heart!

23 JULY

"And He has said to me, 'My grace is sufficient for you, for power is perfected in weakness...' " (2 Corinthians 12:9a, NASB).

The NLT says, " '...My grace is all you need. My power works best in weakness.' So now I am glad to boast about my weaknesses, so that the power of Christ can work through me."

I've been saving this "gem" to share with you. They are the words of Lady Culross to John Livingston, a Covenanter Pastor: "Since God has put His work into your weak hands, look not for long ease here: You must feel the full weight of your calling: a weak man with a strong God."

I found those words so encouraging and I had to pass them on to you!

May the Lord Jesus bless your day in a very big way!

JULY 24

"...People do not live by bread alone, but by every word that comes from the mouth of God" (Matthew 4:4b).

Someone has said, "Nothing is as infectious as example." The Lord knows we learn best through examples. Recently I read part of Leonard E. LeSourd's reflections about his late wife Catherine Marshall's great love for God's Word. I was inspired by her delight in the Bible. You may know that she is the author of *Christy, A Man Called Peter, Something More,* and many other Christian books. Her husband shares her hunger for the Word of God:

> Bibles were scattered throughout our house... all editions, plus reference books and concordances. We often went to bed, turned out the light, and listened to a chapter of Scripture on tape. If she could have found a way to spread Bible passages on a slice of bread, Catherine would have devoured it.
>
> When upset or under spiritual assault or in physical pain, Catherine would go to her office, kneel by her chair, and open her Bible... She would read, then pray, then read, then pray some more. She liked to pray with the Bible clutched in her hands... She would rest her case on its promises. Catherine didn't read the Bible for solace or inspiration,

but to have an encounter with the Lord... I think these were the most intense moments of her life... Catherine's passion for the Word permeated her whole life. It undergirded her writing. It formed a base for us as a married team in the making of family decisions. It provided substance to her counseling of people through the mail. I'm convinced it was also the basis for her inner vitality, her charisma, and the mantle of authority she wore with some reluctance.[64]

25 July

"All your children shall be taught by the LORD, And great shall be the peace of your children" (Isaiah 54:13, ESV).

Kids should have top priority in our lives. Dr. James Dobson has said, "Children must be valued as our most priceless possession." Children and grandchildren are the future of the church. Every investment of time, energy, money and emotion will more than payoff, in this world and in eternity. The people of Israel always considered teaching and discipling their children a very high priority. They guarded family time and established family traditions which helped them maintain their identity as God's people for thousands of years.

God had given them their instructions through Moses: "Place these words on your hearts. Get them deep inside you... Teach them to your children. Talk about them wherever you are, sitting at home or walking in the street; talk about them from the time you get up in the morning until you fall into bed at night" (Deuteronomy 11:18a-19, MSG).

This is still God's plan! Here are some things to teach your children:

- Teach your children that you think they are special – I've always told my kids, "You're the best daughter in the whole-wide world!" "You're the best son in the whole-wide world!" Spend some time with your children doing the things that they like to do. Our children's first glimpse into God's love is the love we show them.

- Teach your children that you love them – One of the best ways love is communicated is through patient, consistent and purposeful discipline. The Bible tells us that if we do not discipline our children we do not love them (Proverbs 13:24). God shows us His love by consistently disciplining throughout our lives (Hebrews 12:5-11). Biblical discipline is not practiced in anger or rage, it is always administered in love.

- Teach your children right and wrong and to obey – Kids want to know boundaries and what is right and wrong. While your children are young, teach them clearly what is morally right and wrong. Teach them modesty, and to always tell the truth, and to look away from evil. The Ten Commandments are a good guide for morality (with the exception of the Fourth Commandment, which is not a moral issue, but the sign of the Old Covenant). These Nine Commandments are all repeated in the New Testament.

- Teach your kids to love God's Word and God's church – Reward your children lavishly and frequently for memorizing God's Word. Encourage them with prizes, money and words of praise for every step they take in internalizing God's Word. Make Sunday the best day of the week! Don't burden them with tons of chores; instead, make it a day when you do special things together, get

together with good friends, and eat special food.
- Teach your kids by your example – Our faith is caught even easier than it is taught. Nothing is as powerful an advantage and blessing to your children than for you to live your life sold-out to the Lord Jesus Christ!

26 JULY

"Then Peter called to him, 'Lord, if it's really you, tell me to come to you, walking on the water.' 'Yes, come,' Jesus said. So Peter went over the side of the boat and walked on the water toward Jesus. But when he saw the strong wind and the waves, he was terrified and began to sink. 'Save me, Lord!' he shouted. Jesus immediately reached out and grabbed him. 'You have so little faith,' Jesus said. 'Why did you doubt me?'" (Matthew 14:28-31).

A while back Leslie had put a piece of paper with a sticky note in my box at the office that read: "Hi honey—thought you'd like this quote—Leslie."

My heart was stirred as I read a portion of pioneer missionary William Carey's sermon in Nottingham. I'll share it with you, updating the text:

"Clear lots of ground for your tents! Make your tents large. Spread out! Think big! Use plenty of rope, drive the tent pegs deep" (Isaiah 54:2, MSG).
- Expect great things from God!
- Attempt great things for God!
- Dare to have a bolder program!
- Dwell in an abundant world!
- Launch out into the deep!

May God give you a clear picture of the kind of expansion He wants to do in your life. Let His work spread out in every direction—think big! The Lord really wants to use you in the Kingdom cause!

July 27

In Paul's second letter to the new believers in Thessalonica he writes: "For you know that you ought to imitate us. We were not idle when we were with you. We never accepted food from anyone without paying for it. We worked hard day and night so we would not be a burden to any of you. We certainly had the right to ask you to feed us, but we wanted to give you an example to follow" (2 Thessalonians 3:7-9).

In this verse he uses the word "model," *tupos* in Greek, which is a "type or an example." The word originally referred to the impression left by a die. God wants our example to be like a "spiritual die," something that would leave a lasting impression on others.

God calls you to be an example that other people can follow in your faith, love, purity, and beliefs. You're called to be that example at home, school, work, and after work.

General George C. Marshall understood what leading by example was all about when he took command of the Infantry School at Fort Benning, Georgia. Finding the post to be in a generally run-down condition, he did something only a real leader's heart would conceive. Rather than issue orders for specific improvements, or bark commands, he simply got out his own paintbrushes, lawn equipment, etc., and went to work

grace today

on his personal quarters. The other officers and men, first on his block and then throughout the post, did the same thing; the General's influence trickled down, and Fort Benning was cleaned up from the top down.

When God changes you, other changes fall into place.

You have a blessed day, filled with Jesus' peace.

28 JULY

"And now, a word to you who are elders in the churches. I, too, am an elder and a witness to the sufferings of Christ. And I, too, will share in his glory when he is revealed to the whole world. As a fellow elder, I appeal to you: Care for the flock that God has entrusted to you. Watch over it willingly, not grudgingly—not for what you will get out of it, but because you are eager to serve God. Don't lord it over the people assigned to your care, but lead them by your own good example" (1 Peter 5:1-3).

A healthy church isn't led by "lording," it's led by example. Church leaders and all of us who are involved in serving Jesus are never called to be any greater than our Master, and He washed feet, fixed breakfasts for large groups, took time for children, cared about details, and constantly looked for ways to bless the people He served. Jesus is a "serving-Savior."

Jesus is the model. Remember what He said, "So Jesus called them together and said, 'You know that the rulers in this world lord it over their people, and officials flaunt their authority over those under them. But among you it will be different. Whoever wants to be a leader among you must be your servant,

and whoever wants to be first among you must be the slave of everyone else. For even the Son of Man came not to be served but to serve others and to give his life as a ransom for many' " (Mark 10:42-45).

Why don't you pause a moment and pray with me: "Lord, today as I serve You I want to have a serving-heart like Yours. I want to live for others and to remember that it's not all about me, it's all about You, Jesus, and serving the people You place in my life this day!"

JULY 29

"Stay alert! Watch out for your great enemy, the devil. He prowls around like a roaring lion, looking for someone to devour" (1 Peter 5:8).

A jackhammer is 100 decibels, but a lion's roar is 114 decibels! When the enemy roars, you're going to feel it for sure! His tactics are fear and intimidation, tools he has used quite successfully for thousands of years. The devil is a "man-eater" waiting to pounce on the unsuspecting or the immature. The way lions work is they look for prey that is lagging behind, sick, young or thirsty. This is the easiest hunt, the quickest way to dinner!

The devil works in just the same way. He looks for those who are distracted by the world or spiritually immature, and for those who have become separated from the rest of the flock.

The message today is "Stay Alert!" This isn't the time to be spiritually sleeping, lounging around or preoccupied with the world. Our enemy is focused, and the Lord tells us to stay focused, too.

Grace today

30 JULY

As I was spending time with the Lord a while back, I was captivated with the thought, "Read the Bible, not just to *cover* ground, but to *gain* ground." Reading large amounts for familiarity is good, but reading for comprehension is vital.

"I have hidden your word in my heart, that I might not sin against you" (Psalm 119:11).

"Your words were found and I ate them, and Your words became for me a joy and the delight of my heart; for I have been called by Your name, O LORD God of hosts" (Jeremiah 15:16, NASB).

The Message paraphrase puts it, "When your words showed up, I ate them—swallowed them whole. What a feast! What delight I took in being yours..."

31 JULY

"And through your faith, God is protecting you by his power until you receive this salvation, which is ready to be revealed on the last day for all to see. So be truly glad. There is wonderful joy ahead, even though you have to endure many trials for a little while. These trials will show that your faith is genuine. It is being tested as fire tests and purifies gold—though your faith is far more precious than mere gold. So when your faith remains strong through many trials, it will bring you much praise and

glory and honor on the day when Jesus Christ is revealed to the whole world" (1 Peter 1:5-7).

It is said that in ancient times the refiner would melt the gold ore down and skim from the surface the impurities as they surfaced. He knew the refining process was over when the surface was clean and he could see his own face reflected on the molten gold. Then he would put out the fire.

Several times the Bible uses this analogy for God's work in our lives. It is a work of refining and reflecting, heating and purifying, the work of the Master Who desires to see Himself reflected in us:

- Steel is iron plus fire.
- Diamonds are carbon plus heat and pressure.
- Linen is flax plus a cleansing bath, the comb that separates, the flail that pounds and the shuttle that weaves.

Years ago Cortland Meyers said, "Human character must have a 'plus' attached to it."

Whatever your "plus" is right now, entrust it to God, He *is* working to make you more like Jesus.

"And we know that God causes all things to work together for good to those who love God, to those who are called according to His purpose" (Romans 8:28, NASB).

God in His infinite wisdom and complete power works every detail of our lives into something good.

Here's a little nugget I dug out for you. Did you know that the term "work together" is a chemist's or pharmacist's term? This is actually saying that the Lord knows the exact measure of the ingredients that is best for each of us. He is skillfully, expertly mixing our lives for our good and His glory!

Rest secure in His loving plan for you!

"So humble yourselves under the mighty power of God, and at the right time he will lift you up in honor" (1 Peter 5:6).

Who is writing this to us? The Apostle Peter, who knew all about being humbled under the mighty power of Jesus. He had the distinction of being the only disciple to be publicly rebuked by the Lord Jesus on more than one occasion!

D. L. Moody quipped, "Be humble or you will stumble."

Surely, we can all be encouraged by Peter. Though Peter was impetuous in his early ministry and even failed at one point, our Lord restored him and then used him to write Holy Scripture.

grace today

God has a Kingdom plan for you, too!

The Amplified Bible translates our passage uniquely: "Therefore humble yourselves [demote, lower yourselves in your own estimation] under the mighty hand of God, that in due time He may exalt you."

Take a "demotion" today, so God can lift you up tomorrow.

3 AUGUST

"...You accepted what we said as the very word of God—which, of course, it is. And this word continues to work in you who believe" (1 Thessalonians 2:13b).

When Billy Graham was asked "Would you do [have done] anything differently?" He says:
- I would study more.
- I would read the Bible more.
- I would pray more.

He continued, "I've let other things interfere with that." We hear you Billy!

Let's pray, "Lord, thanks for the transparency of Your servant. We want to spend more time with You."

Think about what you will do to study more, read the Bible more, and pray more.

The Lord bless you, you are precious in His sight!

A while back during some time with the Lord, I read three sentences about clear-headed leadership that really blessed me. I pass them on to you in the hope that you will clearly hear a word of encouragement from our Lord Jesus.

"You are in the line of battle, and crisis is at hand. To falter a moment would be to imperil some holy interest. Other lives would be harmed by your pausing, holy interests would suffer, should your hands be folded."[65]

The Apostle Paul moved on, through difficulties, disappointments, troubles and suffering. He refused to be stopped in his call and in his work for the Lord. He had a determination to press on, no matter what!

"...I press on so that I may lay hold of that for which also I was laid hold of by Christ Jesus" (Philippians 3:12b, NASB).

"I press on toward the goal for the prize of the upward call of God in Christ Jesus" (Philippians 3:14, NASB).

"...Let us press on to maturity..." (Hebrews 6:1, NASB).

It's not time to kick back and play, or to relax or be diverted from our devotion to Christ and His Church. Press on! Press on! Press on! Jesus is praying for you, His Spirit is empowering you! We'll be going home soon!

"...But I keep going on, trying to grasp that purpose for which Christ Jesus grasped me... But I do concentrate on this: I forget all that lies behind me and with hands outstretched to whatever

grace today

lies ahead I go straight for the goal—my reward the honour of my high calling by God in Christ Jesus" (Philippians 3:12b-14, Phillips).

5 AUGUST

"No longer do I call you slaves, for the slave does not know what his master is doing; but I have called you friends, for all things that I have heard from My Father I have made known to you" (John 15:15, NASB).

The purpose of the Bible is to reveal God and His ways. God wants to know you, but he also wants YOU to know Him! This is an unimaginable privilege! You have a personal invitation from God to know Him. There's a difference between knowing information and facts about God, and knowing God personally. It would be the difference between knowing all the facts and stats about your favorite actor, and actually knowing them as a friend. God really wants you to know Him.

Now, here's the bottom line: He makes Himself knowable through His Word. This is the only way you can develop a friendship with Him. Are you ready?

> BIBLE + TIME + PRAYER/OBEDIENCE = FELLOWSHIP WITH GOD = FRIENDSHIP WITH GOD!

Read Psalm 25:14 in these two translations and a paraphrase:
- "The secret of the LORD is for those who fear Him, and He will make them know His covenant" (NASB).

- "The LORD is a friend to those who fear him. He teaches them his covenant."
- "God-friendship is for God-worshipers; they are the ones he confides in" (MSG).

AUGUST 6

Alien—Belonging to a foreign country. Hello, fellow alien! No, I am not trying to insult you; I've just been reminded that we Christians aren't permanent residents of this world.

"Dear friends, I warn you as 'temporary residents and foreigners' [aliens] to keep away from worldly desires that wage war against your very souls" (1 Peter 2:11).

We are aliens of earth. We are not instructed to become aliens; we already are aliens because of the miracle of new birth.

1 Peter 1:3 says, "...we have been born again..."

We are new creatures, "Therefore if anyone is in Christ, he is a new creature; the old things passed away; behold, new things have come" (2 Corinthians 5:17, NASB).

We are now people who are fully alive, body, soul and spirit! Jesus said, "...that which is born of the Spirit is spirit" (John 3:6, NASB).

We live here, but we don't belong here. "...You are a chosen people. You are royal priests, a holy nation, God's very own possession..." (1 Peter 2:9b).

Grace today

Our citizenship is in heaven, "But we are citizens of heaven, where the Lord Jesus Christ lives. And we are eagerly waiting for him to return as our Savior" (Philippians 3:20).

This is why the world is not always a friendly place for real Christians:

> "The world would love you as one of its own if you belonged to it, but you are no longer part of the world. I chose you to come out of the world, so it hates you" (John 15:19).

A portion of the epistle to Diognetus from the second century summarizes this well: "Christians are not distinguished from the rest of mankind by either country, speech or customs... They reside in their respective countries, but only as aliens. They take part in everything as citizens and put up with everything as foreigners. Every foreign land is their home, and every home a foreign land... They find themselves in the flesh, but do not live according to the flesh. They spend their days in earth, but hold citizenship in heaven."

7 AUGUST

We are living as "foreigners" or "aliens" in this world. Aliens are not permanent residents, but temporary ones "passing through" a territory on their way home.

How does this affect the way we live? What does an alien lifestyle look like? Here we go: "Dear friends, I warn you as 'temporary residents and foreigners' to keep away from worldly desires that wage war against your very souls" (1 Peter 2:11).

Our real homeland is heaven; we are simply on a short trip through a foreign land right now.

Here is a story I read that illuminates this truth: A story is frequently told of a wealthy man who once visited a very famous rabbi. Because the rabbi was so well-known, the rich man expected to find him living in a very fancy house with all kinds of expensive luxuries. Instead, to his surprise, the wealthy visitor discovered the rabbi living in very plain circumstances. The rabbi's study contained only a simple desk, a lamp, and a few chairs.

"Where is all your furniture?" asked the surprised guest.

"Where is all of yours?" countered the rabbi.

"I am just a visitor passing through town," explained the magnate. "When I'm just traveling, I don't take all my furniture with me."

"It's the same with me," replied the rabbi. "I am just a visitor in this world. I don't have the time to collect a lot of furniture" (Source Unknown).

> Knowing Whose I am,
> Helps me to handle what I have,
> In the light of where I am going.

Let's store up treasure in heaven. See how much you can invest in your eternal home this week!

GRace today

8 AUGUST

An alien lifestyle requires endurance. The world we're living in is actually at war with our homeland.

Jesus prayed for us regarding this battle. "I have given them your word. And the world hates them because they do not belong to the world, just as I do not belong to the world. I'm not asking you to take them out of the world, but to keep them safe from the evil one" (John 17:14-15).

Not only is there a battle from without, there is a battle from within. Our flesh (the part of us that stills wars against our new nature) still lures us to cling to the things of the world.

"Do not love this world nor the things it offers you, for when you love the world, you do not have the love of the Father in you. For the world offers only a craving for physical pleasure, a craving for everything we see, and pride in our achievements and possessions. These are not from the Father, but are from this world. And this world is fading away, along with everything that people crave. But anyone who does what pleases God will live forever" (1 John 2:15-17).

Remember, this battle will soon be over; we have a glorious hope in the light of our sojourn. "But we are citizens of heaven, where the Lord Jesus Christ lives. And we are eagerly waiting for him to return as our Savior" (Philippians 3:20).

May the Lord Jesus give you special courage and determination as you "fight the good fight of faith" today.

"Nevertheless, God's solid foundation stands firm, sealed with this inscription: 'The Lord knows those who are his,' and, 'Everyone who confesses the name of the Lord must turn away from wickedness' " (2 Timothy 2:19, NIV).

There's a story that has circulated for years about a soldier in the army of Alexander the Great who had been caught leaving his post without permission. He was brought before the man, who at that time had conquered the world, who addressed him: "I understand that your name is also Alexander. Is that correct?"

The man said, "It is, sir."

"Then I will ask you, are you guilty of all the crimes of which you are accused?"

"I am guilty, sir."

"Then you will have to change your name or change your ways."

When people take Jesus' Name—everyone, including Jesus, expects them to live for Jesus.

Because you are a Christian, what you do reflects on Jesus and His people. You bear *THE NAME*—may God give you the grace to "do it proud!"

"Oh, what joy for those whose disobedience is forgiven, whose sin is put out of sight! Yes, what joy for those whose record the LORD has cleared of guilt, whose lives are lived in complete honesty!" (Psalm 32:1-2).

grace today

10 AUGUST

"Give all your worries and cares to God, for he cares about you" (1 Peter 5:7).

"Casting all your care upon Him, for He cares for you" (NKJV).

Our work is to unload care. God's work is to take care.

"Then Jesus said, 'Come to me, all of you who are weary and carry heavy burdens, and I will give you rest' " (Matthew 11:28).

We serve a God who takes our cares from us. He died so our burdens wouldn't kill us!

Jesus not only takes our cares, He also takes care of us. "...Anyone who is thirsty may come to me! Anyone who believes in me may come and drink! For the Scriptures declare, 'Rivers of living water will flow from his heart' " (John 7:37-38).

What a God we serve! He is unlike any other. He doesn't place burdens *on* us, He removes burdens *from* us! "Thank You, Jesus, for Your faithful love and care for me."

"Live carefree before God; he is most careful with you" (1 Peter 5:7, MSG).

11 AUGUST

"Casting the whole of your care [all your anxieties, all your worries, all your concerns, once and for all] on Him, for He cares for you affectionately and cares about you watchfully" (1 Peter 5:7, AMP).

What does this mean for us today?

"Cares" – Worries, anxieties, fretting, crossing bridges before we come to them.

"All" – The entire worry, not just part of it.

"Cast" – Depositing something permanently.

"Because He cares for you" – For it is a care from Him concerning you, "for you are His concern!"

Peter knew personally that Jesus cares for His people. Jesus pulled him out of many raging storms.

F. B. Meyer provided great practical insight on how to cast our cares. "Treat cares as you treat sins. Hand them over to Jesus one by one as they occur. Commit them to Him. Roll them upon Him. Make them His. By an act of faith look to Him, saying, 'This, Lord, and this, and this, I cannot bear. Thou hast taken my sins: take my cares: I lay them upon Thee, and trust Thee to do for me all, and more than all, I need. I will trust and not be afraid.' "[66]

AUGUST 12

"Praise the Lord; praise God our savior! For each day he carries us in his arms" (Psalm 68:19).

There are times in life when we wonder if God really does care about us, especially during times of pain, suffering, busyness, burnout, or tiring service.

The Bible says the truth will set us free. Here is the truth about God's care for you:

- "Blessed be the Lord, who daily bears our burden, the God who is our salvation" (Psalm 68:19, NASB).

grace today

- "Give your burdens to the LORD, and he will take care of you. He will not permit the godly to slip and fall" (Psalm 55:22).
- "Look at the birds. They don't plant or harvest or store food in barns, for your Heavenly Father feeds them. And aren't you far more valuable to him than they are?" (Matthew 6:26-27).
- "What is the price of two sparrows—one copper coin? But not a single sparrow can fall to the ground without your Father knowing it. And the very hairs on your head are all numbered. So don't be afraid; you are more valuable to God than a whole flock of sparrows" (Matthew 10:29-31).

13 AUGUST

Think about John the Baptist's words: "He must increase, but I must decrease" (John 3:30, NASB).

One of the evidences of the work of God's Spirit in our lives is that Jesus increases and we decrease.

Dr. Andrew Bonar, a fine Bible teacher and pastor, once commented that he could always tell when Christians were growing. He said that in proportion to their growth in grace they would: elevate Jesus, talk less of what they were doing, and become smaller and smaller in their own estimation, until, he said, "like the morning star, [they] faded away before the rising sun."[67]

May your prayer be: "He must increase, but I must decrease."

"On that day a fountain will be opened for the dynasty of David and for the people of Jerusalem, a fountain to cleanse them from all their sins and impurity" (Zechariah 13:1).

Are you thirsty? When was the last time you had a drink of water? You probably didn't have to go very far for it, and had no concern about drinking it. We take having a drink of water for granted, but did you know that more people die each year from unsafe drinking water than from all forms of violence, including war? There are more than one billion people on earth who do not have clean, safe water to drink; that's nearly one in every five. In Ethiopia, only 18 percent of the population have access to safe water; in Sudan, it's 45 percent; in the United States, it's 99 percent.[68]

There's an even greater need: the need for the water of life! If you have had a drink, you'll never be the same! Britain now has a "Minister of Water" who regulates water use in that nation. May you be a "Minister of Water" to those who are spiritually dying of thirst.

"...Anyone who is thirsty may come to me! Anyone who believes in me may come and drink! For the Scriptures declare, 'Rivers of living water will flow from his heart' " (John 7:37-38).

AUGUST **15**

"...the son of Samuel" (1 Chronicles 6:33c, NASB).

Here's the question for today's Bible quiz: What's the name of the prophet Samuel's grandson?

grace today

Here's a clue: He was a famous singer.

His name is Heman! And after studying about him, I want to be a Heman (no, not a "he-man!").

Heman was the son of Joel, and grandson of the prophet Samuel. He was referred to as "the Singer" in 1 Chronicles 6:33, "...From the sons of the Kohathites were Heman the singer, the son of Joel, the son of Samuel" (NASB). Think about the godly grandpa he had. Heman was an answer to Samuel's prayers and a blessing to all of God's people. Thank the Lord for godly grandparents!

As Israel's foremost worship leader, Heman formed a choir that included his fourteen sons, all of whom also assisted their father in the Lord's service. The Scriptures say that God "...honored him with fourteen sons and three daughters" (1 Chronicles 25:5). The record continues: "Under their father's supervision they were in charge of leading the singing and providing musical accompaniment in the work of worship in the sanctuary of God" (1 Chronicles 25:6, MSG).

Heman was also King David's "seer" or counselor. He was called the "Ezrahite" or wise person. He and the other worship leaders, Asaph and Jeduthun, were men so renowned for their wisdom that they were sought out by none other than King David himself (2 Chronicles 29:14, 30; 35:15).

It's sweet to think that David, who was a man after God's own heart (Acts 13:22), surrounded himself with men who had the same kind of hearts (1 Kings 4:31).

God gave Heman a wise and worshipful heart. He led his family

in such a way that they all followed him in ministry, serving the Lord right alongside him. He really is a hero of the faith, a real "HE-MAN!"

AUGUST 16

"For my soul has had enough troubles..." (Psalm 88:3a, NASB).

Heman was a "He-man" because he persevered in trials. Psalm 88, the saddest of all the Psalms, was written by Heman, who obviously suffered constantly.

You can't really know Heman until you know what he went through:

> "Now hear my prayer; listen to my cry. For my life is full of troubles, and death draws near. I am as good as dead, like a strong man with no strength left. They have left me among the dead, and I lie like a corpse in a grave. I am forgotten, cut off from your care. You have thrown me into the lowest pit, into the darkest depths. Your anger weighs me down; with wave after wave you have engulfed me. You have driven my friends away by making me repulsive to them. I am in a trap with no way of escape. My eyes are blinded by my tears. Each day I beg for your help, O LORD; I lift my hands to you for mercy... Can they proclaim your faithfulness in the place of destruction? Can the darkness speak of your wonderful deeds? Can anyone in the land of forgetfulness talk about your righteousness? O LORD, I cry out to you. I will keep on pleading day by day. O LORD, why do you reject me? Why do you turn your face from me? I have been sick and close to death since my youth. I stand helpless and desperate before your terrors. Your fierce anger has overwhelmed

me. Your terrors have paralyzed me. They swirl around me like floodwaters all day long. They have engulfed me completely... Darkness is my closest friend." (Psalm 88:2-18).

Wow—this man went through years of constant pain, depression, rejection, sickness, tears, isolation, and yet he remained faithful to God. His desperate cries—a reality for many believers—are forever recorded in the Bible. Through his long ordeal he continued to look to the Lord, remaining constant in faith, always acknowledging God's sovereignty and hand in everything that came his way. He is really a spiritual brother to Job who said, "Though he slay me, yet will I hope in him..." (Job 13:15a, NIV).

"For my soul has had enough troubles..." (Psalm 88:3a, NASB).

A HE-MAN IS:
- A man his family follows (seventeen kids).
- A worshipper.
- Wise (Psalm 88—Heman the Ezrahite).
- A leader (led the worship, administered the temple priests and wrote the worship manual: Psalm 88 title).
- One who perseveres through trials (Psalm 1).

17 AUGUST

Today I want to remind you that you may come boldly into God's throne room.

"...Let us come boldly to the throne of our gracious God. There we will receive his mercy, and we will find grace to help us when we need it most" (Hebrews 4:16).

The Amplified Bible brings out the best:

> "Let us then fearlessly and confidently and boldly draw near to the throne of grace (the throne of God's unmerited favor to us sinners), that we may receive mercy [for our failures] and find grace to help in good time for every need [appropriate help and well-timed help, coming just when we need it]."

The Message paraphrases:

> "So let's walk right up to him and get what he is so ready to give. Take the mercy, accept the help."

A poor man showed up at the White House, weeping at its gate during Lincoln's presidency. Young Tad Lincoln who was playing on the lawn went over and asked him what was the matter.

"My son is to be shot at dawn and only Mr. Lincoln can help. But these soldiers won't let me in to see him."

"I'll take you to him!" shouted Tad. "He's my father! He'll see me anytime!"

Dear one, God is your Father. He'll hear you anytime. Have you prayed lately? Your Heavenly Father is waiting to hear from you. The door is always open to you! "...We have boldness and confident access through faith in Him" (Ephesians 3:12, NASB).

If you would like, take a few moments to review the lyrics to "What A Friend We Have In Jesus." You'll be interested to read the fourth verse, which is rarely sung:

What a Friend we have in Jesus,
    All our sins and griefs to bear!
What a privilege to carry
    Everything to God in prayer!
O what peace we often forfeit,
    O what needless pain we bear,
All because we do not carry
    Everything to God in prayer.

Have we trials and temptations?
    Is there trouble anywhere?
We should never be discouraged;
    Take it to the Lord in prayer.
Can we find a friend so faithful
    Who will all our sorrows share?
Jesus knows our every weakness;
    Take it to the Lord in prayer.

Are we weak and heavy laden,
    Cumbered with a load of care?
Precious Savior, still our refuge,
    Take it to the Lord in prayer.
Do your friends despise, forsake you?
    Take it to the Lord in prayer!
In His arms He'll take and shield you;
    You will find a solace there.

Blessed Savior, You have promised
    You will all our burdens bear
May we ever, Lord, be bringing
    All to You in earnest prayer.
Soon in glory bright, unclouded
    There will be no need for prayer
Rapture, praise and endless worship
    Will be our sweet portion there.

"As the deer longs for streams of water, so I long for you, O God" (Psalm 42:1).

"Whoever has the Son has life; whoever does not have God's Son does not have life. I have written this to you who believe in the name of the Son of God, so that you may know you have eternal life" (1 John 5:12-13).

Christians often feel insecure about their salvation. Often this happens because they lack understanding about salvation and security in Christ.

If you've never been clearly taught on these subjects, you could think that your relationship with Christ is like every human relationship we enter into, based on some kind of conditional acceptance. It would only be natural to assume that salvation is the same way, right?

But the awesome truth is that God loves us and accepts us unconditionally!

Remember, God saved us knowing full-well what we would be!

Sometimes insecurity's source is diabolical. Satan aims for the heart. He knows that an insecure Christian is an easy target for discouragement.

grace today

19 AUGUST

"If I had not confessed the sin in my heart, the Lord would not have listened" (Psalm 66:18).

Nothing will cause you to lose your joy and assurance faster than trying to hide sin or hanging onto sin in your life!

Let's pray David's Prayer together:

"Have mercy on me, O God, because of your unfailing love. Because of your great compassion, blot out the stain of my sins. Wash me clean from my guilt. Purify me from my sin. For I recognize my rebellion; it haunts me day and night. Against you, and you alone, have I sinned; I have done what is evil in your sight. You will be proved right in what you say, and your judgment against me is just. For I was born a sinner—yes, from the moment my mother conceived me. But you desire honesty from the womb, teaching me wisdom even there. Purify me from my sins, and I will be clean; wash me, and I will be whiter than snow. Oh, give me back my joy again; you have broken me—now let me rejoice. Don't keep looking at my sins. Remove the stain of my guilt. Create in me a clean heart, O God. Renew a loyal spirit within me. Do not banish me from your presence, and don't take your Holy Spirit from me. Restore to me the joy of your salvation, and make me willing to obey you" (Psalm 51:1-12).

If there is anything the Lord shows you that is between you and Him, confess it and turn from it right now and receive the cleansing the Lord offers you. The Lord brings up these things to restore us in our fellowship with Him.

"I have written this to you who believe in the name of the Son of God, so that you may know you have eternal life" (1 John 5:13).

Here is the remedy for the insecurity blues: Hold onto the facts!

Remember what Jesus said in John 5:24: "Truly, truly, I say to you, he who hears My word, and believes Him who sent Me, has eternal life, and does not come into judgment, but has passed out of death into life" (NASB).

The Gospel of John declares: "But to all who believed him and accepted him, he gave the right to become children of God" (John 1:12).

I will never tire of hearing these awesome words of assurance:

"Since we believe human testimony, surely we can believe the greater testimony that comes from God. And God has testified about his Son. All who believe in the Son of God know in their hearts that this testimony is true. Those who don't believe this are actually calling God a liar because they don't believe what God has testified about his Son. And this is what God has testified: He has given us eternal life, and this life is in his Son. Whoever has the Son has life; whoever does not have God's Son does not have life. I have written this to you who believe in the name of the Son of God, so that you may know you have eternal life" (1 John 5:9-13).

There were probably times when Noah was in the ark that he didn't feel saved, but he was safe!

grace today

21 AUGUST

"Come, let us worship and bow down. Let us kneel before the LORD our maker..." (Psalm 95:6).

One of the ways you can know for sure you are a child of God is that you love other children of God.

If you are struggling with having assurance of your salvation, it may be due to a missing ingredient in your spiritual life: Fellowship!

You've got to hang around God's people!

Let's look at Hebrews 10:23-25 from several translations:

- NASB: "Let us hold fast the confession of our hope without wavering, for He who promised is faithful; and let us consider how to stimulate one another to love and good deeds, not forsaking our own assembling together, as is the habit of some, but encouraging one another; and all the more as you see the day drawing near."
- NLT: "Let us hold tightly without wavering to the hope we affirm, for God can be trusted to keep his promise. Let us think of ways to motivate one another to acts of love and good works. And let us not neglect our meeting together, as some people do, but encourage one another, especially now that the day of his return is drawing near."
- Amplified: "So let us seize and hold fast and retain without wavering the hope we cherish and confess and our acknowledgement of it, for He Who promised is reliable (sure) and faithful to His word. And let us consider and give attentive, continuous care to watching

over one another, studying how we may stir up (stimulate and incite) to love and helpful deeds and noble activities, Not forsaking or neglecting to assemble together [as believers], as is the habit of some people, but admonishing (warning, urging, and encouraging) one another, and all the more faithfully as you see the day approaching."

It dawned on me that this isn't a suggestion, it's a command; a clear directive for Christians, not an option. Fellowship was required by the Lord in the Old Covenant, and it is required in the New Covenant as well.

Warren Wiersbe comments on this: "...Fellowship with God must never become selfish. We must also fellowship with other Christians in the local assembly. Apparently, some of the wavering believers had been absenting themselves from the church fellowship. It is interesting to note that the emphasis here is not on what a believer gets from the assembly, but rather on what he can contribute to the assembly. Faithfulness in church attendance encourages others and provokes them to love and good works. One of the strong motives for faithfulness is the soon coming of Jesus Christ..."[69]

May the Lord give you strong assurance as you follow Him, and may He bless your fellowship with God's people!

AUGUST 22

"For I will not presume to speak of anything except what Christ has accomplished through me... in the power of the Spirit..." (Romans 15:18-19, NASB).

grace today

Here's another secret of the Christian life: offer your inadequacy to God.

- Stop making excuses for not serving the Lord.
- Stop trying to do it in the flesh.

Paul gives us a great definition of what serving the Lord is in verses 18-19: ministry is what Christ accomplishes through us! Ministry happens when the power of the Holy Spirit works through us.

In his book, *On Being A Servant Of God,* Warren Wiersbe says, "The trouble with too many of us is that we think God called us to be manufacturers when He really called us to be distributors. He alone has the resources to meet human needs; all we can do is receive His riches and share them with others. 'Silver and gold I do not have,' Peter announced, 'but what I do have I give you' (Acts 3:6). When it comes to ministry, all of us are bankrupt, and only God is rich. Like Paul, we are 'as poor, yet making many rich' (2 Corinthians 6:10)."[70]

We aren't called on by God to come up with something from ourselves to minister to others.

We're simply to receive from the Lord and pass what He gives us on to others! (See Matthew 14:15-21 with John 6:1-14).

This principle of "Distribution" Jesus taught to His disciples on two occasions; once at the feeding of the five thousand and another time at the feeding of the four thousand (five loaves and two fish).

"Lord, we ask that You will distribute Your supply through us!"

"But if we confess our sins to him, he is faithful and just to forgive us our sins and to cleanse us from all wickedness" (1 John 1:9).

One day Thomas Jefferson and some of his friends were riding on horseback cross-country. They came to a stream that was flooded and had to cross it. At the water's edge was a man who was traveling on foot, obviously waiting for someone to help him across the swollen stream.

He waited at the edge until several from the party crossed and then asked the President to help him across. Jefferson took him on the back of his horse and carried him across the stream. On the other side, one of the men asked, "Tell me, why did you select the President for this favor?" The man answered, "I didn't know he was the President. All I know is that on some faces is written the answer 'no' and on some the answer 'yes.' His face said 'yes!' "

Here's what I want you to know today: God has a yes-face! When you confess your sins to Him, He is faithful and just to forgive you. He removes your guilt and your sins from you forever!

"He has removed our sins as far from us as the east is from the west" (Psalm 103:12).

He will cover up your sins: "How blessed is he whose transgression is forgiven, whose sin is covered!" (Psalm 32:1, NASB).

grace today

He will put your sins out of His mind forever! "...And I will forgive their wickedness, and I will never again remember their sins" (Jeremiah 31:34b).

24 AUGUST

"Then God looked over all he had made, and he saw that it was very good!" (Genesis 1:31).

Are you having to listen to your teacher or professor talk about the "theory" of evolution? Hang in there. The God who died for you also created you! Hold onto your faith.

God looked over all creation, including humankind, and declared it was good. Let's think about how good, how utterly amazing His creation truly is! Let me share something I read years ago:

> A human body ...is a masterpiece of exquisite design. Beautifully "engineered," it is governed by several hundred control systems—each interacting with the others to maintain perfect overall balance. Man's brain has 10 billion nerve cells to record what he sees and hears. His skin has more than 2 million tiny sweat glands—about 3,000 per square inch—all part of an intricate network that regulates body temperature. A "pump" in his chest makes his blood cells travel 168 million miles a day, or 6,720 times around the world! The lining of his stomach contains 35 million glands secreting juices to aid the chemical processes which sustain his life. The marvels of the human body are beyond comprehension!

....most new products don't operate efficiently until all the "bugs" are ironed out... Just think, the first time God put a human body together, it worked![71]

"I will give thanks to You, for I am fearfully and wonderfully made; wonderful are Your works, and my soul knows it very well" (Psalm 139:14, NASB).

"Thank you for making me so wonderfully complex! Your workmanship is marvelous—how well I know it" (Psalm139:14).

God is awesome and worthy of our praise, today and forevermore!

AUGUST 25

"Thank you for making me so wonderfully complex! Your workmanship is marvelous—how well I know it" (Psalm 139:14).

The "theory" of evolution assumes that "simple" cells just evolved. But the "simple" cells aren't so simple. Today's message is a different kind of devotional; it's devotional-ammo—"Anti-Evolution Ammo."

Hey students of all ages, those who want a defense for your faith in the Creator-God, read on!

Let's take a little extra time to look at the simplest of cells, E. coli:

...the phylogenetic tree is built on the premise that life evolved from a simple cell, but that "simple cell" has yet to be found. Would Darwin have ever even formulated his

theory if he had possessed an electron microscope and been aware of the complexity and design of cells too small to be seen by the naked eye?

E. coli is placed on the lowest branch of the tree, assumed to be early in terms of evolution. Invisible to the naked eye, measuring 2 micrometers long and 0.8 micrometers in diameter, it is a marvelous example of design and complexity.

The cell is enclosed within a double wall, or membrane. Within this membrane are about 2,400,000 proteins, 1,800 kinds of molecules, and 14,000 messenger RNA's. Add to that 22,000,000 lipid molecules and 280,000,000 small metabolites. All these jostle together in the cytoplasm which is 75 percent water, but they all have a purpose and work harmoniously...

A similar coordination is present in the tiny bacterium. All the proteins and molecules share in its internal metabolism. Their work is encoded in its genes. It is estimated that those instructions equal about ten pages in the Encyclopedia Britannica.

Metabolism requires energy, and energy in E. coli is provided by electrical power generated by the cell. An alternative energy source is also available, if required. Electricity drives its external flagella, which rotate like propellers. The "propeller shaft" penetrates through the membrane and into the cytosol by means of a bushing and can propel the little bug at a speed of about ten to twenty cell lengths per second.

Besides this, the direction in which the cell is driven is "computerized." The flagella all rotate together in a counterclockwise direction when the cell is in forward gear, but when its "computerized" sensing mechanism informs it that the gradient to which it is heading has changed, a "switch" is thrown, and the flagella change gears and begin a clockwise rotation. This results in what is called a "tumbling motion," and the cell changes direction.

Of course, I am writing metaphorically. The pictures elicited may be unreal, but the facts are correct. Such is just a brief introduction to this simple cell![72]

May our Heavenly Father, our Creator-GOD, give you new strength today!

"Do you not know? Have you not heard? The Everlasting God, the LORD, the Creator of the ends of the earth does not become weary or tired. His understanding is inscrutable. He gives strength to the weary, and to him who lacks might He increases power" (Isaiah 40:28-29, NASB).

AUGUST 26

"My child, listen to me and do as I say, and you will have a long, good life. I will teach you wisdom's ways and lead you in straight paths" (Proverbs 4:10-11).

The importance of getting our directions from God cannot be overstated.

Look at what Proverbs 3:5-6 says about this: "Trust in the LORD with all your heart; do not depend on your own understanding. Seek his will in all you do, and he will show you which path to take."

There's a special promise in God's Word for us in Psalm 32:8: "The LORD says, 'I will guide you along the best pathway for your life. I will advise you and watch over you.' "

A. W. Tozer lends insight: "The Lord would seem to be more concerned with where we are going rather than how fast. A steady pace in the right direction will lead to the right goal at last, but if the life is aimed at the wrong goal, speed will only take us further astray in a shorter time."

The problem with our world/society is that we are all going so fast that we often don't stop to think where we're going!

27 AUGUST

"My child, listen to me and do as I say, and you will have a long, good life. I will teach you wisdom's ways and lead you in straight paths" (Proverbs 4:10-11).

Here's another spiritual secret: God blesses *His* plans, not ours!

Too often, we offer our plans to God and ask Him to bless them. Or even more frequently, we don't even offer our plans to God until things aren't going well.

This surely wasn't how Jesus modeled life. He would seek guidance from Father in Heaven. Luke tells us that "...Jesus

Himself would often slip away to the wilderness and pray" (Luke 5:16, NASB).

A lot of times we fail because we are not in the right place! We're not in the place of God's blessing, either through misdirected steps, or because we are practicing a sinful lifestyle that the Lord will not bless.

God is very concerned about the direction of your life. That's why He is communicating with you. That's why His Word was written!

Romans 15:4-6 says: "For whatever was written in earlier times was written for our instruction, so that through perseverance and the encouragement of the Scriptures we might have hope. Now may the God who gives perseverance and encouragement grant you to be of the same mind with one another according to Christ Jesus, so that with one accord you may with one voice glorify the God and Father of our Lord Jesus Christ" (NASB).

This passage indicates that the "historical" portions of the Bible are more than history to us; they are to be living examples from which we are to draw strength.

AUGUST 28

"...I focus on this one thing..." (Philippians 3:13b).

Paul got his direction from the Lord, and then he never turned back! He didn't doubt, nor did he turn aside. He didn't try to do everything either! He focused on one thing, living with laser-like effectiveness.

Grace today

He says, "...I focus on this one thing: Forgetting the past and looking forward to what lies ahead, I press on to reach the end of the race and receive the heavenly prize for which God, through Christ Jesus, is calling us" (Philippians 3:13b-14).

Paul remarked in his first letter to the Corinthians that "...Christ did not send me to baptize, but to preach the gospel..." (1 Corinthians 1:17, NASB).

A. W. Tozer wrote: "A great economizing of time and effort can be effected by learning what we should do and then sticking to it, quietly refusing to be turned aside from our task."

Take a minute and think about how you can focus more on what you do best for God.

29 AUGUST

"...My grace is sufficient for you, for my power is made perfect in weakness" (2 Corinthians 12:9a, NIV).

There are times when our weaknesses and inadequacies are all part of God's plan for our lives.

Paul describes his own experience of chronic weakness in 2 Corinthians, "To keep me from becoming conceited because of these surpassingly great revelations, there was given me a thorn in my flesh, a messenger of Satan, to torment me. Three times I pleaded with the Lord to take it away from me. But he said to me, 'My grace is sufficient for you, for my power is made perfect in weakness.' Therefore I will boast all the more gladly about my weaknesses, so that Christ's power may rest on me. That is why,

for Christ's sake, I delight in weaknesses, in insults, in hardships, in persecutions, in difficulties. For when I am weak, then I am strong" (2 Corinthians 12:7-10, NIV).

One of the things you see is that there are times, as in Paul's situation, when weakness is a great asset.

Oswald Chambers said, "God comes in where my helplessness begins." Our weaknesses make us appreciate God's strength!

Let God come in today! May our Lord Jesus bless you with His strong encouragement!

AUGUST 30

"For we are God's masterpiece. He has created us anew in Christ Jesus, so we can do the good things he planned for us long ago" (Ephesians 2:10).

A friend shared with me this insight—see if it fits you!

> If part of the Holy Spirit's job in the past has been to create something out of nothing, then to create something out of your life is not going to be His most difficult task! I am frustrated by people who have no difficulty believing that God could create the universe, but do have difficulty believing God can do something worthwhile with them. The One who brought things into being in the first place will live within you and make your life His workshop.[73]

"Lord, set up Your workshop right here in my heart. I believe You can do something big in me! In Jesus' Name, Amen!"

grace today

31 AUGUST

"So let's not get tired of doing what is good. At just the right time we will reap a harvest of blessing if we don't give up" (Galatians 6:9).

Sometimes we need to be encouraged to press on in the face of adversity. I think you will be encouraged today to continue serving God, by looking at John Wesley's example. He was the founder of the Methodist Church.

From the Diary of John Wesley:

> Sunday, A.M., May 5
> Preached in St. Anne's. Was asked not to come back anymore.
>
> Sunday, P.M., May 5
> Preached in St. John's. Deacons said, "Get out and stay out."
>
> Sunday, A.M., May 12
> Preached in St. Jude's. Can't go back there, either.
>
> Sunday, A.M., May 19
> Preached in St. Somebody Else's. Deacons called special meeting and said I couldn't return.
>
> Sunday, P.M., May 19
> Preached on street. Kicked off street.
>
> Sunday, A.M., May 26
> Preached in meadow. Chased out of meadow as bull was turned loose during service.

Sunday, A.M., June 2
Preached out at the edge of town. Kicked off the highway.

Sunday, P.M., June 2
Afternoon, preached in a pasture. Ten thousand people came out to hear me.

(Source Unknown)

Sometimes we wonder how we can find the strength to continue hour after hour, day after day, week after week, month after month, year after year... Look to Jesus!

"Think of all the hostility he endured from sinful people; then you won't become weary and give up" (Hebrews 12:3).

Keep on keeping on!

"Guard your heart above all else, for it determines the course of your life" (Proverbs 4:23).

A. W. Tozer was a great pastor and insightful theologian. His writings continue to stir the Church to blazing commitment to Jesus Christ. I would recommend any and all of his books to you.

Here are his "Rules of Self-Discovery":
- What we want most.
- What we think about most.
- How we use our money.
- What we do with our leisure time.
- The company we enjoy.
- Whom and what we admire.
- What we laugh at.[74]

"Watch over your heart with all diligence, for from it flow the springs of life" (Proverbs 4:23, NASB).

"Avoid all perverse talk; stay away from corrupt speech. Look straight ahead, and fix your eyes on what lies before you. Mark out a straight path for your feet; stay on the safe path. Don't get sidetracked; keep your feet from following evil" (Proverbs 4:24-27).

The Lord bless you as you walk this day for Jesus' glory.

grace today

2 SEPTEMBER

"Dear brothers and sisters, when troubles come your way,
consider it an opportunity for great joy" (James 1:2).

Here is some help to understand your trials:
- Trials are temporary – They come "...for a little while"
  (1 Peter 1:6).
- Trials are necessary – "If there's no pain, there's no gain."
  There's never any growth apart from brokenness.
- Trials are varied – They come to us in many forms.
- Trials are valuable – They develop or refine our faith
  (1 Peter 1:7).
- All our trials are controlled – There are limits to how much
  God will allow us to suffer.

No matter what you are going through, Jesus is with you. You
are never alone. I pray you feel His presence very near right now.

3 SEPTEMBER

"For you know that when your faith is tested, your endurance
has a chance to grow. So let it grow, for when your endurance
is fully developed, you will be perfect and complete, needing
nothing" (James 1:3-4).

James tells us that we should rejoice in our trials because they're
productive.

He tells us one thing our trials produce is endurance. That means
"staying power," "hanging-in-there-ness"—in spite of trouble or
adversity.

Endurance will do two things for you. If you let it have its full course, it will "make you perfect"—verse 4. This means, "totally grown up or mature" in Christian character.

Endurance, if allowed to have its full course in your life, will also make you "complete, needing nothing." The word, "complete" was used of the animals that were offered as sacrifices that were without blemish or defect!

The more suffering that we are under, the closer to perfection and completion we come! "Lord, I will rejoice!"

SEPTEMBER 4

"...Lord, teach us to pray..." (Luke 11:1b).

One of the major reasons prayers are not answered is because they miss the target.

Picture your prayers as an arrow. When we pray, we launch the arrow; the target is God's will. One of the secrets to answered prayer is practice and patience.

The Apostles James and John give some major reasons why prayers go off target and never get answered:

- We don't ask – God says, "...You do not have, because you do not ask" (James 4:2b, NASB).
- We ask with wrong motives – "...Yet you don't have what you want because you don't ask God for it. And even when you ask, you don't get it because your motives are all wrong—you want only what will give you pleasure"

(James 4:2b-3). Lots of prayers are offered to God with selfish motives.

- We ask with guilty consciences – "Dear friends, if we don't feel guilty, we can come to God with bold confidence" (1 John 3:21). Jesus will cleanse you with His blood; confess your sins to Him (1 John 1:8-9; 2:1-2).

- We ask while disobedient – "And we will receive from him whatever we ask because we obey him and do the things that please him" (1 John 3:22). A key to answered prayer is doing what God has told you to do in His Word. Sometimes answers to prayers are withheld because of disobedience to God. David wrote about this kind of experience: "If I had not confessed the sin in my heart, the Lord would not have listened. But God did listen! He paid attention to my prayer. Praise God, who did not ignore my prayer or withdraw his unfailing love from me" (Psalm 66:18-20).

- We pray out of God's will – "This is the confidence which we have before Him, that, if we ask anything according to His will, He hears us. And if we know that He hears us in whatever we ask, we know that we have the requests which we have asked from Him" (1 John 5:14-15, NASB). The Amplified Bible says: "And this is the confidence (the assurance, the privilege of boldness) which we have in Him: [we are sure] that if we ask anything (make any request) according to His will (in agreement with His own plan), He listens to and hears us. And if (since) we [positively] know that He listens to us in whatever we ask, we also know [with settled and absolute knowledge] that we have [granted us as our present possessions] the requests made of Him."

Make any adjustments the Lord shows you and launch those prayer arrows!

"God replied to Moses, 'I AM WHO I AM. Say this to the people of Israel: I AM has sent me to you'" (Exodus 3:14).

"I was regretting the past and fearing the future. Suddenly my Lord was speaking. 'My name is I AM.' He paused, I waited. He continued. 'When you live in the past with its mistakes and regrets it is hard. I am not there. My name is not, I WAS. When you live in the future with its problems and fears it is hard. I am not there. My name is not, I WILL BE. But when you live in this moment, it is not hard. I am here. My name is I AM.'"[75]

Today, consider the many ways Jesus promises to be the greatest I AM in your life:
- I AM the I AM – John 8:24, 28, 58.
- I AM the Good Shepherd – John 10:11.
- I AM the Resurrection and the Life – John 11:25.
- I AM the Way, the Truth and the Life – John 14:6.
- I AM the Bread of Life – John 6:35.
- I AM the Door – John 10:9 (NASB).
- I AM the Light of the World – John 8:12.
- I AM the True Vine – John 15:1 (NASB).

The Lord Jesus is everything you need; you can lean on Him!

"...Can a mother forget her nursing child? Can she feel no love for the child she has borne? But even if that were possible, I would not forget you!" (Isaiah 49:15).

grace today

God cannot, and God will not, forget you! He has paid for you with the life of His Son. You are preciously valuable to Him, and you always will be.

You are not just a number in God's flock; He knows you intimately; He knows your face; you are uniquely valuable to God.

It is said that there is a tribe of people in a far-off land that knows nothing of arithmetic. They never count. A man asked one of them how many sheep he had. "Don't know," came the reply. "Then how do you know if one is missing?" he asked. "Because of the face that I would miss."

You are a person that God loves, a face that He would miss.

7 SEPTEMBER

"Look here, you who say, 'Today or tomorrow we are going to a certain town and will stay there a year. We will do business there and make a profit.' How do you know what your life will be like tomorrow? Your life is like the morning fog—it's here a little while, then it's gone. What you ought to say is, 'If the Lord wants us to, we will live and do this or that' " (James 4:13-15).

A lot of people are living without foresight—not planning for their future—planning everything—but eternity!

They have lots of goals, plans and ideas—they're on their way— but they've left out a very important part of their journey—God!

James must have overheard a number of business people in his congregation thinking this same way:

- "This is what I want, this is how I'm going to achieve it, and this is how I'm going to plan my life accordingly."
- "We've made a feasibility study..."
- "We've taken a demographical study..."
- "According to our most recent polls..."
- "Looking at the numbers—there's no way..."

That all sounds so good, but without considering God and His plans, it is foolish living according to James.

Don't get me wrong. There's nothing wrong with planning, but if we make our plans without God, we're being arrogant and foolish.

We begin to think that we're the captain of the ship and master of our destiny. The thinking kind of goes like this: "All we have to do is make an informed decision and it's a sure thing!"

The people James is talking about here were probably good, honest people, but they'd left God out of their plans. They were living like practical atheists.

SEPTEMBER 8

We want to bring God into our plans because we're aware that life is short—we don't know how long we'll live.

Life is short, it's transitory. We don't even know if we'll be around tomorrow, but God is eternal!

grace today

"You are just a vapor that appears for a little while and then vanishes away" (James 4:14b, NASB).

Vapor is a term used for a "puff of smoke," "steam" rising from hot water, or "breath" coming from your nose on a cold morning. It describes something that's not permanent. It appears and then it disappears.

A university student asked Billy Graham a question a while ago. He asked, "At your age what is the greatest surprise in your life?" Billy Graham answered, "The greatest surprise of life to me at my age is the brevity of life. How quick it's all over."

"Your life is like the morning fog—it's here a little while, then it's gone" (James 4:14b).

The universal testimony of people and of Scripture is that life is brief and fragile.

9 SEPTEMBER

"...I have stilled and quieted my soul" (Psalm 131:2, ASV).

How would you like to have a vacation every day?

Try this: take five minutes midday and close your eyes and go with the Lord somewhere in the Scripture. Read or remember a passage and go there with Jesus. Don't study, just be still, quiet your soul.

These mini-vacations are free—and they're freeing!

Being still is not a waste of time; it will actually extend your time and keep you tuned into the Master!

Chuck Swindoll said, "I cannot be the man I should be without times of quietness. Stillness is an essential part of growing deeper."[76]

What we need:
- A quiet time.
- A quiet heart.
- A quiet place.

See if the Lord doesn't have a message for you in this verse: "For thus said the Lord God, the Holy One of Israel: In returning [to Me] and resting [in Me] you shall be saved; in quietness and in [trusting] confidence shall be your strength..." (Isaiah 30:15, AMP).

SEPTEMBER 10

The world's largest library is the Library of Congress in Washington, DC with over 25 million books. The top ten largest libraries in the world have over 164 million books! If you lived to be eighty you'd have to read 5,620 books a day, twenty-four hours a day, from birth, to read them all!

Can you imagine all the subjects you'd read about? There's a lot of knowledge out there, and that's not even considering the info in cyberspace!

The Bible is the record of Jesus' life, death and resurrection. It is a subject that can never be exhausted. The Apostle John ends his

twenty-one chapter Gospel with these words: "Now there are also many other things that Jesus did. Were every one of them to be written, I suppose that the world itself could not contain the books that would be written" (John 21:25, ESV).

Wow, this puts things into graphic perspective. The four Gospels are very important and contain the most important message you could ever read.

Enjoy them, read them, and start with the Gospel of John. Nothing beats the New Living Translation for readability.

11 September

Do you have any idea how to pronounce: Chargoggagoggmanchaugagoggchaubunagungamaug?

It's America's longest single place name; it's actually a lake near Webster, Massachusetts. They say it's pronounced, "char-gogg-a-gogg (pause) man-chugg-a-gog (pause) chau-bun-agung-a-maug." In the Native American language of the region it means, "You fish on your side, I'll fish on mine, and no one fishes in the middle."[77]

We have one word for that in the English language: "ownership." The Bible teaches that rather than holding onto things tightly and demanding our rights, we ought to hold things loosely and share what we have with others. What's the biblical precedent for this? God's love. "God so loved the world that He GAVE..." Our love is never more like God's than when we give sacrificially.

"Teach those who are rich in this world not to be proud and not to trust in their money, which is so unreliable. Their trust should be in God, who richly gives us all we need for our enjoyment. Tell them to use their money to do good. They should be rich in good works and generous to those in need, always being ready to share with others" (1 Timothy 6:17-18).

Believers in the New Testament Church didn't know how to say, "Chargoggagoggmanchaugagoggchaubunagungamaug;" instead they said, "Love."

SEPTEMBER 12

"...The disciples were first called Christians in Antioch" (Acts 11:26b, NASB).

Did you know that the United States of America was named after a real person? Yes, it's true. His name was Amerigo Vespucci (Italy, 1451-1512). Though no one remembers Amerigo, everyone knows America.

A very large group of people are named after someone who will never be forgotten—Christians! As a believer, you carry the name of Jesus Christ on you; actually, you are one of Jesus' representatives on earth. You may be the only "Jesus" many people have ever encountered.

His Name is upon you—it's a good, honored, powerful, exalted Name!

"...God elevated him to the place of highest honor and gave him the name above all other names, that at the name of Jesus every

knee should bow, in heaven and on earth and under the earth, and every tongue confess that Jesus Christ is Lord, to the glory of God the Father" (Philippians 2:9-11).

13 September

Have you found that you pray better and with more passion and for longer periods of time when you pray with others?

A few years ago David Bryant studied all the scriptural accounts of people praying and found that roughly ninety percent of the time, people prayed with other people, not by themselves. Even the Lord's Prayer is corporate: "Our Father... give us today our daily bread..." (Matthew 6:9-11, NIV).

When we pray according to Jesus' will, we can expect Him to answer our prayers: "If you abide in Me, and My words abide in you, ask whatever you wish, and it will be done for you" (John 15:7, NASB).

I like the way The Message paraphrases this same verse: "But if you make yourselves at home with me and my words are at home in you, you can be sure that whatever you ask will be listened to and acted upon."

What a great promise! I'm going to pray more!

14 September

"For whatever was written in former days was written for our instruction, that through endurance and through the

encouragement of the Scriptures we might have hope" (Romans 15:4, ESV).

The Bible has a two-fold purpose in our lives:
1. It instructs us as to how to know and love God.
2. It encourages us.

The result is we live with hope! The Greek word translated "hope" is *elpizo*. Rather than conveying the idea of wishful thinking, it means having "a confident expectation." Sometimes it is also translated, "trust." The instruction and encouragement from the Word results in hope in a believer's life.

It's been said that a person can live about forty days without food, about three days without water, and about eight minutes without air—but only one second without hope.

Your situation is not hopeless. You will find in God and His Word the comfort and hope you need.

"Now may the God of hope fill you with all joy and peace in believing, so that you will abound in hope by the power of the Holy Spirit" (Romans 15:13, NASB).

SEPTEMBER 15

One of the Scriptures that helps me the most day-to-day is Philippians 4:6-7. I especially like the way the NLT puts it:

> "Don't worry about anything; instead, pray about everything. Tell God what you need, and thank him for all he has done. Then you will experience God's peace, which

exceeds anything we can understand. His peace will guard your hearts and minds as you live in Christ Jesus."

Someone has said, "Worry is like a rocking chair. It gives you something to do but doesn't get you anywhere."[78]

Here you go: The antidote for worry is to pray about everything, investing that "worry" time into "trust" time. This basically means telling God what you need and expecting Him to take care of you. You are His child, after all!

The result will be a deep-seated, unshakeable peace that guards your heart and mind.

"Don't fret or worry. Instead of worrying, pray. Let petitions and praises shape your worries into prayers, letting God know your concerns. Before you know it, a sense of God's wholeness, everything coming together for good, will come and settle you down. It's wonderful what happens when Christ displaces worry at the center of your life" (Philippians 4:6-7, MSG).

16 SEPTEMBER

"I appeal to you, dear brothers and sisters, by the authority of our Lord Jesus Christ, to live in harmony with each other. Let there be no divisions in the church. Rather, be of one mind, united in thought and purpose" (1 Corinthians 1:10).

The guy on the deserted island was finally rescued! He'd been there for a long time. He fell on his knees and thanked the captain of the ship for rescuing him. But the captain said, "Wait

a minute, are there other people on this island?" "No," the guy responded, "That first hut is the house I live in, the second hut is the church I go to, and the third hut is the church I used to go to."

Conflict in the church is nothing new!

The New Testament honestly records the conflicts that the early Church experienced.

In chapter eleven of 1 Corinthians Paul says, "...I hear that there are divisions among you when you meet as a church, and to some extent I believe it" (1 Corinthians 11:18).

Sadly, the Church at Corinth isn't the only church that has had divisions and quarrels. There are many churches today that are stalled and diverted by division. This is usually a sign of spiritual immaturity.

One of the evidences of Christian maturity will be a growing oneness of mind, a unity of mind and purpose!

When you think about it, unity is a miracle of the Holy Spirit! Unity can't be legislated by people; it can only be created by the Holy Spirit and maintained by God's people as He focuses us around our Lord Jesus Christ. Because we're one in our fellowship in Jesus, we should be one in our fellowship with each other.

Our responsibility is not to create unity, it's not to obtain unity, it's to maintain unity!

17 September

"...Being diligent to preserve the unity of the Spirit in the bond of peace" (Ephesians 4:3, NASB).

Our duty is not to create unity in the church, nor is it to obtain unity, but it is to "...preserve the unity of the Holy Spirit in the bond of peace."

To "preserve" means to "keep watch" or "keep guard over."

What would you think if Jesus were physically with you today and someone began to attack Him, and pulled out a knife and began to try to slash Him to death?

What would any of us who love the Lord do? We'd rush to protect Him, we'd rush to preserve Him; we'd take the hit for Him if necessary.

Well, that should be our same response to anyone who would attempt to attack and divide the Church, because the Church is Jesus' body on earth! Disunity in the Church is an attack on our Lord.

A man went over to a friend's house, and everyone in the family recited their favorite Bible verse. The youngest daughter quoted John 3:16: "For God so loved the world, that He gave His only begotten Son, that whosoever believes in Him should not perish but have *internal* life."

No one corrected her. Everyone realized the truth is that eternal life should bring internal life as well.

SEPTEMBER 18

"Above all, you must live as citizens of heaven, conducting yourselves in a manner worthy of the Good News about Christ. ...standing together with one spirit and one purpose, fighting together for the faith, which is the Good News" (Philippians 1:27).

Satan's strategy is to divide and conquer; ours is to maintain unity.

I've observed that divisions cannot happen easily in churches that are filled with people who have the Lord's perspective.

This reminds me of something I once read:

> A man visiting the countryside near Edinburgh, Scotland took pictures of the fences bordering the farm properties. In one print his wife was seen standing beside one of the fences. A few months later he took his children to Scotland to show them the same fences, but they could not be seen. A visitor explained, "You must have been here in the spring; now it's harvest time and the grain is grown so high it blocks the fences."[79]

Are you in competition with some other believer? Do you feel like someone is stepping on your turf? Get a harvest mentality. There's so much to do; we don't have time to worry about fences!

Remember, conflicts and divisions disappear when we get the Lord's perspective.

grace today

19 SEPTEMBER

"For You, Lord, are good, and ready to forgive, and abundant in lovingkindness to all who call upon You" (Psalm 86:5, NASB).

How do we actually drop the charges against those who have offended us?

At the outset you have to understand that real forgiveness doesn't come naturally. It's actually the life of Jesus being extended through you.

Forgiveness is dropping the charges against those who have hurt you or offended you or insulted you or mocked you or abused you or ignored you or neglected you. This step is not optional.

I think the Lord knew we'd like to skip this step; that's why He taught us to pray: "Forgive us our debts, as we also have forgiven our debtors" (Matthew 6:12, NASB).

Jesus gave His own divine commentary on this phrase a few verses later when He said, "If you forgive those who sin against you, your Heavenly Father will forgive you. But if you refuse to forgive others, your Father will not forgive your sins" (Matthew 6:14-15).

Jesus emphasized this teaching again to His disciples in Mark 11:25-26, "Whenever you stand praying, forgive, if you have anything against anyone, so that your Father who is in heaven will also forgive you your transgressions. [But if you do not forgive, neither will your Father who is in heaven forgive your transgressions]" (NASB).

Is Jesus teaching that we earn forgiveness of our sins by forgiving others? Obviously, no, we are forgiven wholly by Jesus' sacrifice for us and our faith in Him (Acts 10:43; Ephesians 1:7), but our forgiveness of others shows that we have received Jesus' forgiveness. It is the nature of God to forgive (Numbers 14:18), and we share His divine nature (2 Peter 1:4).

September 20

Paul makes this very practical application of forgiveness: "Be kind to one another, tender-hearted, forgiving each other, just as God in Christ also has forgiven you" (Ephesians 4:32, NASB).

If we have really experienced God's forgiveness, we will extend God's forgiveness to others: "Make allowance for each other's faults, and forgive anyone who offends you. Remember, the Lord forgave you, so you must forgive others" (Colossians 3:13).

Ultimately unforgiveness leads to bondage and an emotional isolation. Jesus illustrated this principle in the Parable of the Unmerciful Servant:

> Then Peter came to him and asked, "Lord, how often should I forgive someone who sins against me? Seven times?" "No, not seven times," Jesus replied, "but seventy times seven! Therefore, the Kingdom of Heaven can be compared to a king who decided to bring his accounts up to date with servants who had borrowed money from him. In the process, one of his debtors was brought in who owed him millions of dollars. He couldn't pay, so his master ordered that he be sold—along with his wife, his children, and everything he owned—to pay the debt. But the man fell down before his

master and begged him, 'Please, be patient with me, and I will pay it all.' Then his master was filled with pity for him, and he released him and forgave his debt. "But when the man left the king, he went to a fellow servant who owed him a few thousand dollars. He grabbed him by the throat and demanded instant payment. His fellow servant fell down before him and begged for a little more time. 'Be patient with me, and I will pay it,' he pleaded. But his creditor wouldn't wait. He had the man arrested and put in prison until the debt could be paid in full. When some of the other servants saw this, they were very upset. They went to the king and told him everything that had happened. Then the king called in the man he had forgiven and said, 'You evil servant! I forgave you that tremendous debt because you pleaded with me. Shouldn't you have mercy on your fellow servant, just as I had mercy on you?' Then the angry king sent the man to prison to be tortured until he had paid his entire debt. That's what my Heavenly Father will do to you if you refuse to forgive your brothers and sisters from your heart" (Matthew18:21-35).

In this parable Jesus is warning us that:
- Unforgiveness is torture.
- Unforgiveness enslaves.
- Unforgiveness imprisons.

If we do not forgive, we will be enslaved and isolated by our own bitterness and resentment.

21 SEPTEMBER

Forgiveness is a choice. Forgiveness is not an emotion or a feeling; it's a decision of the will. It's a very definite choice!

A friend asked Clara Barton: "How can you forgive that person? Don't you remember what they did to you?" "No," she replied, "I distinctly remember forgetting it!"

Proverbs 19:11 says "Sensible people control their temper; they earn respect by overlooking wrongs."

Even if you do not feel like it, forgive the person who has offended you; this is what God wants you to do. Choosing to forgive them is not saying that what they did to you was okay, it's taking the spiritual step to do what God wants you to do. God will bless this step. You are on the road to freedom!

Make a conscious decision to continue to extend the forgiveness as layer by layer the Holy Spirit reveals the offense to you.

SEPTEMBER 22

We forgot the cross!

I was at a retreat center in Arizona a while back and saw a new wooden cross out in front of the office building. When I asked the staff where it had come from, they explained that it was brought up by a group who held a beautiful retreat about the cross. They had used the cross as the centerpiece of their program—and then when they packed up to go home—they left the cross behind!

Wow! Isn't that the way it so often goes—we glory in the cross and then we forget to take it home with us.

Jesus said, "...If anyone wishes to come after Me, he must deny himself, and take up his cross and follow Me" (Mark 8:34b, NASB).

grace today

23 SEPTEMBER

God's Word is powerful!

Billy Graham has been one of the most successful evangelists in the history of the church. His method was simple: Let God's Spirit use God's Word.

Billy Graham said, "I have used from twenty-five to one hundred passages of Scripture with every sermon and learned that modern man will surrender to the impact of the Word of God."[80]

The truth is: "...the word of God is alive and powerful. It is sharper than the sharpest two-edged sword, cutting between soul and spirit, between joint and marrow. It exposes our innermost thoughts and desires" (Hebrews 4:12).

Open God's Word for yourself and experience its power today. I'm praying that the Lord gives you a hunger for His Word.

24 SEPTEMBER

"For the love of Christ controls us, because we have concluded this: that one has died for all, therefore all have died..." (2 Corinthians 5:14, ESV).

At three o'clock one afternoon about two thousand years ago, we all died! We were ruined thousands of years before this without our participation when Adam sinned (Romans 5:12). At Calvary,

again without participating personally, we were saved from the ruination of sin through the death of Jesus Christ. Now Jesus invites everyone to come to Him. Jesus said, "...Every sin and blasphemy can be forgiven..." (Matthew 12:31a).

"...and he died for all, that those who live might no longer live for themselves but for him who for their sake died and was raised..." (2 Corinthians 5:15, ESV).

Belonging to the Lord always leads to living for the Lord.

"Therefore, if anyone is in Christ, he is a new creation. The old has passed away; behold, the new has come..." (2 Corinthians 5:17, ESV).

This is a remarkable verse sharing an incredible truth. If you are "in Christ" you are a "new creation"! This could be actually translated, "a new species"!

"For our sake he made him to be sin who knew no sin, so that in him we might become the righteousness of God" (2 Corinthians 5:21, ESV).

We trade places with Jesus. God made Him to be sin, what He was not, in order that we might be made righteous, something we are not!

We are "complete in Christ," and "accepted in the Beloved," and "there is therefore now no condemnation for those who are in Christ Jesus" (Colossians 2:10; Ephesians 1:6, NKJV; Romans 8:1, ESV).

25 SEPTEMBER

Think of the people that God has used to serve Him who didn't have any great qualifications:

- What degree did Moses have? Perhaps he had a B.S.D. degree (Back Side of the Desert)!
- David, a S.K.G.S. degree, (Sheep-Keeper and Giant Slayer)!
- Esther, a B.Q. degree (Beauty Queen)!
- Amos, an F.P. degree (Fig Picker)!

What degree would you have? It could get pretty funny when you think about it. The reality is, God can use you, yes you! "For consider your calling, brethren, that there were not many wise according to the flesh, not many mighty, not many noble" (1 Corinthians 1:26, NASB).

Notice it says, "not many noble;" it doesn't say, "not any noble!" Lady Huntington, a precious sister who lived during the early part of the twentieth century, a member of the British nobility, used to say that she was saved by an *M*! She said, "If this verse said, 'not *any* mighty, not *any* noble,' I would have been lost! But the Lord put an *M* in front of 'any,' so it says, 'not *many* noble!'"

I'm encouraged! For God to use you, you don't need educational degrees, powerful financial backing, or influential connections.

God wants to use you!

26 SEPTEMBER

"...But God has chosen the foolish things of the world to shame the wise, and God has chosen the weak things of the world to

shame the things which are strong, and the base things of the world and the despised God has chosen, the things that are not, so that He may nullify the things that are" (1 Corinthians 1:27-28, NASB).

The way the Lord uses us and the way He chooses to work may seem absurd and illogical to us.

One of the reasons God does this, is because He wants it to be clearly visible, in what we do for Him, and in what He does with us, that it is Him doing it and that it is not us! It is not our wisdom, it's not our plan, and obviously, not our strength!

Dwight L. Moody was tremendously used of God about one hundred years ago! After his death, a good friend and associate wrote a book entitled, *Why God Used D. L. Moody.*

In that book there's an account of one of the greatest awakenings of the nineteenth century, which began when Mr. Moody and singer Ira Sankey came to Cambridge University in England.

When Moody arrived at Cambridge, members of the faculty and student body were outraged that this backwoods American preacher would dare to appear and speak in what was considered to be the very heart of culture of the English world.

APPLICATION: Do you ever feel like God calls you to serve outside of your comfort zone? How do you react when initially you aren't received? Would you be tempted to doubt that God sent you?

Let's finish the story of Moody tomorrow...

27 SEPTEMBER

"...But God has chosen the foolish things of the world to shame the wise, and God has chosen the weak things of the world to shame the things which are strong..." (1 Corinthians 1:27, NASB).

Sometimes God stretches us by using us in areas that are way outside the boundaries of our comfort zones.

Let's continue where we left Mr. Moody and Mr. Sankey...

Everyone knew very well that Moody "murdered" the King's English. Someone once said that Moody was the only man he had ever heard who could pronounce "Jerusalem" in one syllable!

The non-Christian university students arrived for the chapel service determined that, when Moody began to speak, they would "boo" him off the platform.

Here's what happened: Moody began by asking Sankey to sing. He was a great musician and really had a way with people; whenever he sang, audiences quieted down and listened to him. As soon as he finished, Moody stepped to the edge of the platform and, looking directly at the students, he said these remarkable words, "Young gentlemen, don't ever think God don't love you, for He do!"

The students were dumbfounded by that beginning. Moody went on, and in a few minutes later he again said, "Don't ever think God don't love you, for He do!" Something about the very ungrammatical structure of these words captured them.

Moody's intense earnestness spoke right to their hearts, beyond all the external things. Moody went on to lead many to Christ, and a great awakening came to Cambridge University through this man who spoke to tens of thousands, even though he slaughtered his grammar!

Wow! "Never think God don't love you, for He do!"

And: "Never think that God can't use you, for He do!"

May the strong grace of Jesus bless you this day!

SEPTEMBER 28

"This foolish plan of God is wiser than the wisest of human plans, and God's weakness is stronger than the greatest of human strength" (1 Corinthians 1:25).

Our usefulness to God and for God is not derived from our abilities, but upon God's power!

When God wanted to choose a couple to be the founders of a mighty nation, whom did He choose? Significantly, not Mr. and Mrs. Fertility, but Abram and Sarai, a childless couple, struggling with infertility issues.

When God wanted to deliver His chosen people from Egyptian slavery, He didn't pick someone from Pharaoh's palace; that's what *we* would have done. Instead, He chose an eighty-year-old fugitive! Moses was looking after sheep in the wilderness.

Another God-pick was David. When God chose David to be Israel's second king, He passed over all those "most likely to succeed" and anointed the youngest son of Jesse, a boy who was tending sheep, a boy whom his family even forgot they had! (1 Samuel 16).

Are you beginning to get the idea that God's way isn't our way? He doesn't think like we think. He sees potential in the impossible and advantage in weakness. God loves to work in ways and through people who, in their very use, bring Him glory!

"Father, I'm going to stop thinking of why You can't use me to serve You. I give You the things that I think disqualify me or make me the least likely to succeed. I'm available; I'd do anything I knew You were asking me to do. In Jesus' good Name I pray. Amen!"

29 SEPTEMBER

"For I am with you..." (Acts 18:10a).

As Paul faced fear, he could be sure the Lord was with Him because His word is His promise.

God gave Paul a specific promise for his fear: "...Don't be afraid! Speak out! Don't be silent! For I am with you, and no one will attack and harm you, for many people in this city belong to me" (Acts 18:9-10).

When you're fearful, remember that you have the same assurance of God's promises!

There are three thousand promises in the Word of God—that's eight a day, three hundred and sixty-five days a year! There's a promise to meet any and all of our needs!

Here's what to do: Believe the promises of God and act on them!

Remember, you have God's antidote for spiritual paralysis:
- His Presence.
- His Promises.
- His Power.

September 30

"...We can know the wonderful things God has freely given us" (1 Corinthians 2:12b).

Having a hard time being thankful? Just look at who you used to be (before Christ) and who you are today because of what Christ has done for you. Wow, that will put you on your knees in thanksgiving pretty fast, won't it?

Speak aloud these spiritual blessings that are yours in our Lord Jesus Christ:
- I am saved from God's wrath forever!
- I accept the things of God.
- I can understand the Word.
- I can say "no" to sin (I am no longer a slave of sin).
- I think about God.
- I understand spiritual things.
- I am no longer a child of wrath.
- I am a part of God's family.
- The "old man" is dead.

grace today

- I have a new nature!
- I am alive to God!
- The Holy Spirit literally lives in me!
- The same power that raised Jesus Christ from the dead works in me!

This new spiritual life, this new creation, cannot be called a "natural" life—it's a supernatural life!

"With all this going for us, my dear, dear friends, stand your ground. And don't hold back. Throw yourselves into the work of the Master, confident that nothing you do for him is a waste of time or effort" (1 Corinthians 15:58, MSG).

Don't be discouraged! God remembers you and your service for Him!

The NASB puts it this way; "Therefore, my beloved brethren, be steadfast, immovable, always abounding in the work of the Lord, knowing that your toil is not in vain in the Lord."

"Toil" means "to labor to the point of exhaustion."

Hebrews 6:10 says: "For God is not unjust so as to forget your work and the love which you have shown toward His name, in having ministered and in still ministering to the saints" (NASB).

Frankly, I'm just blown away by this verse, aren't you? Nothing, absolutely nothing you've done for the Lord Jesus has been forgotten! That's just so encouraging!

In 2 Chronicles 15:7, Azariah the Prophet encouraged King Asa with these words: "But you, be strong and do not lose courage [let your hands drop], for there is reward for your work" (NASB).

Eighteen times in the New Testament Jesus encourages us that there are rewards coming! Wow! Jesus rewards us for serving Him, even though our service is because He is working through us! (Philippians 2:13). That's just more grace than I can imagine!

grace today

2 OCTOBER

"I see God... the Holy One coming... His coming is as brilliant as the sunrise. Rays of light flash from his hands, where his awesome power is hidden" (Habakkuk 3:3-4).

"You've done everything you can. You need to leave it in God's hands now..." Has anyone ever said that to you? Have you ever said that to someone? I wonder if we really know what we're saying?

What does it mean to "leave things in God's hands?" What kind of a place would "God's hands" be? Are we really safe in God's hands?

This is a study that has really blessed me; I could hardly wait to share it with you!

Here's what the Bible has to say about God's hands:

- God's hand secures us – "And I give them eternal life, and they shall never lose it or perish throughout the ages. [To all eternity they shall never by any means be destroyed.] And no one is able to snatch them out of My hand" (John 10:28, AMP).
- God's hand protects us – "Do not fear, for I am with you; Do not anxiously look about you, for I am your God. I will strengthen you, surely I will help you, surely I will uphold you with My righteous right hand" (Isaiah 41:10, NASB).
- God's hand brings fulfillment – "He said, 'Blessed be the LORD, the God of Israel, who spoke with His mouth to my father David and has fulfilled it with His hand...' " (1 Kings 8:15, NASB). "You have kept your promise to your servant David, my father. You made that promise

with your own mouth, and with your own hands you have fulfilled it today" (2 Chronicles 6:15).
- God's hand corrects us – "Therefore humble yourselves under the mighty hand of God, that He may exalt you at the proper time" (1 Peter 5:6, NASB).

We'll continue this study tomorrow...

OCTOBER 3

Let's look at some more things the Bible says about God's hands:
- God's hand supports us – "Do not fear, for I am with you; do not anxiously look about you, for I am your God. I will strengthen you, surely I will help you, surely I will uphold you with My righteous right hand" (Isaiah 41:10, NASB). "My soul clings to you; your right hand upholds me" (Psalm 63:8, ESV). "The LORD sustains all who fall, and raises up all who are bowed down" (Psalm 145:14, NASB).
- God's hand strengthens us – "...I was strengthened according to the hand of the LORD my God upon me, and I gathered leading men from Israel to go up with me" (Ezra 7:28b, NASB).
- God's hand abundantly provides for us – "O LORD our God, all this abundance that we have provided to build You a house for Your holy name, it is from Your hand, and all is Yours" (1 Chronicles 29:16, NASB). "This Ezra went up from Babylon, and he was a scribe skilled in the law of Moses, which the LORD God of Israel had given; and the king granted him all he requested because the hand of the LORD his God was upon him" (Ezra 7:6, NASB). "...And the king granted them to me because the good hand of my God was on me" (Nehemiah 2:8b, NASB).

- Your future is in His hands – "My future is in your hands..." (Psalm 31:15a).

You are safe in God's hands! What a place to be!

4 OCTOBER

God's hands are a place of incredible power and awesome majesty.

"I see God... the Holy One coming... His coming is as brilliant as the sunrise. Rays of light flash from his hands, where his awesome power is hidden" (Habakkuk 3:3-4).

- God's hands are good – "For on the first of the first month he began to go up from Babylon; and on the first of the fifth month he came to Jerusalem, because the good hand of his God was upon him" (Ezra 7:9, NASB). "According to the good hand of our God upon us..." (Ezra 8:18a, NASB). "...And the king granted them to me because the good hand of my God was on me" (Nehemiah 2:8b, NASB).
- Being in God's hands is a place of satisfaction – "The eyes of all look to you in hope; you give them their food as they need it. When you open your hand, you satisfy the hunger and thirst of every living thing" (Psalm 145:15-16).
- God's hands shape us – "And yet, O LORD, you are our Father. We are the clay, and you are the potter. We all are formed by your hand" (Isaiah 64:8).
- God's hands guide us – "If I ride the wings of the morning, if I dwell by the farthest oceans, even there your hand will guide me, and your strength will support me" (Psalm 139:9-10).

"I see God... the Holy One coming... His coming is as brilliant as the sunrise. Rays of light flash from his hands, where his awesome power is hidden" (Habakkuk 3:3-4).

- God's hand delivers us from enemies – "Remember that you were once slaves in Egypt, but the LORD your God brought you out with his strong hand and powerful arm..." (Deuteronomy 5:15). "We broke camp at the Ahava Canal on April 19 and started off to Jerusalem. And the gracious hand of our God protected us and saved us from enemies and bandits along the way" (Ezra 8:31). I also like the way the NASB translates this: "...and the hand of our God was over us, and He delivered us from the hand of the enemy and the ambushes by the way."

- God's hand unites us for obedience – "At the same time, God's hand was on the people in the land of Judah, giving them all one heart to obey the orders of the king and his officials, who were following the word of the LORD" (2 Chronicles 30:12).

- God's hands are mighty and awesome in power – "Lord GOD, You have begun to show Your servant Your greatness and Your strong hand; for what god is there in heaven or on earth who can do such works and mighty acts as Yours?" (Deuteronomy 3:24, NASB). "Or has a god tried to go to take for himself a nation from within another nation by trials, by signs and wonders and by war and by a mighty hand and by an outstretched arm and by great terrors, as the LORD your God did for you in Egypt before your eyes?" (Deuteronomy 4:34, NASB). "and he said, 'O LORD, the God of our fathers, are You not God in the heavens? And are You not ruler over all the kingdoms of

the nations? Power and might are in Your hand so that no one can stand against You' " (2 Chronicles 20:6, NASB).

You truly are in great hands!

6 October

"For no one can lay any foundation other than the one we already have—Jesus Christ" (1 Corinthians 3:11).

Christianity is Christ! Anything that the Church grows into must be built upon Him. A good, solid foundation is absolutely essential for Christian growth.

A foundation determines:
- Size and design.
- Strength.
- Longevity.

Jesus is our foundation, and He will never move! Our foundation is not faulty; it is firm!

The only structure ever erected on a foundation of solid gold is the Gate of the Fortress of Purandhar, India. The Rajah of Bedar, who built it in 1290, was informed by his craftsmen that the site was a veritable quagmire into which any structure would collapse.

In his desperation, this extremely wealthy man listened to a dream in which he was advised to build the gate upon a golden underpinning. He excavated two great cavities in the marshy ground. Each of the excavations measured 35 feet square and 112

feet deep. The royal treasury was emptied of 50,000 gold bricks, weighing 4,320 grains each.

This precious hoard, totaling 37,500 pounds, worth more than $16 million dollars, was lowered into the ground to form the fabulous foundation upon which the gate was built. Both the gate and the 14-karat gold treasure upon which it rests are still there.

Jesus is our precious foundation!

OCTOBER 7

God's plans are good!

" 'For I know the plans I have for you,' says the LORD. 'They are plans for good and not for disaster, to give you a future and a hope' " (Jeremiah 29:11).

God has plans for your life! He knows all about it—we don't! We don't know what He's up to!

God's plans for your life have been prepared from all eternity! They are eternal plans!

God's plans are not static, though they are eternal, He is constantly thinking about you today! The Hebrew actually reads, "For I know the plans that I am planning for you." God is always thinking about us!

Psalm 139:17-18 says, "How precious are your thoughts about me, O God. They cannot be numbered! I can't even count them; they outnumber the grains of sand!..."

God's plan is a good plan! I've shared this verse with people who are in desperate financial difficulties, and they gasp because in the NASB it says "...plans for welfare..." But it also goes on to say, "and not for calamity."

Note that the word, "welfare" means "shalom" or "peace" or "wholeness!"

8 OCTOBER

"Let a man regard us in this manner, as servants of Christ and stewards of the mysteries of God" (1 Corinthians 4:1, NASB).

How do you think others view you? The Apostle Paul wanted to be known as a servant. A genuine servant of Christ is characterized by humility. He or she is not concerned about status, but service.

Paul told the folks in Corinth to regard him this way: not as an apostle par excellence, but as a "servant."

The Greek word he used that's translated "servants" is *uperetes,* which means "an under-rower."

The Roman war galleys were common sights to the Corinthians. These war galleys were propelled mainly by rowing. Everyone knew that the lowest deck of the galley was filled with two long rows of benches where dozens of oarsmen, usually slaves, sat chained to the ship and to each other.

The oarsmen generally were prisoners of war or criminals. Many of them would never see freedom again.

It was common for several men to handle each oar, as their combined weight was needed to raise the oar out of the water, and their combined strength was needed to pull it.

In front of them, sitting on a raised platform, was the captain of the ship; the galley slaves fixed their eyes on him and did whatever the captain commanded.

"Under-rowers," "Galley slaves"—that's the word Paul chooses to describe himself.

Paul is saying, "We're not supermen, we're servants of Christ—our eyes are fixed on Jesus, and we do whatever He tells us to do! Whatever He tells us to say, we say! Our responsibility is to follow His orders!"

We are "servants of Christ." We're "under-rowers" helping to propel the ship of grace over the water of time until we reach our harbor safe in heaven.

OCTOBER 9

"For even the Son of Man came not to be served but to serve others and to give his life as a ransom for many" (Mark 10:45).

I want to be like Christ! What is Christ like? Understanding our Lord means understanding what servant-hood really is all about.

Jesus says, "The greatest among you must be a servant. But those who exalt themselves will be humbled, and those who humble themselves will be exalted" (Matthew 23:11-12).

grace today

What was in Jesus' mind when He came to serve? He was showing us that the way up is actually down! If you want to stand tall in God's church, you have to learn to be on your face before Him.

Obviously, this is just the opposite of this world's system.

Ministry means service. It means opening your eyes and seeing what needs to be done and doing it! It means that we consider no job to be beneath us nor too unimportant for us.

Unless you're an aviation buff, Charles Lawrence isn't a name you're likely to know. He is credited with developing the engine for "The Spirit of St. Louis," the aircraft Charles Lindbergh flew non-stop from Long Island to Paris in 1927.

After the record-setting flight, Charles' friends held a dinner in honor of his achievement. At the dinner, in response to the attention he received, he made an excellent observation: "This is nice, and I appreciate it very much, but who ever heard of Paul Revere's horse?"

There's a great deal of wisdom in his words. Lawrence understood that his role was minor; he had merely helped provide a usable vehicle. The real achievement was Lindbergh's. He made the necessary sacrifices and he flew the mission.

10 OCTOBER

"But we don't need to write to you about the importance of loving each other, for God himself has taught you to love one another. Indeed, you already show your love for all the believers... Even so, dear brothers and sisters, we urge you to love them even more" (1 Thessalonians 4:9-10).

We can never love each other too much. Earlier Paul said, "...may the Lord make your love for one another and for all people grow and overflow, just as our love for you overflows" (1 Thessalonians 3:12). One paraphrase puts it this way: "And may the Master pour on the love so it fills your lives and splashes over on everyone around you..." (MSG).

Part of the ministry of the Holy Spirit in this New Covenant is to teach us to love one another, "For God himself has taught you to love one another."

Loving other Christians is one of the identifying marks of an authentic disciple of Jesus.

"So now I am giving you a new commandment: Love each other. Just as I have loved you, you should love each other. Your love for one another will prove to the world that you are my disciples" (John 13:34-35).

The world will recognize that we're really followers of Jesus when they see us loving one another.

OCTOBER 11

"Though they stumble, they will never fall, for the LORD holds them by the hand" (Psalm 37:24).

How do you respond when you fail? What's a believer's response?
- Go immediately to Jesus. Refuse to believe that He is mad with you.
- Apply grace liberally to the wound! Agree with God and own up to your sin, admit your weakness, accept God's forgiveness, and ask for His strength.

grace today

- Forgive yourself. What do you expect of yourself when you're not walking in the Spirit? Perhaps you think you could do more without the Lord's strength than the Lord thought you could do? Really, nothing you do surprises Him—you just surprised yourself. Now you can trust yourself less and trust God more.
- Get with God's people. Failure doesn't disqualify you from fellowship. God's people love you.
- Make restitution when it's appropriate and where it's possible.
- Build barriers that will keep you from falling into the same hole again.
- Hold onto your hope in Christ!

12 OCTOBER

"God blesses those who are merciful, for they will be shown mercy" (Matthew 5:7).

Jesus says that "...in the way you judge, you will be judged; and by your standard of measure, it shall be measured to you" (Matthew 7:2, NASB).

We experienced God's mercy when we trusted in Christ. God didn't give us what we deserved. Now, Jesus asks us to have a merciful heart to other people. Show your family members mercy. Live mercifully at work. Drive with mercy on the freeways!

God's mercy is always tied to His grace. Mercy is not getting what we deserve, but grace is getting what we don't deserve.

"Mercy relates to the negative; grace relates to the positive. In relation to salvation, mercy says, 'No hell,' whereas grace says, 'Heaven,' Mercy says, 'I pity you;' grace says, 'I pardon you.' "[81]

When we pray "Lord Jesus Christ, have mercy upon me, a sinner," Jesus will grant that request, but He expects us to pass on that mercy to others.

The Apostle Paul never lost sight of the mercy that God had shown him. "This is a trustworthy saying, and everyone should accept it: 'Christ Jesus came into the world to save sinners' — and I am the worst of them all. But God had mercy on me so that Christ Jesus could use me as a prime example of his great patience with even the worst sinners. Then others will realize that they, too, can believe in him and receive eternal life" (1 Timothy 1:15-16).

OCTOBER 13

"God blesses those whose hearts are pure, for they will see God" (Matthew 5:8).

God loves purity of heart. This isn't talking about being sinless (1 John 1:8), but it is talking about having and maintaining the truth within. It means serving God with single-heartedness and not sharing space in our hearts with the world.

God's plan is that we stay pure by:
- Being fortified by His Word – "How can a young person stay pure? By obeying your word... I have hidden your word in my heart, that I might not sin against you" (Psalm 119:9, 11).

grace today

- Making a covenant with our eyes – It's important that we guard the eye gate! "I made a covenant with my eyes not to look lustfully at a girl" (Job 31:1, NIV). Watch what you watch. For some it means turning off the TV or canceling the cable service. You can't "control" the temptation. The Word tells us to "...flee youthful lust" (2 Timothy 2:22, NASB). Install software on you computer to keep out pornography and to report your computer activity to an accountability partner.

I'm praying that the Lord keeps you strong.

14 OCTOBER

Today we're going to look at how to be a good spiritual coach.

We don't learn well all by ourselves. Most people don't learn spiritual truths in isolation. Wisely, the Book of Proverbs counsels, "Iron sharpens iron, so one man sharpens another" (Proverbs 27:17, NASB).

The New Testament models this method of producing the next generation of believers. Paul was Timothy's spiritual coach. Barnabas was Paul's mentor at the beginning of his spiritual journey.

This New Testament method of growth has been lost to many Christians for generations.

Here are six things to look for when you're choosing a spiritual coach:
1. Look for someone who has a longing for the Lord like you want to have. They have the close walk with Jesus that you would like to have.

2. Look for someone who walks humbly before God and people.
3. Look for someone who is wise in the Word.
4. Look for someone who models integrity.
5. Look for someone who is still spiritually growing themselves. Paul indicates that the relationship should be mutually encouraging: "For I long to visit you so I can bring you some spiritual gift that will help you grow strong in the Lord. When we get together, I want to encourage you in your faith, but I also want to be encouraged by yours" (Romans 1:11-12).
6. Look for someone who "fits" your personality. Maybe you have a similar background, or you have common interests, or shared experiences of some kind.

OCTOBER 15

"The master said, 'Well done, my good and faithful servant. You have been faithful in handling this small amount, so now I will give you many more responsibilities. Let's celebrate together!'" (Matthew 25:23).

God's servants are faithful. Here are some of the ways we live faithfully:

*   We finish what we start for the Lord.
*   We keep our word.
*   We are serious in our preparation for service.
*   We put the Lord ahead of our own desires. He always comes first.

A faithful person can be counted on.

grace today

16 OCTOBER

"So they arrived at the other side of the lake, in the region of the Gerasenes" (Mark 5:1).

The disciples not only arrived at the other side of the lake, going through the storm, but they came out more mature, more complete, fuller of faith.

Here are some of the lessons we can learn through their storm:
- The storm will not last forever!
- The Lord's "slumber" is not indifference to me.
- I'm not the only one going through storms.
- The Lord will finish the work He began in me.
- I can have Jesus' very own peace.
- The boat is not going to sink!

"I took my troubles to the LORD; I cried out to him, and he answered my prayer" (Psalm 120:1).

17 OCTOBER

Take some time today and look up these verses that show the power of the Word of God:
- It breaks hard hearts – Jeremiah 23:29.
- It convicts of sin – Acts 2:37.
- It regenerates – 1 Peter 1:23; James 1:18.
- It produces faith – Romans 10:17.
- It cleanses – Ephesians 5:26.
- It builds us up – Acts 20:32.
- It makes us wise – Psalm 119:130; 2 Timothy 3:15.
- It gives us assurance of our salvation – 1 John 5:13.

- It gives us joy – Jeremiah 15:16; John 15:11.
- It revives us – Psalm 119:25, 37, 40, 50, 93, 107, 149, 154, 156.

Note that this work of transformation is the work of a lifetime!

As one person said, "When you're through changing, you're through! You'll be in heaven!"

OCTOBER 18

"But now the LORD says: Be strong... Be strong... Be strong... for I am with you, says the LORD of Heaven's Armies" (Haggai 2:4).

The Living God, your Father in Heaven, is always with us. We're never alone. God is with you; you don't have to be afraid!

"...The Lord is near. Be anxious for nothing..." (Philippians 4:5b-6a, NASB).

When the wicked triumph and injustice wins, when the world goes wrong and right is trampled under might, be reassured that God sees it all and is in control of all! God will not be mocked (Galatians 6:7). He has appointed a day to judge all things.

Acts 17:31 says: "...He has fixed a day in which He will judge the world in righteousness through a Man whom He has appointed, having furnished proof to all men by raising Him from the dead" (NASB).

"The knowledge that we are never alone calms the troubled sea of our lives and speaks peace to our souls."[82]

19 OCTOBER

"Hallelujah! For the Lord our God, the Almighty, [omnipotent, KJV] reigns" (Revelation 19:6b, NASB).

God is omnipotent. Omni means "all," and potent means "power," so God has unlimited power.

In fact, God is referred to as the "Almighty" fifty-eight times in the Bible (El Shaddai, God Almighty). He is the "Mighty God." This title, "Almighty" is only used of the Lord and no one else in the Bible. Because God is Almighty, all-powerful, nothing is too difficult for God.

The truth of God's onmi-power or omnipotence rings throughout the Scripture. All power belongs to God. I like the way A. W. Tozer puts it. He says God has "...an incomprehensible plentitude of power, a potency that is absolute."[83]

"The LORD merely spoke, and the heavens were created. He breathed the word, and all the stars were born. He assigned the sea its boundaries and locked the oceans in vast reservoirs. Let the whole world fear the LORD, and let everyone stand in awe of him. For when he spoke, the world began! It appeared at his command" (Psalm 33:6-9).

20 OCTOBER

"Hallelujah! For the Lord our God, the Almighty, [omnipotent, KJV] reigns" (Revelation 19:6b, NASB).

"So, God is all powerful. I guess I know that. So what?"

Well, His power directly affects you! It directly affects all of us because God's power saves us!

"For I am not ashamed of the gospel, for it is the power of God for salvation to everyone who believes..." (Romans 1:16, NASB).

"For the word of the cross is foolishness to those who are perishing, but to us who are being saved it is the power of God" (1 Corinthians 1:18, NASB).

Without that power we wouldn't be saved. There'd be no way we'd be drawn to Him if He didn't have the power.

"No one can come to Me unless the Father who sent Me draws him..." (John 6:44a, NASB).

Think of it: it's because of God's power, and only God's power, that we are saved!

Thinking about God's omnipotence leads me to worship. When I think of how powerful He is, not only in the universe, but displayed in my life, I am overcome with awe and praise.

"...I heard something like a loud voice of a great multitude in heaven, saying, 'Hallelujah! Salvation and glory and power belong to our God'... Then I heard something like the voice of a great multitude and as the sound of many waters and like the sound of mighty peals of thunder, saying, 'Hallelujah! For the Lord our God, the Almighty, reigns' " (Revelation 19:1, 6, NASB).

grace today

21 October

"Stop being angry! Turn from your rage! Do not lose your temper—it only leads to harm" (Psalm 37:8).

When someone rages at you, stay calm.

Proverbs 10:19 says: "When there are many words, transgression is unavoidable, but he who restrains his lips is wise" (NASB).

Talk about practical application!

Listen to this counsel from Ecclesiastes 10:4: "If your boss is angry at you, don't quit! A quiet spirit can overcome even great mistakes."

22 October

If we are not "doing the Word," we can become hearers only and deceive ourselves. The Apostle James says: "And remember, it is a message to obey, not just to listen to. So don't fool yourselves" (James 1:22, TLB).

The most satisfying life is one of active service for the Lord. Doing good things, good works, can't save us, but we were saved to do good things! (See Ephesians 2:10).

A lot of people think they'll just take a break from serving the Lord. "It will only be for a few weeks," they say. I've talked to them, but all too often those weeks have become years. Determine to do what the Lord shows you in His Word. Be a doer of the Word!

"...I know every thought that comes into your minds" (Ezekiel 11:5b).

Our Father in Heaven knows us, so we can be honest.

"The eyes of the LORD are in every place, watching the evil and the good" (Proverbs 15:3, NASB).

One of the things that is important to tell our children is that the Lord sees everything they do. There is nothing He does not see. He knows everything.

We need to remind ourselves of this! Why is it people never think about God *before* sinning, but are so God-conscious *after* sinning?

"O God, you know how foolish I am; my sins cannot be hidden from you" (Psalm 69:5).

God knows all our sins. Moses wrote, "You spread out our sins before you—our secret sins—and you see them all" (Psalm 90:8).

No matter now hard people try to get away from God, they never can! God knows all things. People think that just because they are getting away with something, it must be that God doesn't care, or He doesn't see. Just because there isn't immediate judgment doesn't mean that you're getting away with anything! There's no secret that you can keep from God. His perfect knowledge extends to the heart (see 1 Samuel 16:7).

David said: "And you, Solomon my son, know the God of your father and serve him with a whole heart and with a willing mind, for the LORD searches all hearts and understands every plan and thought..." (1 Chronicles 28:9, ESV).

God says: "I, the LORD, search the heart, I test the mind..." (Jeremiah 17:10, NASB).

24 OCTOBER

"If we claim we have no sin, we are only fooling ourselves and not living in the truth. But if we confess our sins to him, he is faithful and just to forgive us our sins and to cleanse us from all wickedness" (1 John 1:8-9).

Another way that God shows His faithfulness to us is that He is faithful to forgive us. What a relief it is to know that God's forgiveness is tied to His faithfulness. You don't have to worry about whether God is going to forgive you one time, but not another. God is faithful to forgive us all the time. The Gospel is all about forgiveness.

Years ago, I read the words of a hymn that really encouraged me. I don't know the melody, I've never sung it, but the lyrics beautifully express the Gospel of forgiveness. Though the lyrics are old, the truth they express is just what we need today:

> I hear the accuser roar
>   Of ills that I have done;
> I know them well, and thousands more,
>   Jehovah findeth none.

Though the restless foe accuses—
  Sins recounting like a flood,
Ev'ry charge our God refuses;
  Christ has answered with His blood!

The only way to have the guilt of sin lifted is to ask Jesus to wash us clean.

OCTOBER 25

"For God is Spirit, so those who worship him must worship in spirit and in truth" (John 4:24).

One of the ways that we can offer extraordinary worship to our Lord Jesus Christ is by offering Jesus our minds.

God wants us to worship Him intelligently.

Some people almost make you believe that the less you know, the better you worship. But the very opposite is true. Actually, the more you know about Jesus and His Word, the more extraordinary your worship will be!

The more you know Him, and the better you understand who He is and what He is like, the deeper your worship will be.

When you see and begin to understand the attributes of God, worship is ignited in your heart!

26 OCTOBER

"Give your burdens to the LORD, and he will take care of you..." (Psalm 55:22a).

He is with us in every trial and difficulty; He's there to carry every burden and to support us. He wants to be our "burden-bearer."

There is not one day you will live that the Lord is not with you, whether you are consciously aware of it or not. The Lord is with us, carrying our burdens, and carrying us!

"He lifts the burdens from those bent down beneath their loads" (Psalm 146:8b, TLB).

"Praise the Lord; praise God our savior! For each day he carries us in his arms" (Psalm 68:19).

Sometimes we feel like we just can't bear our circumstances any longer. We think that if one more thing happens to us we will be destroyed. However, God can use these things to press us in closer to Him if we will not resist His work in our lives.

My prayer for you is that our strong Savior, Jesus, lifts the burden that you've been carrying. It's too much for you!

27 OCTOBER

"Dear brothers and sisters, pattern your lives after mine, and learn from those who follow our example" (Philippians 3:17).

The NASB puts it, "Join in following my example..."

"Let me be your example here, my brothers: let my example be the standard by which you can tell who are genuine Christians among those about you" (Phillips).

There's big power in example.

Will Houghton was a preacher who became the President of Moody Bible Institute during the 1940's. He played a large role in the conversion of an agnostic who was contemplating suicide. The skeptic was desperate, but he decided that if he could find a minister who lived his faith, he would listen to him. So he hired a private detective to watch Houghton. When the investigator's report came back, it revealed that this preacher's life was above reproach; he was for real. The agnostic went to Houghton's church, accepted Christ, and later sent his daughter to Moody Bible Institute.

It's interesting that the Italian word for influence is influenza. When we think of that word, we think of something that's highly contagious. That's exactly the point—someone is watching you!

OCTOBER 28

Proverbs 28:13 says, "People who conceal their sins will not prosper, but if they confess and turn from them, they will receive mercy."

Note the next verse, "Blessed are those who fear to do wrong, but the stubborn are headed for serious trouble" (verse 14).

Let our prayer be: "Lord, may I always have a tender conscience and a reverent fear of sin and wrong doing. Please keep my feet on the right side of the street, and today I chose to say 'NO' to sin and 'YES' to righteousness. In Jesus' Name, Amen!"

God bless you today as you live for Jesus.

29 OCTOBER

"So I urge you to imitate me" (1 Corinthians 4:16).

A brief, simple, but expressive eulogy was pronounced by Martin Luther upon a pastor at Zwickau in 1522, named Nicholas Haussmann.

"What we preach, he lived," said the great reformer.

Years ago someone said, "I wouldn't give much for your religion unless it can be seen. Lights do not talk, but they do shine."

That kind of sounds like something someone else has said: "Let your light shine before men in such a way that they may see your good works, and glorify your Father who is in heaven" (Matthew 5:16, NASB).

30 OCTOBER

"How great is our Lord! His power is absolute! His understanding is beyond comprehension!" (Psalm 147:5).

The overwhelming testimony of the Bible is that God knows all things!

In Hannah's song of thanksgiving, these words are recorded for us, "...For the LORD is a God of knowledge..." (1 Samuel 2:3b, NASB).

The Apostle Paul declared, "Oh, the depth of the riches both of the wisdom and knowledge of God! How unsearchable are His judgments and unfathomable His ways!" (Romans 11:33, NASB).

Through Isaiah the prophet, God said, "Why do you say, O Jacob, and assert, O Israel, 'My way is hidden from the LORD, and the justice due me escapes the notice of my God?' Do you not know? Have you not heard? The Everlasting God, the LORD, the Creator of the ends of the earth does not become weary or tired. His understanding is inscrutable [incomprehensible]" (Isaiah 40:27-28, NASB).

Job said, "With Him are wisdom and might; to Him belong counsel and understanding" (Job 12:13, NASB).

"Who has directed the Spirit of the LORD, or as His counselor has informed Him?" (Isaiah 40:13, NASB).

"For who has known the mind of the Lord, or who has been his counselor?" (Romans 11:34, ESV).

"He counts the number of the stars; He gives names to all of them. Great is our Lord and abundant in strength; His understanding is infinite" (Psalm 147:4-5, NASB).

We can trust God with our lives!

31 OCTOBER

"Watch out! Don't do your good deeds publicly, to be admired by others, for you will lose the reward from your Father in heaven" (Matthew 6:1).

When people love you, they will give you a "heads up." Here are some of the Bible's "heads ups" for us.

We should beware of:

- Hypocrisy – "Beware of these teachers of religious law! For they like to parade around in flowing robes and love to receive respectful greetings as they walk in the marketplaces. And how they love the seats of honor in the synagogues and the head table at banquets. Yet they shamelessly cheat widows out of their property and then pretend to be pious by making long prayers in public. Because of this, they will be severely punished" (Luke 20:46-47).
- People – "But beware! For you will be handed over to the courts and will be flogged with whips in the synagogues" (Matthew 10:17).
- Popularity – "Woe to you when all men speak well of you, for their fathers used to treat the false prophets in the same way" (Luke 6:26, NASB).
- Greed – "Then he said, 'Beware! Guard against every kind of greed. Life is not measured by how much you own' " (Luke 12:15).
- False Prophets – "Beware of false prophets who come disguised as harmless sheep but are really vicious wolves" (Matthew 7:15). "I am warning you ahead of time, dear friends. Be on guard so that you will not be carried away by the errors of these wicked people and lose your own secure footing" (2 Peter 3:17).

"Then those who feared the Lord talked often one to another; and the Lord listened and heard it, and a book of remembrance was written before Him of those who reverenced and worshipfully feared the Lord and who thought on His name. And they shall be Mine, says the Lord of hosts, in that day when I publicly recognize and openly declare them to be My jewels [My special possession, My peculiar treasure]. And I will spare them, as a man spares his own son who serves him" (Malachi 3:16-17, AMP).

Those who fear/revere the Lord speak often to one another about the Lord! And you know what? The Lord loves to stand around the corner listening!

Our words about the Lord mean so much to Him that it sounds like He journals them! He is so blessed by it that He writes it down in a scroll/book of remembrance!

I keep special cards or letters that have been given or sent to me over the years. Sometimes I've wondered if I was overly sentimental or something, but now I know that my Lord can relate to that.

Remember that the Lord loves you very much!

"Blessed and holy are those who share in the first resurrection. For them the second death holds no power, but they will be priests of God and of Christ and will reign with him a thousand years" (Revelation 20:6).

Lady Anne Grimston did not believe in the resurrection of the dead. When she was on her deathbed in her mansion, she said to a friend, "I shall live again as surely as a tree will grow from my body!"

Not long thereafter, she died and was buried in a beautiful marble tomb. The grave was marked by a large marble slab and surrounded by an iron railing.

Years later the marble slab was found to be moved a little. Then it cracked, and through the crack a small tree began to grow. The tree continued to grow, tilting the stone and breaking the marble slabs until today. It has surrounded the tomb with its roots and has torn the railing out of the ground with its four massive trunks.

Today, the tree that cracked Lady Anne Grimston's grave is one of the largest trees in England.

The Bible says the day is coming when every grave will be cracked wide open!

When Jesus returns for His Church, the graves of every believer who has died and gone to be with the Lord will be cracked open! They will be resurrected!

This is the first resurrection!

The Bible says that this is the resurrection you want to be in! Enjoy this verse in the Amplified translation, as we await this awesome truth. "Blessed [happy, to be envied] and holy [spiritually whole, of unimpaired innocence and proved virtue] is the person who takes part [shares] in the first resurrection!

Over them the second death exerts no power or authority, but they shall be ministers of God and of Christ [the Messiah], and they shall rule along with Him a thousand years" (Revelation 20:6, AMP).

NOVEMBER 3

"When everything is ready, I will come and get you, so that you will always be with me where I am" (John 14:3).

Our Lord is coming! Maranatha!

We are witnessing, living as we do at the end of the age, the collapse of civilization. It is obvious that we are moving quickly toward the end of the world.

Science has no answer for our problems. It can only define them.

There is only one ray of hope that shines through the darkness of this world's awful, terminal problems. It is the blessed hope that Jesus Christ gave us in John 14:1-3:

> "Don't let your hearts be troubled. Trust in God, and trust also in me. There is more than enough room in my Father's home. If this were not so, would I have told you that I am going to prepare a place for you? When everything is ready, I will come and get you, so that you will always be with me where I am."

Jesus promised to come back and take us to be with Him forever!

Knowing that Jesus may return at any moment gives us hope.

Whatever trouble or hard times we may be in, the truth is, it might all be over today!

Soon the Lord will descend from heaven with a shout, and with the voice of the archangel, and with the trumpet of God!

4 November

"When everything is ready, I will come and get you, so that you will always be with me where I am" (John 14:3).

When we are discouraged, we need to remind one another of an ancient Aramaic word the church said to encourage one another: "Maranatha!" It means, "Our Lord is Coming!"
- When we are in pain, "Maranatha!"
- When we are in poverty, "Maranatha!"
- When we are in plenty, "Maranatha!"
- When we are in sorrow, "Maranatha!"

Paul said, "Therefore comfort one another with these words..." What words? These words:

> "For the Lord himself will come down from heaven with a commanding shout, with the voice of the archangel, and with the trumpet call of God. First, the Christians who have died will rise from their graves. Then, together with them, we who are still alive and remain on the earth will be caught up in the clouds to meet the Lord in the air. Then we will be with the Lord forever" (1 Thessalonians 4:16-17).

"The Lord isn't really being slow about his promise, as some people think. No, he is being patient for your sake. He does not want anyone to be destroyed, but wants everyone to repent" (2 Peter 3:9).

Jesus is coming back. Then a time of trouble, like the world has never seen before, will begin.

People say, "Where's the promise of His coming?" "There's plenty of time."

What's holding up the Lord's return? Maybe He's waiting for you!

The only hope that this world has is Divine intervention, the return of Jesus Christ!

But, "Oh," you say, "That's just a fire escape!" You'd better believe it is! If the building's on fire, who's going to fault you for using the fire escape?

We who look for our Lord's soon return are not pessimistic, we are realistic! We know and are convinced that the only hope of this world is the return of the Lord Jesus Christ!

You may remember old Harry Truman, not the president, but the caretaker of the recreation lodge on Spirit Lake, five miles north of Mount St. Helens in Washington. All during that spring of 1980, Harry had been warned to leave the area. The experts were certain that the mountain was about to erupt, but he refused to listen to the warnings to leave the smoking mountain. He had stupidly asserted that the mountain wouldn't dare blow up on him!

grace today

But the mountain did blow up! What remorse and regret must have flashed through Harry Truman's mind in that brief instant before he was enveloped in the wrath of that mountain's spectacular eruption. He had waved his fist in the face of all those who had warned him and said, "I'll be here till hell freezes over!"

I'm sure Harry would love to be able to repent now, but it's too late. The mountain blew up! It's all over.

What about you? The mountain is just about ready to blow! There is a way off—Jesus has the free gift of salvation for you.

6 NOVEMBER

"Dear brothers and sisters, pattern your lives after mine, and learn from those who follow our example" (Philippians 3:17).

"You may write my life across the skies. I have nothing to conceal." These were the words of 58-year-old preacher Charles Spurgeon shortly before his death. He wasn't afraid to have anyone look into his life, it was an open book.[84]

At the end of Samuel the prophet's life, he could look back and say the same thing, "I've lived a life of integrity." Here's a portion of his farewell address to Israel:

> Then Samuel addressed all Israel: "I have done as you asked and given you a king. Your king is now your leader. I stand here before you—an old, gray-haired man—and my sons serve you. I have served as your leader from the time I was a boy to this very day. Now testify against me in the

presence of the LORD and before his anointed one. Whose
ox or donkey have I stolen? Have I ever cheated any of you?
Have I ever oppressed you? Have I ever taken a bribe and
perverted justice? Tell me and I will make right whatever
I have done wrong." "No," they replied, "you have never
cheated or oppressed us, and you have never taken even
a single bribe." "The LORD and his anointed one are my
witnesses today," Samuel declared, "that my hands are
clean." "Yes, he is a witness," they replied. "...As for me,
I will certainly not sin against the LORD by ending my
prayers for you. And I will continue to teach you what is
good and right" (1 Samuel 12:1-5, 23).

Psalm 24:4 gives some integrity basics in describing people
of integrity; they are: "Only the clean-handed, only the pure-
hearted; men who won't cheat, women who won't seduce"
(MSG).

"Lord, help me to live this day in integrity. I want to be whole
and undivided in my service for You. Please fill me with the
Holy Spirit's power. In Jesus' Name, Amen!"

NOVEMBER 7

"...I will lead a life of integrity in my own home" (Psalm 101:2b).

Look at this passage in the Psalms, the "I WILLS" of integrity:

"I will be careful to live a blameless life—when will you
come to help me? I will lead a life of integrity in my own
home. I will refuse to look at anything vile and vulgar. I hate
all who deal crookedly; I will have nothing to do with them.

grace today

I will reject perverse ideas and stay away from every evil. I will not tolerate people who slander their neighbors. I will not endure conceit and pride. I will search for faithful people to be my companions. Only those who are above reproach will be allowed to serve me. I will not allow deceivers to serve in my house, and liars will not stay in my presence. My daily task will be to ferret out the wicked and free the city of the LORD from their grip" (Psalm 101:2-8).

Former Senator Alan Simpson said, "If you have integrity, nothing else matters. If you don't have integrity, nothing else matters."[85]

8 NOVEMBER

Have you ever rejoiced over *not* being able to find something? Generally, we're glad when we find things we have lost. But there's one thing we're happy we'll never find—our sin!

When we come to Jesus, this is what happens to our sins:
- He banishes them – "He does not punish us for all our sins; he does not deal harshly with us, as we deserve... He has removed our sins as far from us as the east is from the west" (Psalm 103:10, 12).
- He bars them from His sight – "Lo, for my own welfare I had great bitterness; it is You who has kept my soul from the pit of nothingness, for You have cast all my sins behind Your back" (Isaiah 38:17, NASB).
- He buries them in the depths of the sea – "Once again you will have compassion on us. You will trample our sins under your feet and throw them into the depths of the ocean!" (Micah 7:19).

- He blots them out – "I—yes, I alone—will blot out your sins for my own sake and will never think of them again" (Isaiah 43:25).

Jesus didn't come to be a sacrifice to *cover* sin! John the Baptist said, "...Behold, the Lamb of God who takes away the sin of the world!" (John 1:29b, NASB).

Our sins are not just covered up, they have been completely eradicated!

NOVEMBER 9

"When Jesus had tasted it, he said, 'It is finished!' Then he bowed his head and released his spirit" (John 19:30).

Aren't all religions essentially the same? Have you ever thought that, or had someone ask you that?

Actually, after having studied comparative religions for years, I have come to the conclusion that there is only a difference of two letters between Christianity and all others religions on the earth, the letters "N" and "E"—two letters that change eternity.

The way to heaven, as taught by all other religions on earth could be summarized by one word: "DO!"

Christianity's way to heaven could also be summarized by one word: "DONE!"

We are saved by a finished work! Jesus finished the work of our salvation!

grace today

That's why on the cross He shouted, "IT IS FINISHED!" When He said that on the cross, He meant what He said! The work of salvation was finished! It was done!

The Old Testament priest's work was never done. As you look at the furnishings in the temple, there was no place for him to sit down and rest. He was not to sit down. His work was never done!

But when Jesus Christ came and offered Himself as the atoning sacrifice for our sins, the Bible tells us that when He ascended into heaven, He sat down at the right hand of God!

The reason He could sit down was because He had finished the work of our salvation!

It is Jesus' good works that save us! His doing, His dying, His rising again!

Note that we are not saved by what Christ is doing in us. We are saved only and wholly by what Christ did for us at the cross!

10 NOVEMBER

"...Your heavenly Father already knows all your needs." (Matthew 6:32b).

Because God is omniscient, He knows all things. He knows what we need and will always supply us.

"...Your heavenly Father already knows all your needs. Seek the Kingdom of God above all else, and live righteously, and he will give you everything you need." (Matthew 6:32b-33).

Emil Brunner said, "God's knowledge is not objective and impersonal, but 'interested.' ...His knowledge is the expression of His sympathy, His care, His planning, and His love. He 'knows what we have need of before we ask Him.' "

Knowing that God knows everything takes the stress out of life. We don't have to worry because someone is taking care of us who knows everything that we need.

"And my God will supply all your needs according to His riches in glory in Christ Jesus" (Philippians 4:19, NASB).

NOVEMBER 11

"...Your heavenly Father already knows all your needs." (Matthew 6:32b).

Our Father knows what we need and will always supply us.

> God declares: "Remember the former things long past, for I am God, and there is no other; I am God, and there is no one like Me, declaring the end from the beginning, and from ancient times things which have not been done, saying, 'My purpose will be established, and I will accomplish all My good pleasure' " (Isaiah 46:9-10, NASB).

God knows our days even before we have lived them!

> "I knew you before I formed you in your mother's womb. Before were born I set you apart and appointed you as my prophet to the nations" (Jeremiah 1:5).

grace today

God knows us intimately before we are born!

> "You saw me before I was born. Every day of my life was recorded in your book. Every moment was laid out before a single day had passed" (Psalm 139:16).

We can trust Him to take care of our future!

12 NOVEMBER

"Then all the officials of the king of Babylon came and took seats in the Middle Gate: Nergal-Sharezer of Samgar, Nebo-Sarsekim a chief officer, Nergal-Sharezer a high official and all the other officials of the king of Babylon" (Jeremiah 39:3, NIV).

Who would have thought that some guy's strange name in Jeremiah 39 would someday confirm the authenticity and the integrity of the Scripture? But that is exactly what has happened.

Recently a small clay tablet unearthed in the 1920's near Baghdad with an ancient cuneiform inscription was finally translated. The two-inch tablet, dating from King Nebuchadnezzar II of Babylon, names a Babylonian officer by the name of Nebo-Sarsekim who, according to Jeremiah 39:3, was present at the Babylonian siege of Jerusalem.

Here's the Biblical record: "...In the ninth year of Zedekiah king of Judah, in the tenth month, Nebuchadnezzar king of Babylon marched against Jerusalem with his whole army and laid siege to it. And on the ninth day of the fourth month of Zedekiah's eleventh year, the city wall was broken through. Then all the officials of the king of Babylon came and took seats in the Middle

Gate: Nergal-Sharezer of Samgar, Nebo-Sarsekim a chief officer, Nergal-Sharezer a high official and all the other officials of the king of Babylon" (Jeremiah 39:1-3, NIV).

The recently translated clay tablet is actually a receipt for a gift of gold that Nebo-Sarsekim gave to a temple in the ancient city of Babylon. It records his name, his title as "an officer," and the amount of his gift.

What does this mean? It means:
- You can trust the Bible in even the smallest details it records to be accurate and correct.
- The Bible story was not "made up;" it is an accurate history, down to the seemingly "incidental" details of the names and ranks of those who sat in counsel after Jerusalem was captured.

The Lord has preserved the Bible for us today because it is His Word and He wants us to trust what it says.

NOVEMBER 13

Continued from yesterday... One more thing:

God is actively revealing the accuracy of His Word in these last days. In the last one hundred years, the science of archeology has produced thousands of evidences that the Bible record is reliable. There has not been one archeological discovery that has contradicted the text of Scripture! With the discovery of the Dead Sea Scrolls, for instance, evidence was produced that revealed the Old Testament we have today is just as accurate as it was five hundred years before Christ!

grace today

Yesterday we read about a recent discovery by Michael Jursa, associate professor at the University of Vienna. It was made during his research trip to the British Museum to study its collection of more than 100,000 cuneiform tablets; this little tablet caught his attention. He reported it was so well preserved, it took him only a few minutes to decipher it. (Incidentally, he is one of only a few people in the world who can translate and read cuneiform script). Apparently, no one else had ever made the connection with Jeremiah's record.

Only God could use a 2,600-year-old receipt to establish His Word!

God is into the details.

Pray with me: "Lord, thanks for being involved in the details, from the microscopic to the mega-issues of the universe. Thank You for Your detailed plan for my life, and for the guidance Your Word offers me. I love You, Lord. In Jesus' Name, Amen."

"I rejoice in your word like one who discovers a great treasure" (Psalm 119:162).

14 NOVEMBER

"The underground waters stopped flowing, and the torrential rains from the sky were stopped" (Genesis 8:2).

A global flood is not just a myth, it's history. The fossil and geological record evidences a sudden, cataclysmic disaster on a worldwide scale. When we were at the Museum of Natural History in New York City, we saw the fossilized remains of dinosaurs on display.

One of them was so well preserved that we saw the pattern of the scales of its fossilized skin. Fossilized eggs were also on display that had obviously been suddenly buried in such a way that they did not decay, and they were still nested together with the mother still sitting on the eggs! It was actually kind of funny to look at the displays and see the obvious, and then read the signs "explaining" what had happened. The explanations didn't make sense. They appeared to be convoluted. Many of them did have reference to some kind of a "flood" or sudden burial in water.

It didn't take us long to connect the dots, but those who postulate the hypothesis of evolution seem to be oblivious to the obvious, whether they're looking through a microscope or gazing through a telescope.

It takes much more faith to believe them, than to believe the Bible record. God destroyed the world with a flood, and only one family survived. Noah really did build an ark.

Read Genesis 7:17-8:4 for a quick summary of the historical record.

November 15

Noah really did build an ark to preserve his family. There really was a worldwide flood, as Jesus testified:

> "When the Son of Man returns, it will be like it was in Noah's day. In those days, the people enjoyed banquets and parties and weddings right up to the time Noah entered his boat and the flood came and destroyed them all" (Luke 17:26-27).

grace today

Here's a quick summary of the historical record:

> "For forty days the floodwaters grew deeper, covering the ground and lifting the boat high above the earth. As the waters rose higher and higher above the ground, the boat floated safely on the surface. Finally, the water covered even the highest mountains on the earth, rising more than twenty-two feet above the highest peaks. All the living things on earth died—birds, domestic animals, wild animals, small animals that scurry along the ground, and all the people. Everything that breathed and lived on dry land died. God wiped out every living thing on the earth—people, livestock, small animals that scurry along the ground, and the birds of the sky. All were destroyed. The only people who survived were Noah and those with him in the boat. And the floodwaters covered the earth for 150 days" (Genesis 7:17-24).

We can trust God's Word!

16 NOVEMBER

Noah really did build an ark to preserve his family. There really was a worldwide flood, as Genesis testified:

> "But God remembered Noah and all the wild animals and livestock with him in the boat. He sent a wind to blow across the earth, and the floodwaters began to recede. The underground waters stopped flowing, and the torrential rains from the sky were stopped. So the floodwaters gradually receded from the earth. After 150 days, exactly five months from the time the flood began, the boat came to rest on the mountains of Ararat" (Genesis 8:1-4).

Genesis 8:2 mentions "the fountains of the deep" (NASB) which contributed greatly to a vast amount of water that covered the world and created the oceans as we know them. I recently read an article that confirms the Bible record that there are "fountains of the deep." "Scientists scanning the deep interior of the Earth have found evidence of a vast water reservoir beneath eastern Asia that is at least the volume of the Arctic Ocean. The discovery marks the first time such a large body of water has [been] found in the planet's deep mantle."[86]

Proverbs, in its wisdom, says, "I was there when he set the heavens in place, when he marked out the horizon on the face of the deep, when he established the clouds above and fixed securely the fountains of the deep" (Proverbs 8:27-28, NIV)

November 17

"You are my hiding place; You preserve me from trouble; You surround me with songs of deliverance. Selah" (Psalm 32:7, NASB).

"Trust in Him at all times, O people; pour out your heart before Him; God is a refuge for us. Selah" (Psalm 62:8, NASB).

Each of these Psalms contains a word that I used to skip over without a thought. Do you notice it now? It's the word "Selah." I didn't think much about it until the day I found out it means "pause."

When David wrote his worship music, he masterfully inserted moments of silence in the songs... times of reflection... giving the soul time to catch up with the words.

Begin enjoying the God-ordained pauses of His Scripture.

God orders our steps and even our pauses...

18 NOVEMBER

The Psalms contain a word that I used to skip over without a thought. It's the word "Selah," which means "pause." David masterfully inserted moments of silence and reflection in his worship songs.

Read the following Psalm out loud and take time during the interludes to pray your own response to God, or to listen to what the Holy Spirit speaks to you during this quiet pause. Take time to "pray the spaces."

> "Say to God, 'How awesome are your deeds! Your enemies cringe before your mighty power. Everything on earth will worship you; they will sing your praises, shouting your name in glorious songs.' Interlude [Selah]

> "Come and see what our God has done, what awesome miracles he performs for people! He made a dry path through the Red Sea, and his people went across on foot. There we rejoiced in him. For by his great power he rules forever. He watches every movement of the nations; let no rebel rise in defiance. Interlude [Selah]

> "Let the whole world bless our God and loudly sing his praises. Our lives are in his hands, and he keeps our feet from stumbling. You have tested us, O God; you have purified us like silver... We went through fire and flood, but

you brought us to a place of great abundance... Interlude [Selah]

"Come and listen, all you who fear God, and I will tell you what he did for me. For I cried out to him for help, praising him as I spoke... Praise God, who did not ignore my prayer or withdraw his unfailing love from me" (Psalm 66:3-20).

God orders our steps and even our pauses... I hope that reading the Scripture this way was a blessing to you.

May today be a day when the blessings you receive right now linger in your mind and pop up to encourage you at just the right time.

NOVEMBER 19

Today, I really want to encourage you who have very difficult people in your lives. I know God has a special word for you right now. Carefully, prayerfully read each of these verses and hear the special message the Lord has for you:

"For strangers are attacking me; violent people are trying to kill me. They care nothing for God. Interlude [Selah]

"But God is my helper. The Lord keeps me alive!

"May the evil plans of my enemies be turned against them. Do as you promised and put an end to them.

"I will sacrifice a voluntary offering to you; I will praise your name, O LORD, for it is good.

"For you have rescued me from my troubles and helped me to triumph over my enemies" (Psalm 54:3-7).

- Isn't it amazing how the Lord gives us just what we need, just when we need it most?

20 NOVEMBER

I think a person's Bible often tells a story. It tells a story about the person who owned it for many years. When I'm asked to share in a memorial service for someone, I often ask to see their Bible, and for many Christians, their Bible preaches the message. On many instances, I've seen texts underlined or notes written in the margins that speak more eloquently of their faith than I could ever speak.

As a child, I noticed my grandmother wrote little messages in the fly leafs of her Bible, a practice that I've continued. Here's one of those "treasures":

> Sow a thought and you reap an act;
> Sow an act and you reap a habit;
> Sow a habit and you reap a character;
> Sow a character and you reap a destiny.[87]

"Don't be misled: No one makes a fool of God. What a person plants, he will harvest. The person who plants selfishness, ignoring the needs of others—ignoring God!—harvests a crop of weeds. All he'll have to show for his life is weeds! But the one who plants in response to God, letting God's Spirit do the growth work in him, harvests a crop of real life, eternal life" (Galatians 6:7-8, MSG).

Think about this: "What am I planting?" "What am I cultivating?" I'll harvest in proportion to what I've planted.

"Lord, break up the hard soil of my heart and plant patience, love, and peace. Let there be a crop of real life growing in me. In Jesus' Name, Amen."

NOVEMBER 21

"Know, recognize, and understand therefore that the Lord your God, He is God, the faithful God..." (Deuteronomy 7:9a, AMP).

God is faithful. That's not a promise, it's reality. Our believing in the faithfulness of God doesn't make God anymore faithful than He has always been; it changes the way we live! So face this day and every situation this day brings, knowing that your faithful Father is ruling and over-ruling on your behalf.

I'm encouraged every time I read the words of J. Hudson Taylor, pioneer missionary to China, "All of God's greats have been weak men who did great exploits for God because they reckoned on His being faithful."[88]

"Lord, thank You for being a faithful Father to me."

NOVEMBER 22

"Give thanks to the LORD and proclaim his greatness. Let the whole world know what he has done... Give thanks to the LORD, for he is good! His faithful love endures forever" (1 Chronicles 16:8, 34).

grace today

There are lots of things we can thank God for. Have you thought of thanking God for the things that can never be taken away from you?

Thank God for what we cannot lose: Eternal life!

"I give them eternal life, and they will never perish. No one can snatch them away from me, for my Father has given them to me, and he is more powerful than anyone else. No one can snatch them from the Father's hand" (John 10:28-29).

The Amplified Bible puts it this way: "And I give them eternal life, and they shall never lose it or perish throughout the ages. [To all eternity they shall never by any means be destroyed.] And no one is able to snatch them out of My hand. My Father, Who has given them to Me, is greater and mightier than all [else]; and no one is able to snatch [them] out of the Father's hand."

Read how Eugene Peterson renders these verses in The Message: "I give them real and eternal life. They are protected from the Destroyer for good. No one can steal them from out of my hand. The Father who put them under my care is so much greater than the Destroyer and Thief. No one could ever get them away from him."

Thank God you will also never lose His love!

"Long ago the LORD said to Israel: "I have loved you, my people, with an everlasting love. With unfailing love I have drawn you to myself" (Jeremiah 31:3).

"...Israel, out looking for a place to rest, met God out looking for them!" God told them, "I've never quit loving you and never

will. Expect love, love, and more love!" (Jeremiah 31:2b-3, MSG).

And we will never lose the Lord's presence!

Jesus said, "...And be sure of this: I am with you always, even to the end of the age" (Matthew 28:20b).

NOVEMBER 23

"In everything give thanks..." (1 Thessalonians 5:18a, NASB).

This is one of the keys to living a peaceful, tranquil Christian life.

This means that we give thanks for the good that Father in Heaven is accomplishing *through* everything.

We can give thanks for everything because we know nothing can touch us that God hasn't allowed for some good purpose for our lives or for the lives of others.

Though we can't control the good or bad things that come into our lives, we can control our response to them.

All that pioneer missionary to India, Amy Carmichael, wanted to do was serve God, but she experienced repeated health problems. There were times when she was so sick she couldn't get out of bed. During one of those times she said, "Nothing in life can harm you, only your response." She wasn't controlled by invading circumstances.

Years ago, Tim Hansel had a mountain climbing accident that has left him in chronic, never-ending pain. In his pain he wrote

a book that has encouraged hundreds of thousands of people through their difficult times, it's called, *You Gotta Keep Dancin*. Look at just one sentence from this book. Hansel says: "If you can't change circumstances, change the way you respond to them."[89]

24 NOVEMBER

"For to me, to live is Christ and to die is gain" (Philippians 1:21, NASB).

"General," said a major, "I always observe that the people who have a lot to say about being ready to shed their last drop of blood are amazingly particular about the first drop." That's so true. The only things really worth living for are the things worth dying for. What would those things be in your life?

Knowing we have eternal life gives us the ability to live for the things that really matter and to let go of this life, if necessary. Billy Graham said, "If you're ready to die, then you're ready to live!"

25 NOVEMBER

"...Speak, LORD, your servant is listening..." (1 Samuel 3:9b).

I think it's a good idea, and a biblical one, to always ask God's help in understanding His Word before I start reading it. Since the Bible is spiritual, it can only be understood with spiritual help.

I borrow my prayer from David, "Open my eyes to see wonderful things in your Word" (Psalm 119:18, TLB).

This teaches us to turn to the Lord of the Word before we turn to the Word of the Lord.

My prayer for you is that God will place the "key" of understanding in your hand today as you read His Word. Jesus said, "Turning to the disciples, He said privately, 'Blessed are the eyes which see the things you see...' " (Luke 10:23, NASB).

Let's put this into action right now; pray: "Lord, open my eyes to see wonderful things in Your Word... Speak, LORD, your servant is listening..." (Psalm 119:18, TLB; 1 Samuel 3:9b).

NOVEMBER 26

"Let the wicked leave their way of life and change their way of thinking. Let them turn to the LORD, our God; he is merciful and quick to forgive" (Isaiah 55:7, TEV).

How many times have you said, "I really needed to hear that"?

What I need to hear most is that God loves me, accepts me, forgives me, and that I have the security of having eternal life. I've found it true that "we preach best what we need to hear most." The reason why you can share the message of God's love and grace is because you know *you* need it! Thus, when you talk about it, you have the ring of authenticity. People know you're being genuine and that the Lord has changed your life.

grace today

"This is a trustworthy saying, and everyone should accept it: 'Christ Jesus came into the world to save sinners'—and I am the worst of them all. (NOTE: We might argue with Paul at this point!) But God had mercy on me so that Christ Jesus could use me as a prime example of his great patience with even the worst sinners. Then others will realize that they, too, can believe in him and receive eternal life. All honor and glory to God forever and ever! He is the eternal King, the unseen one who never dies; he alone is God. Amen" (1 Timothy 1:15-17).

I'm praying that the Lord blesses you today and that you live in a way that brings honor and glory to God. Just one more thing: hang in there; Jesus is in control of everything that is happening today!

27 NOVEMBER

It's very easy for us to underestimate God. He is able to do more than we could ever imagine. "For nothing is impossible with God" (Luke 1:37, NASB). God is faithful. He is reliable. He has committed Himself to us in word and deed and through His powerful Word accomplished His plan for us and for the world. One translation puts it: "For no word of God shall be void of power" (ASV).

God promised Abraham that He would do the impossible for him: "Is anything too difficult for the LORD? At the appointed time I will return to you, at this time next year, and Sarah will have a son" (Genesis 18:14, NASB).

Even though Job experienced huge sorrow and loss, he knew this truth: "I know that You can do all things, and that no purpose of

Yours can be thwarted" (Job 42:2, NASB).

I want to share this text with you from several translations:

> "I know that You can do all things, and that no thought or purpose of Yours can be restrained or thwarted" (AMP).

> "I know that you can do anything, and no one can stop you" (NLT).

> "I know that you can do all things and that no plan of yours can be ruined" (NCV).

Jeremiah lived his life with the same bedrock faith: "O Sovereign LORD! You made the heavens and earth by your strong hand and powerful arm. Nothing is too hard for you!" (Jeremiah 32:17). The NASB puts it, "...Nothing is too difficult for You!"

Jesus lived His life on earth with this same confidence and consciousness: "And looking at them Jesus said to them, 'With people this is impossible, but with God all things are possible' " (Matthew 19:26, NASB).

NOVEMBER 28

"...the LORD looks at the heart" (1 Samuel 16:7b).

Matthew 6:4; 6:6, 6:18 (NASB) all have something in common. They tell us that God rewards unseen devotion. Look at these statements with me:

- Matthew 6:3-4 – "But when you give to the poor, do not let your left hand know what your right hand is doing, so that

your giving will be in secret; and your Father who sees what is done in secret will reward you"

- Matthew 6:6 – "But you, when you pray, go into your inner room, close your door and pray to your Father who is in secret, and your Father who sees what is done in secret will reward you."
- Matthew 6:17-18 – "But you, when you fast, anoint your head and wash your face so that your fasting will not be noticed by men, but by your Father who is in secret; and your Father who sees what is done in secret will reward you."

God is with you in this quiet moment. Nothing you do goes unnoticed and will never go unrewarded.

29 NOVEMBER

"...For apart from me you can do nothing" (John 15:5b).

This verse is a "proof" text. It has been proven true in my life; how about yours? I cannot do anything (that really matters) apart from Jesus. When I try to live on my own, disconnected from the source of life and nourishment, I dry up as fast as a branch would wither cut off from the vine in the desert heat. We can bear up under a lot of heat and stress if we stay plugged-in to the Vine.

What you're doing right now is part of that life. The Lord speaks to you, and you respond to Him and grow spiritually. You're going to be busy today, but you have to stay "plugged-in" or you'll find yourself wilting in spirit.

Jesus said: "Yes, I am the vine; you are the branches. Those who remain in me, and I in them, will produce much fruit. For apart from me you can do nothing" (John 15:5).

NOVEMBER 30

"Day and night I have only tears for food, while my enemies continually taunt me, saying, 'Where is this God of yours?' " (Psalm 42:3).

"I can't understand why I have to go through all of this." The many times I have heard this, I always feel like anything I say is not enough. I don't have the answers, and we certainly aren't going to have the complete picture this side of heaven.

Let me share an insight the Lord gave me which isn't the typical "canned" response; something that I've found very helpful in my own experience: "God never wastes a sorrow."

We serve a God who never disengages from us; "…You have collected all my tears in your bottle. You have recorded each one in your book" (Psalm 56:8b).

"That's why we can be so sure that every detail in our lives of love for God is worked into something good" (Romans 8:28, MSG).

"Forgetting the past and looking forward to what lies ahead, I press on to reach the end of the race and receive the heavenly prize for which God, through Christ Jesus, is calling us" (Philippians 3:13b-14).

You're going to make it! Don't give up, and don't stop now!

One of the things I have pasted into the flyleaf of my Bible is the story of Jim Elliot. After graduating from Wheaton College, he went to be a missionary to Ecuador. When he tried to reach out to the Auca Indians, he was martyred, along with four other men. Before he died, he had written these words in his journal, "He is no fool who gives what he cannot keep to gain what he cannot lose."

Reading Elliot's words always inspires me to keep a loose grip on things that are so easily lost and to hang onto the things that can never be taken away.

Don't let anyone keep you from living with eternity's priorities always in view. "Only one life, 'twill soon be past; only what's lived for Christ will last."

The Lord bless you with His strong grace and strength, and may He refresh you today!

"I shall delight in Your statutes; I shall not forget Your word" (Psalm 119:16, NASB).

grace today

It's been said that the Psalms are the language of the heart.

Spurgeon believed that you have to read the Psalms to know how good they are: "...Happy [is] he who for himself knows the secret of the Psalms."[90]

I want to encourage you to read Psalms and Proverbs daily. Read a Psalm each day and the chapter of Proverbs that corresponds to the day of the month; there are thirty-one Proverbs, one for every day!

You will grow in wisdom and in worship, and you will find your soul satisfied with God. He has so many things to offer those who diligently seek Him.

Let's pray together: "Lord, open my eyes that I may see wonderful things from Your Word. Give me an increased hunger for You. Today I'm struggling. There are lots of things opposing me. Please give me peace and vindicate me. In Jesus' Name, Amen!"

3 December

"That God is on one side and all the people on the other side, and Christ Jesus, himself man, is between them to bring them together, by giving his life for all mankind" (1 Timothy 2:5-6b, TLB).

Have you ever been given wrong directions? Ever taken a wrong turn? It is so frustrating and such a waste of time.

Wouldn't it be great if there was only one path in life? No energy spent on making the right choice? Wow, that sure would free up time and energy!

In Europe, many towns and villages still bear the marks of walls that surrounded them in the Middle Ages. Streets near these old walls are curved and sometimes wind up in a dead end. I heard about one traveler who was in one of these villages and got lost. He came up to a man walking down the street and asked help finding directions. When the stranger directed him, the traveler was still a little doubtful. "Is that the best way?" he asked. The stranger answered, "It is the only way. If you follow the other turn, it will bring you back here."

What a great illustration of the way to God. Go through Jesus Christ and His death on the cross. "Is that the best way?" someone might ask. "It is the only way." Any other turn will take you, not back to where you are, but off into outer darkness of separation from God.

Jesus is the link between earth and heaven. He can take hold of man with one hand and take hold of God with the other because He is God and man.

"Then he said, 'I tell you the truth, you will all see heaven open and the angels of God going up and down on the Son of Man, the one who is the stairway between heaven and earth' " (John 1:51).

Take a few moments and connect these verses with Genesis 28:10-17.

4 DECEMBER

"You must have the same attitude that Christ Jesus had" (Philippians 2:5).

Paul holds up the example of Jesus as a model for us to follow. G. K. Chesterton once said: "The problem with Christianity is not that it has been tried and found wanting, but that it has been found difficult and left untried."

Nowhere could this be more true than when we look at this passage in Philippians 2:5-11: "Have this mind among yourselves, which is yours in Christ Jesus, who, though he was in the form of God, did not count equality with God a thing to be grasped, but made himself nothing, taking the form of a servant, being born in the likeness of men. And being found in human form, he humbled himself by becoming obedient to the point of death, even death on a cross. Therefore God has highly exalted him and bestowed on him the name that is above every name, so that at the name of Jesus every knee should bow, in heaven and on earth and under the earth, and every tongue confess that Jesus Christ is Lord, to the glory of God the Father" (ESV).

Paul is quoting what many think is an early Christian hymn (verses 6-11), and some think that Paul himself may even have written it.

Jesus took seven steps down. Can you identify them in verses 6-8? Would we be willing to take steps down? Would we be willing to step down?

"Who, although He existed in the form of God, did not regard equality with God a thing to be grasped..." (Philippians 2:6, NASB).

Jesus didn't hold on to His right to act and be worshipped as God, or to exercise His power and unlimited knowledge.

Jesus was "equal" with God. The Greek word, "equal" here refers to something that's exactly the same in size, quality, quantity, and character.
- Jesus is in every sense equal to God.
- Jesus was God without effort!

The Bible teaches that Jesus has always been God. Though He is "the Son of God," He is also "God the Son." Jesus pre-existed as God.

Look at what Jesus says in John 8:56-58:

> "Your father Abraham rejoiced as he looked forward to my coming. He saw it and was glad." The people said, "You aren't even fifty years old. How can you say you have seen Abraham?" Jesus answered, "I tell you the truth, before Abraham was even born, I AM!"

Jesus claimed to be God many times:

> "For this reason therefore the Jews were seeking all the more to kill Him, because He not only was breaking the Sabbath, but also was calling God His own Father, making Himself equal with God" (John 5:18, NASB).

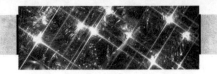

"The Jews answered Him, 'For a good work we do not stone You, but for blasphemy; and because You, being a man, make Yourself out to be God' " (John 10:33, NASB).

"Philip said to Him, 'Lord, show us the Father, and it is enough for us.' Jesus said to him, 'Have I been so long with you, and yet you have not come to know Me, Philip? He who has seen Me has seen the Father; how do you say, "Show us the Father" '?" (John 14:8-9, NASB).

6 December

Though Jesus was God and was worshiped as the second Person of the glorious Trinity, He took the form of a "bond servant."

"But [He] emptied Himself, taking the form of a bond-servant, and being made in the likeness of men" (Philippians 2:7, NASB).

The word "emptied" is the word from which we get the term "kenosis," the doctrine of Christ's self-emptying in His incarnation.
- Jesus did not empty Himself of Deity.
- He didn't exchange Deity for humanity.

But it was Jesus' death on a cross that especially gave Him the outward appearance of a slave. We're told that so many slaves were crucified in the Roman Empire that crucifixion was called the "slaves' punishment."[91]

Jesus emptied Himself by choice. What do you think motivated Him? What choices can we make today that show our heart's response to God's love?

Jesus emptied Himself in two ways.

First, Jesus covered His divine glory. Isaiah 53:2 says, "For He grew up before Him like a tender shoot, and like a root out of parched ground; He has no stately form or majesty that we should look upon Him, nor appearance that we should be attracted to Him" (NASB). Jesus only displayed His divine glory once while He was on earth in human flesh. That was in His transfiguration (Matthew 17:1-4; John 1:14).

Second, Jesus did not use His divine attributes to benefit Himself. He laid aside His divine privileges and voluntarily submitted to limitations that all human beings have. He refused to use His divine attributes to make His life easier!

Although He was omniscient, omnipresent, and omnipotent in His deity, He allowed His humanity to grow in wisdom, kept His body in one place at a time, took time to walk all over Israel, and allowed human beings to arrest Him, torture Him, and crucify Him!

"For God is working in you, giving you the desire and the power to do what pleases him" (Philippians 2:13).

Bible teacher, C. I. Scofield said, "Christian experience is not something which is going on around the believer, but something which is going on in him... Right Christian experience is the

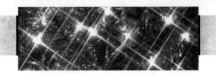

outworking, whatever one's circumstances may be, of the life, nature and mind of Christ living in us."

This means that the Christian life is not the achievement of some kind of spiritual effort, but a divine effect.

Jesus never told people to try to live as He lived by imitation, but to let Him live in them by divine initiative.

I'm praying that you are encouraged by Jesus' strong love today!

9 DECEMBER

"For God so loved the world, that He gave His only begotten Son, that whoever believes in Him shall not perish, but have eternal life" (John 3:16, NASB).

God's love is not conditional, it's continual! Just look at the object of God's love: the world. The world hates Him, the world rejected Him, and the world is full of sinners. God's love is truly an unconditional love:

- Not an, "I'll love you if..."
- Not an, "I'll love when..."
- Not an, "I'll love you as soon as..."
- But, "I love you" ...period, no matter what your condition. God doesn't love you because you are important; you are important because God loves you.

Let's read the lyrics to a beautiful song written nearly one hundred years ago called *The Love of God*.

The Love of God is greater far
    Than tongue or pen can ever tell;
It goes beyond the highest star,
    And reaches to the lowest hell.
The guilty pair, bowed down with care,
    God gave His Son to win;
His erring child He reconciled,
    And rescued from his sin.

Could we with ink the ocean fill,
    And were the skies of parchment made;
Were every stalk on earth a quill,
    And every man a scribe by trade;
To write the love of God above
    Would drain the ocean dry;
Nor could the scroll contain the whole,
    Though stretched from sky to sky.

Oh, love of God, how rich and pure!
    How measureless and strong!
It shall forevermore endure—
    The saints' and angels' song.[92]

December 10

"God loved the world so much that he gave his one and only Son so that whoever believes in him may not be lost, but have eternal life" (John 3:16, NCV).

Notice, God loved, so He gave! We know God loves us because He has given us His only-begotten, His unique Son. It is in the

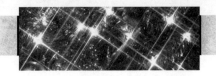

face of the selfless, self-sacrificing Jesus Christ that we learn of God's character.

God does not love us because Jesus died for us; it's the other way around! The Son of God died to redeem us because God loved us so much.

God's giving grows out of His loving!

God loves you! Do you know that? God loves you! He has demonstrated that love for you in Jesus Christ! God loves you!

11 DECEMBER

"And I'm telling the story of God Eternal, singing the praises of Jacob's God" (Psalm 75:9, MSG).

Walter Wink has said, "If Jesus had never lived, we would not have been able to invent him."[93]

How could we ever have come up with a God who righteously condemns sin but clears the sinner?

Who would have ever been able to think that the Creator would become a creature and live among those made of the dust of the earth?

Who would dream that God would step down and pick us up and say, "Where are those who condemn you? ...Neither do I condemn you, go and sin no more..."?[94]

Who could conceive of a God nailed to a Roman cross?

Who would think that someone would rise from the dead and conquer death for us?

No one would have ever come up with this story; it's the Gospel. The word "Gospel" comes from an ancient English word meaning "God's story!" The message of Jesus is Good News from heaven! The story has changed our lives; let's get the story out there!

DECEMBER 12

"Know this: GOD, your God, is God indeed, a God you can depend upon" (Deuteronomy 7:9a, MSG).

God is faithful! That is what He is! It's a part of His nature! Throughout Scripture He is characterized by His faithfulness.

Early in the Bible, Moses declares: "Know therefore that the LORD your God, He is God, the faithful God..." (Deuteronomy 7:9a, NASB).

The word "faithful" (*aman*) literally means "firm, established, lasting, reliable, sure." It's basically the same word as "Amen!"

Look at how the "Song of Moses" refers to the faithfulness of God in Deuteronomy 32:3-4: "I will proclaim the name of the LORD; how glorious is our God! He is the Rock; his deeds are perfect. Everything he does is just and fair. He is a faithful God who does no wrong; how just and upright he is!"

God is the One Person whom you can depend upon to be stable and trustworthy, no matter what! If He has said He will do

grace today

something, He will do it! You can count on that!

In 2 Timothy 2:13 Paul says, "If we are faithless, He remains faithful; for He cannot deny Himself" (NASB).

What a great assurance we have!

13 DECEMBER

God is always faithful in what He says.

"God is not a man, that He should lie, nor a son of man, that He should repent; has He said, and will He not do it? Or has He spoken, and will He not make it good?" (Numbers 23:19, NASB).

Titus 1:2 says God is the "...God, who cannot lie..." (NASB).

Hebrews 6:18 says that "...it is impossible for God to lie..." (NASB).

God is faithful in what He does. He's faithful to:
- Forgive us – Remember 1 John 1:8-9? John is not writing to the unsaved (1 John 5:13). The moment when we took Jesus as our Savior, by His grace, He forgave our sin. Our sins are already forgiven (1 John 2:12).
- Strengthen us and protect us – This is especially true during times of temptation and trial. "But the Lord is faithful, and He will strengthen you and protect you from the evil one" (2 Thessalonians 3:3, NASB).
- Discipline us – The word discipline comes from the word disciple, which means "To train us as His children." The reason why God disciplines us is because He is faithful!

"I know, O LORD, that your regulations are fair; you disciplined me because I needed it. Now let your unfailing love comfort me, just as you promised me, your servant. Surround me with your tender mercies so I may live, for your instructions are my delight" (Psalm 119:75-77).

DECEMBER 14

"Now to Him who is able to keep you from stumbling, and to make you stand in the presence of His glory blameless with great joy, to the only God our Savior, through Jesus Christ our Lord, be glory, majesty, dominion and authority, before all time and now and forever. Amen" (Jude 24-25, NASB).

"Faithful is He who calls you and He also will bring it to pass" (1 Thessalonians 5:24, NASB).

Corrie Ten Boom stated this truth so succinctly: "In God's faithfulness lies eternal security." Erwin Lutzer, Pastor of Moody Memorial Church in Chicago, has said, "God's investment in us is so great He could not possibly abandon us."

If God can keep the universe going, if God can maintain the fixed order of the sun by day and the moon by night, then He is able to keep you! "The LORD will accomplish what concerns me..." (Psalm 138:8a, NASB).

Some three hundred and fifty years ago, William Secker wrote these words: "Though Christians be not kept altogether from falling, yet they are kept from falling altogether."

grace today

15 December

"Who among you fears the LORD and obeys his servant? If you are walking in darkness, without a ray of light, trust in the LORD and rely on your God" (Isaiah 50:10).

It's one thing to know about the faithfulness of God, but another thing to live by it! We all have times in our lives when, based on outward conditions and external situations, it is difficult to believe that God is faithful.

- We're disappointed.
- We're suffering.
- We feel everything is hopeless.

If this is hitting home today, read on. I think you'll resonate with what A. W. Pink has said:

> There are seasons in the lives of all when it is not easy, no not even for Christians, to believe that God is faithful. Our faith is sorely tried, our eyes bedimmed with tears, and we can no longer trace the outworkings of His love. Our ears are distracted with the noises of the world, harassed by the atheistic whisperings of Satan, and we can no longer hear the sweet accents of His still small voice. Cherished plans have been thwarted, friends on whom we relied have failed us, a professed brother or sister in Christ has betrayed us. We are staggered. We sought to be faithful to God, and now a dark cloud hides Him from us. We find it difficult, yea, impossible, for carnal reason to harmonize His frowning providence with His gracious promises. Ah, faltering soul, severely tried fellow pilgrim, seek grace to heed Isa. 50:10, "Who is among you that fears the LORD, That obeys the voice of His servant, That walks in darkness and has no light? Let him trust in the name of the LORD and rely on his God."[95]

Father in Heaven may allow you to suffer, but He can never forget you because He is faithful! God is faithful; that is our encouragement!

December 16

Honesty is important to God. He wants us to face reality, and sometimes that means calling sin, "SIN."

My wife Leslie came up with something a few years ago that is priceless; Calvary's Women's Ministry published it, and I want to share it with you:

The Politically Correct Sins of the Flesh
- I'm not a liar, I'm a Reality Enhancement Engineer.
- I'm not a nag, I'm a Verbally Repetitive Assistant.
- I'm not a gossip, I'm an Information Dissemination Agent.
- I'm not greedy, I'm a Material Acquisitions Specialist.
- I'm not prideful, I'm in Humility Regression.
- I'm not prone to outbursts of anger, I'm in a Persistent Volcanic State of Eruption.
- I'm not a whiner, I'm Contentment Challenged.
- I'm not bossy, I'm a Life Control Director.
- I'm not vengeful, I'm a Repentance Promotion Facilitator.
- I'm not unforgiving, I'm a Personal Error Accumulations Accountant.
- I'm not rebellious, I'm a Submission Avoidance Tactician.[96]

"And why worry about a speck in your friend's eye when you have a log in your own?" (Matthew 7:3).

grace today

"What then? Are we better than they? Not at all; for we have already charged that both Jews and Greeks are all under sin; as it is written, 'THERE IS NONE RIGHTEOUS, NOT EVEN ONE'" (Romans 3:9-10, NASB).

17 DECEMBER

"The wise are cautious and avoid danger; fools plunge ahead with reckless confidence" (Proverbs 14:16).

I had to laugh a while ago when I read the headline in *USA Today*: "British marines storm beach in Spain." That piqued my interest. I didn't know that Great Britain was at war with Spain, at least not in the past hundred years! I read on: "Britain apologized for invading Spain over the weekend by mistake. About 20 Royal Marines went off course in an amphibious exercise and stormed a Spanish beach near the British colony of Gibraltar. They left after residents told them they were in Spain."[97]

Whoops, guess those GPS systems were turned off!

How many times do we storm into situations without getting our directions from GPS—God's Perspective System?

18 DECEMBER

Do you ever wonder how God can use you?

Abram was a nobody when God called him. He did not know God—he worshipped idols.

> "From ancient times your fathers lived beyond the River, namely, Terah, the father of Abraham and the father of Nahor, and they served other gods" (Joshua 24:2b, NASB).

Abram didn't find God; God found him! God is always the initiator, and we are the responders.

> "You are the LORD God, who chose Abram and brought him out from Ur of the Chaldees, and gave him the name Abraham" (Nehemiah 9:7, NASB).

God moved Abram from his familiar, comfortable surroundings. God shapes the ones He loves often by allowing serious, dire situations to come into their lives.

> "The LORD had said to Abram, 'Leave your native country, your relatives, and your father's family, and go to the land that I will show you. I will make you into a great nation. I will bless you and make you famous, and you will be a blessing to others'" (Genesis 12:1-2).

He does this to test us, to train us, and often to show the work He is doing in us. In the process of the trial, God will generally teach us about Who He is and our need of Him.

Henry Blackaby says, "This is always God's pattern: He chooses, He calls, and He shapes a person in an intimate and loving relationship. God reveals Himself and His ways to the one He can trust. God's revelation is not for observation but to enable obedience!"[98]

19 DECEMBER

Do you have any idea how many miles you have traveled over the course of your life? Some websites actually will calculate how many miles that might be.

Abraham's journey, as chronicled in Genesis chapters eleven and twelve, covered thousands of miles. His long "walk" has many similarities to your spiritual journey.

Let me share some of the things I noted about Abraham's walk that parallel ours. First of all, look at the different places he lived.

He first moved from Ur of the Chaldees. Ur means "in darkness." Then he moved to Haran, which was a sort of halfway house, moving on to Shechem. The name Shechem in Hebrew means "shoulder" and reminds me of the time the Lord spoke concerning the tribe of Benjamin, "About Benjamin he said: 'Let the beloved of the LORD rest secure in him, for he shields him all day long, and the one the LORD loves rests between his shoulders' " (Deuteronomy 33:12, NIV). We all need a "Shechem" experience (Genesis 12:6-7).

Then He moved between Bethel and Ai (verse 8). "Bethel" means "house of God;" "Ai" means "ruin." This, too, parallels the Christian experience. We're either looking toward God or being ruined in the flesh. We're living in one or the other.

Abraham walked on to the Negev, which means "the desert."

Where has your journey taken you? Have you been walking in a spiritual desert too long? Maybe it's time to return to Bethel.

"Trust in the LORD with all your heart; do not depend on your own understanding. Seek his will in all you do, and he will show you which path to take" (Proverbs 3:5-6).

Stressing the importance of a good vocabulary, the teacher told her young students, "Use a word ten times, and it shall be yours for life." From somewhere in the back of the room came a small male voice chanting, "Amanda, Amanda, Amanda, Amanda, Amanda, Amanda, Amanda, Amanda, Amanda, Amanda."

Wow, if it were only this easy to get what we want! Many people teach that if you just name what you want and really believe it, God will honor your faith and give it to you. That sounds good. Lots of people begin saying, "Money, money, money, money" and others "health, health, health, health."

As cool as it sounds to think that we can have whatever we want because God is a good God, it is a misrepresentation of the whole counsel of God's Word. What kind of a Father would God be if He gave us everything we desire? Lots of those things may not be good for us. Good fathers often say "no" because they are good fathers and love their children.

God's Word encourages us to ask for God's will to be done, not our will. Yet still, God is a Father Who desires to give. Take some time and look at John 14:13-14; John 15:7; 1 John 5:14-15.

Let's ask ourselves:
- Am I asking God for something and disappointed because He has not given it to me?
- Am I content with God's will?

grace today

- Am I scared of God's will?
- Am I disappointed with God?

"Father, thank You for always giving me what is best for me, even though I am sometimes disappointed or cannot understand Your reasoning. I understand our relationship is based on my trusting that You love me, care for me, and are working everything together for good. In Jesus' Name, Amen."

21 DECEMBER

"God showed how much he loved us by sending his one and only Son into the world so that we might have eternal life through him. This is real love—not that we loved God, but that he loved us and sent his Son as a sacrifice to take away our sins" (1 John 4:9-10).

I've got to share a story I read with you. I read about a Christian coal miner who was injured in the mines at a young age many years ago. He was disabled, and over the years basically watched the dreams he had for his life evaporate. Through the window beside his bed, he could see every one going on with life—marrying, raising families, and eventually having grandchildren.

One day, when this bedridden miner was very old, a young man came to visit him. "I hear that you believe in God and claim that He loves you. How can you believe such things after what has happened to you? Don't you sometimes doubt God's love?"

The old man paused and then smiled. He said, "Yes, it's true. Sometimes Satan comes calling on me in this fallen down old house of mine. He sits right there by my bed where you're sitting

now and points out my window to the men I once worked with who are still strong and active, and Satan asks, 'Does Jesus love you?' "

"Then Satan casts a jeering glance at this little room and points to the nice home of my friends across the street and asks again, 'Does Jesus love you?' "

"Then, Satan points to the grandchild of a friend of mine, a man who has everything I don't have, and Satan waits for a tear in my eye before he whispers in my ear, 'Does Jesus really love you?' "

"Well, what do you say when Satan speaks to you that way?" asked the young man.

The old miner said, "I take Satan by the hand. I lead him in my mind to a hill called Calvary. There, I point to the thorn-crowned head, to the nail-pierced hands and feet, and to the spear-wounded side. Then I tell Satan, 'YES, JESUS LOVES ME!' "

At the cross, God has forever proven His love for you and me!

DECEMBER 22

"God promised this Good News long ago through his prophets in the holy Scriptures. The Good News is about his Son. In his earthly life he was born into King David's family line" (Romans 1:2-3).

The long-awaited Messiah has come!

We can know this for sure because God put a safety feature in the Bible. He revealed to the ancient prophets specific

requirements that anyone claiming to be the Messiah would have to meet.

Because God loves us and doesn't want us to be deceived, He laid down over 300 specific requirements that the true Savior of the world would have to fulfill. The Real Messiah's ID is recorded for us in the Bible!

Here's just a few of the over 300 prophetic requirements that Jesus had to fulfill in order to be the true Messiah. He had to:

- Be born in Bethlehem (Micah 5:2).
- Be miraculously conceived (Isaiah 7:14).
- Be from the tribe of Judah, specifically, the family-line of Jesse (Genesis 49:10; Isaiah 11:10).
- Have his life threatened when He was still only a child (Jeremiah 31:15; Hosea 11:1).
- Live in Nazareth and minister in Galilee (Isaiah 9:1-2; Matthew 2:23).
- Enter Jerusalem on the exact date the ancient prophet Daniel predicted and receive a king's welcome (Daniel 9:25).
- Be betrayed by a friend (Psalm 41:9).
- Be betrayed by His friend for 30 pieces of silver and that money thrown down in the temple and given to the Potter (Zechariah 11:12-13).
- Be pierced in His hands and feet (Psalm 22:16).
- Be hung up for all to laugh at and mock (Psalm 22:7).
- Die and be buried in a rich man's tomb (Isaiah 53:9).
- Rise from the dead three days after He died (Isaiah 53:11; Matthew 20:19; Luke 18:33).

Only Jesus can and has met all the Old Testament requirements to be the Messiah! It's too late for anyone to make this claim now.

December 23

"...So he is first in everything" (Colossians 1:18b).

Though our text is talking about the church and the entire universe, by extension, our Lord Jesus should have first place in our Christmas celebration, wouldn't you agree? There is a growing discomfort in the commercial world with acknowledging Jesus during this season, though He is the reason for the season, the first cause of it all! Without the gift of God's Son, there would be no gifts given and no holiday sales.

I want to encourage you to keep Jesus central in your Christmas celebration and enjoy this time, rather than be stressed out by it.

You are under no law to decorate, to shop or to cook! You have the liberty to slow down and enjoy your family, your church and your Savior. You could even extend your Christmas celebration another day or for another week if you find yourself running out of time. My family has done this for years.

I'm praying that the peace of Jesus Christ keeps you peace-filled and that the joy of Jesus fills every part of your life.

December 24

"For God loved the world so much that he gave his one and only Son, so that everyone who believes in him will not perish but have eternal life" (John 3:16).

Jesus Christ uniquely and completely fulfills every one of the ancient prophecies concerning the Savior of the world; that's why we're so excited about His birth!

grace today

But we're not just excited about His birth, we're excited about His mission!

Though Bethlehem is only about six miles from Jerusalem, it represents one of the most difficult journeys for many people to make in their understanding of Who Jesus is and why He came.

In Bethlehem, we see the manger; but in Jerusalem, we see the cross and the empty tomb.
- The manger shows us the humility of Christ
- The cross shows us the love of Christ.
- And the empty tomb shows us the power of the risen Christ over death.

Only Jesus Christ can make a difference in our world and in our families.

25 DECEMBER

" 'For a child is born to us, a son is given to us...' He will be the '...Prince of Peace' " (Isaiah 9:6).

Merry Christmas! I'm praying that you experience many blessings today and much joy with family and friends! I know that some of you are alone today, and I'm praying that the presence of the Prince of Peace comforts and strengthens you wherever you are, regardless of your circumstances. I like what Frances Roberts said, "Finding God, you have no need to seek peace, for He Himself is your peace."

Here are a few promises from the Prince of Peace that I've selected just for you on this Christmas Day:

" 'For the mountains may move and the hills disappear, but even then my faithful love for you will remain. My covenant of blessing will never be broken,' says the LORD, who has mercy on you" (Isaiah 54:10).

"I am leaving you with a gift—peace of mind and heart. And the peace I give is a gift the world cannot give. So don't be troubled or afraid" (John 14:27).

"Now may the God of peace—who brought up from the dead our Lord Jesus, the great Shepherd of the sheep, and ratified an eternal covenant with his blood—may he equip you with all you need for doing his will. May he produce in you, through the power of Jesus Christ, every good thing that is pleasing to him. All glory to him forever and ever! Amen" (Hebrews 13:20-21).

The promise of the Messiah of Peace:

"But you, O Bethlehem Ephrathah, are only a small village among all the people of Judah. Yet a ruler of Israel will come from you, one whose origins are from the distant past. The people of Israel will be abandoned to their enemies until the woman in labor gives birth... And he will stand to lead his flock with the LORD's strength, in the majesty of the name of the LORD his God. Then his people will live there undisturbed, for he will be highly honored around the world. And he will be the source of peace" (Micah 5:2-5a).

The fulfillment of the prophecy:

"Suddenly, the angel was joined by a vast host of others—the armies of heaven—praising God and saying, 'Glory to God

in highest heaven, and peace on earth to those with whom God is pleased.' When the angels had returned to heaven, the shepherds said to each other, 'Let's go to Bethlehem! Let's see this thing that has happened, which the Lord has told us about.' They hurried to the village and found Mary and Joseph. And there was the baby, lying in the manger. After seeing him, the shepherds told everyone what had happened and what the angel had said to them about this child" (Luke 2:13-17).

26 December

"I am coming soon. Hold on to what you have, so that no one will take away your crown" (Revelation 3:11).

Jesus wants to reward any investment of our lives into His kingdom!

The Bible promises rewards for those who serve the Lord!

What you send up now is going to be there when you get there!

The New Testament reveals that we have the opportunity to receive crowns for investing our lives in Jesus' kingdom!

But we have to order our crowns now!

Eternal investments are People, God's Word and the Gospel.

Martin Luther was an eternal investor. He said: "If we consider the greatness and the glory of the life we shall have when we have risen from the dead, it would not be difficult at all for us

to bear the concerns of this world. If I believe the Word, I shall on the Last Day, after the sentence has been pronounced, not only gladly have suffered ordinary temptations, insults, and imprisonment, but I shall also say: 'O, that I did not throw myself under the feet of all the godless for the sake of the great glory which I now see revealed and which has come to me through the merit of Christ!' "

When we sing, "Crown Him With Many Crowns," stop and think, "Where are those crowns going to come from?"

DECEMBER 27

"Commit everything you do to the LORD. Trust him, and he will help you" (Psalm 37:5).

To "commit" means "to roll off your burden."

Peter reminds us, "Give all your worries and cares to God, for he cares about you" (1 Peter 5:7).

We don't cast off our cares to become careless, but we do it to become "care-less." There are many burdens we take on ourselves that we were never intended to bear. Jesus said: "...my yoke is easy to bear, and the burden I give you is light" (Matthew 11:30).

Before you move on, make sure you stop, pause right now and take inventory: "Am I feeling the weight?" "Is it too heavy for me?" "Is this a fit, or am I carrying something that is mighty heavy?" Give it right now to the Almighty One.

grace today

...Wow! That's better. It feels lighter already!

Know you are prayed for and in Jesus' strong grace!

28 DECEMBER

"Be still in the presence of the LORD, and wait patiently for him to act. Don't worry about evil people who prosper or fret about their wicked schemes" (Psalm 37:7).

God is on your side. One person with God on their side, against a thousand, is still in the majority! "...Greater is He who is in you than he who is in the world" (1 John 4:4b, NASB).

I like the point Charles Spurgeon makes concerning this verse: "What if wicked devices succeed and your own plans are defeated! There is more of the love of God in your defeats than in the successes of the wicked."

I read about the way a little boy misquoted the famous hymn *Trust and Obey,* he said, "Trust and O.K.!"

29 DECEMBER

"Day by day the LORD takes care of the innocent, and they will receive an inheritance that lasts forever" (Psalm 37:18).

God has made such a huge investment in you. He loves you all the time and gives you eternal life! You cannot be separated from His love.

Day by day the Lord takes care of us, "Therefore we do not lose heart. Though outwardly we are wasting away, yet inwardly we are being renewed day by day" (2 Corinthians 4:16, NIV).

Eugene Peterson paraphrases it this way: "So we're not giving up. How could we! Even though on the outside it often looks like things are falling apart on us, on the inside, where God is making new life, not a day goes by without his unfolding grace" (2 Corinthians 4:16, MSG).

Take a moment and pray: "Lord, thank You that this day, today, You will care for me and I will experience Your unfolding grace. Renew my spirit. In Jesus' Name, Amen."

DECEMBER 30

When you don't hang out, you miss out!

"One of the twelve disciples, Thomas (nicknamed the Twin), was not with the others when Jesus came. They told him, 'We have seen the Lord!'..." (John 20:24-25a).

"Let us think of ways to motivate one another to acts of love and good works. And let us not neglect our meeting together, as some people do, but encourage one another, especially now that the day of his return is drawing near" (Hebrews 10:24-25).

Think of some fun ways you can encourage others to come to church with you.

Missing out can lead to doubt!

grace today

"...But he (Thomas) replied, 'I won't believe it unless I see the nail wounds in his hands, put my fingers into them, and place my hand into the wound in his side' " (John 20:25b).

Are you in doubt? Fellowship it out.

"For where two or three have gathered together in My name, I am there in their midst" (Matthew 18:20, NASB).

31 DECEMBER

"...The godly are generous givers" (Psalm 37:21b).

The Bible has a lot to say about generosity, like the blessing pronounced in Proverbs 11:25: "The generous man will be prosperous, and he who waters will himself be watered" (NASB)

The NLT puts it this way: "The generous will prosper; those who refresh others will themselves be refreshed."

You may be thinking, "But I don't have much to give, I can't afford to be generous." This would be my challenge; even if you don't have much, give what you can.

Think about it in light of 2 Corinthians 8:11b-12, "...Give in proportion to what you have. Whatever you give is acceptable if you give it eagerly. And give according to what you have, not what you don't have."

Winston Churchill said, "We make a living by what we get, but we make a life by what we give."

May the strong grace of Jesus and His mighty power strengthen you today and into this New Year!

grace today

Endnotes

<u>January</u>
1. January 5 – Warren Wiersbe, *Wiersbe's Expository Outlines on the New Testament,* (1992).
2. January 7 – *USA Today Snapshots,* 5/22/00.
3. January 25 – Harold Myra and Marshall Shelley, *The Leadership Secrets of Billy Graham,* (Zondervan, 2005), 25-26.
4. January 30 – *Choice Notes on the Psalms,* 165.

<u>February</u>
5. February 9 – <u>Good News Unlimited</u>, He Who Is Christ.
6. February 12 – "Water," *Eternity,* (August 1996), 27; cited by John MacArthur, *Matthew,* 180-181.
7. February 16 – *Real Discipleship,* 33.
8. February 18 – Illustration taken from the article, "Invest Yourself in People," <u>Discipleship Journal</u>, Issue 24, (1984), by Max Melonuk, 7.
9. February 20 – George MacDonald.
10. February 23 – Focus on the Family, "The Pastor's Weekly Briefing," 8/8/96.
11. February 25 – Quoted by Lane T. Dennis, in Sept/Oct 1996, 3, from a forthcoming book by David Sanford of the Luis Palau Evangelistic Association.
12. February 26 – Samuel Fisk, *40 Fascinating Conversion Stories.*

<u>March</u>
13. March 1 – F. B. Meyer, *Elijah,* 81.
14. March 2 – Ibid., 66.
15. March 5 – Billy Graham, *Hope for the Troubled Heart,* (Minneapolis, MN: Grason, 1991), 46.

16. March 6 – Herbert Lockyer, Sr., *Psalms, A Devotional Commentary*, (Grand Rapids, MI: Kregel Publ., 1993), 516.
17. March 6 – Dr. V. Raymond Edman, former Chancellor of Wheaton College (IL).
18. March 7 – Barry and Carol St. Clair, *Ignite the Fire*, (Chariot Victor Publishing, 1999), 153-154.
19. March 12 – Wiley E. Hughes, "Because I Love You," Hillsong.
20. March 15 – Mark S. Wheeler, *The Marks of a Servant*, 17.
21. March 16 – Corrie Ten Boom, *Clippings From My Notebook*, (London: Triangle, SPCK, 1982), 39.
22. March 20 – George Sweeting, *More Than 2,000 Great Quotes and Illustrations*, 197-198.
23. March 24 – *Health News*, 3/2004.
24. March 25 – *USA Today*, 6/16/99.

April
25. April 1 – Paul Aurandt, *More of Paul Harvey's The Rest of the Story*, (New York, NY: Bantam Books, 1980), 134-135.
26. April 3 – Charles Price, *Real Christians*, 110.
27. April 5 – Plummer, 75.
28. April 9 – Joseph Stowell, <u>Moody</u>, July/Aug. 1990, 28.
29. April 12 – Richard L. Strauss, *The Joy of knowing God*, (Neptune, NJ: Loizeaux Brothers, 1984), 55-56.
30. April 21 – Kenneth W. Osbeck, *Amazing Grace: 366 Inspiring Hymn Stories for Daily Devotions*, 335.
31. April 23 – A. W. Tozer, *The Knowledge of the Holy*, 116.
32. April 26 – Alan Redpath, *Victorious Christian Living*, 166.

May
33. May 8 – Clarence E. McCartney, *The Great Texts of the Bible*, 60.
34. May 13 – Herbert Lockyer, *All the Doctrines of the Bible*, 28.
35. May 14 – A. W. Tozer, *The Knowledge of the Holy*, (San Francisco: Harper, 1992), 105.

36. May 16 – R. Kent Hughes, <u>Decision</u>, "The Power That Holds All Things Together," Sept. 1991, 35.
37. May 18 – Mrs. Charles E. Cowman, *Streams in the Desert*, May 1.
38. May 18 – <u>Moody</u>, January 1986, 39.
39. May 20 – A. W.Tozer, *The Knowledge of the Holy*, 87.
40. May 26 – Corrie ten Boom, *Clippings from My Notebook*, (London: Triangle, SPCK, 1982), 28-29.
41. May 27 – *Drapers Book of Quotations*, (Wheaton, IL: Tyndale, 1992), 55.
42. May 29 – A. W. Pink, *The Attributes of God*, (Grand Rapids: Baker, 1975), 37.

June

43. June 3 – D. Martyn Lloyd-Jones, *Faith on Trial*, (Grand Rapids, MI: Eerdmans, 1965), 43-44.
44. June 5 – Evelyn Underhill, *Worship*, (Scranton: Harper and Row, 1936), 3.
45. June 7 – Worthy of Worship, Chicago, IL: Moody Press, 1989), 60-61.
46. June 13 – George Sweeting, <u>Moody</u>, 12/93, 70.
47. June 21 – D. L. Moody, *Secret Power*, (New Kensington, PA: Whitaker House, 1997), 91-92.
48. June 25 – Ibid., 99-100.
49. June 26 – Craig Brian Larson, *Pastoral Grit*, 65.
50. June 26 – Ibid.
51. June 29 – Corrie ten Boom, *Clippings From My Notebook*, (London: Triangle, SPCK, 1982), 25.

July

52. July 4 – Mark Beliles and Stephen McDowell, "Restoring America's Christian History, The Perspective of Providence," <u>SCP Journal</u>, Vol. 17:4, (1993), 25.
53. July 4 – Ibid., 27.

54. July 4 – Peter Marshall and David Manuel, *The Light and the Glory*, (Old Tappan, NJ: Fleming H. Revell, 1977), 309.

55. July 4 – George Bancroft, *History of the United States, Vol. VI*, (Boston: Little, Brown, and CO., 1878), 321. Quoted by Mark Beliles and Stephen McDowell, "Restoring America's Christian History, The Perspective of Providence," <u>SCP Journal</u>, Vol. 17:4, (1993), 27.

56. July 4 – John Wingate Thorton, *The Pulpit of the American Revolution*, (Boston: Gould and Lincoln, 1860). Quoted by Mark Beliles and Stephen McDowell, "Restoring America's Christian History, The Perspective of Providence," <u>SCP Journal</u>, Vol. 17:4, (1993), 27.

57. July 9 – Chuck Swindoll, <u>First Evangelical Free Church of Fullerton Newsbreak</u>, Vol. 14, No. 12, April 3-9, 1994.

58. July 10 – "Franklin Graham: 'My Father's Son,'" Samaritan's Purse, 11.

59. July 13 – Author unknown, (Los Angeles, CA: Free Tract Society, Inc.).

60. July 15 – Charitie Lees Bancroft, (1841-1923).

61. July 19 – Ray Beeson and Ranelda Mack Hunsicker, *The Hidden Price of Greatness*, (Wheaton, IL: Tyndale House Publishers, 1991), 29-31.

62. July 20 – Hugh Ross, <u>Facts and Faith</u>, January, 1999, 4-5. NOTE: We are aware that there are differences of opinion regarding Hugh Ross's theories, we not necessarily endorsing his teachings, but merely quoting this illustration.

63. July 21 – Craig B. Larson, Editor, *Illustrations for Preaching and Teaching*, 197-198.

64. July 24 – W. B. Freeman, *God's Little Devotional Book for Couples*, (Honor Books, 2001), 48-49.

August
65. August 4 – Mrs. Charles E. Cowman, *Streams in the Desert*, March 11.

66. August 11 – F. B. Meyer, *Tried by Fire*, 172.

67. August 13 – Adaptation of D. L. Moody quotation, Paul Lee Tan, *Encyclopedia of 7700 Illustrations, Signs of the Times*, (Rockville, MD: Assurance Publishers, 1979), 571.

68. August 14 – Lori Joseph and Sam Ward, "Water Unsafe in Much of the World," *USA Today Snapshots*, 5/17/01.

69. August 21 – *The Bible Exposition Commentary*, (Chariot Victor Publishing, 1989).

70. August 22 - Warren Wiersbe, *On Being A Servant Of God*, (1993), 5.

71. August 24 – Herbert G. Bosch, <u>Our Daily Bread</u>, Sept. 2nd.

72. August 25 – Lyndon K. McDowell, "The Choice: Assumption or Assurance?," <u>Ministry</u>, 2/2005, 17.

73. August 30 – Charles Price, *Real Christians*, 110.

<u>September</u>

74. September 1 – Howard and William Hendricks, *As Iron Sharpens Iron*, 38.

75. September 5 – Helen Malacoat.

76. September 9 – Chuck Swindoll, quoted by Edythe Draper, *Draper's Book of Quotations for the Christian World*, (Tyndale, 1992), 421.

77. September 11 – Russell Ash, *The Top Ten of Everything 2003*, (DK Publishing, Published in the United States by Dorling Kindersley Publishing Inc. NY, NY), 94.

78. September 15 – Bernard Meltzer, *Draper's Book of Quotations*, (Wheaton, IL: Tyndale, 1992).

79. September 18 – Leslie B. Flynn, *When the Saints Come Storming In*, 85.

80. September 23 – Billy Graham, *Billy Graham: God's Ambassador*, (Time-Life Books with the BGEA, 1999), 51.

grace today

October

81. October 12 – John MacArthur, Jr., *The MacArthur New Testament Commentary*, (Moody Press, 1983-2002).
82. October 18 – A. W. Tozer, *The Knowledge of the Holy*.
83. October 19 – Ibid., 102.

November

84. November 6 – James McGraw, *Great Evangelical Preachers of Yesterday*, (Abingdon Press, 1961), 113.
85. November 7 – <u>Reader's Digest</u>, March 2001, 61.
86. November 16 – *Huge 'Ocean' Discovered Inside Earth*, LiveScience.com, 2/28/07.
87. November 20 – Samuel Smiles, (1812-1904).
88. November 21 – J. Hudson Taylor, (1832-1905).
89. November 23 – Tim Hansel, *You Gotta Keep Dancin*, 37.

December

90. December 2 – Charles Spurgeon, *The Treasury of David, Volume II*, vi.
91. December 6 – Martin Hengel, *Crucifixion*, 51.
92. December 9 – Fredrick M. Lehman, The Love of God, (1917).
93. December 11 – Phillip Yancy, *The Jesus I Never Knew*.
94. December 11 – John 8:10-11.
95. December 15 – A. W. Pink, *The Attributes of God*, 53-54.
96. December 16 – Leslie Martin, Heart and Home Women's Ministry, (Calvary Community Church, 2001).
97. December 17 – *USA Today*, 2/29/02.
98. December 18 – Henry Blackaby and Kerry L. Skinner, *Created to be God's Friend, Workbook; Lessons from the life of Abraham*, (Nashville, TN: Thomas Nelson Publishers, 2000), 120.